AF412295

First Impressions

Early Prints by Forty-six Contemporary Artists

First Impressions

Early Prints by Forty-six Contemporary Artists

Introduction by Elizabeth Armstrong

Essays by Elizabeth Armstrong and Sheila McGuire

Hudson Hills Press, New York

in association with Walker Art Center, Minneapolis

First Impressions

Walker Art Center
Minneapolis, Minnesota
4 June–10 September 1989

Laguna Gloria Art Museum
Austin, Texas
2 December 1989–21 January 1990

Baltimore Museum of Art
Baltimore, Maryland
25 February–22 April 1990

Neuberger Museum, State University of New York
Purchase, New York
21 June–16 September 1990

Major funding for this exhibition was provided by Champion International Corporation.

Note to the reader

Works included in the checklist that are discussed in the text but not illustrated are referred to by their checklist numbers (e.g., cat. no. 39). Measurements given for a work indicate the size of the sheet. The following abbreviations are used in the text: E.A. (Elizabeth Armstrong), S.M. (Sheila McGuire), ULAE (Universal Limited Art Editions), Gemini G.E.L. (Graphic Editions Limited), and NSCAD (Nova Scotia College of Art and Design).

First Edition

© 1989 Walker Art Center. All rights reserved under International and Pan-American Copyright Conventions. No part of this book may be reproduced or utilized in any form or by any means, electronic or mechanical, including photocopying, recording, or by any information storage-and-retrieval system, without permission in writing from Walker Art Center. Inquiries should be addressed to Editor, Walker Art Center, Vineland Place, Minneapolis, MN 55403.

Published in the United States by Hudson Hills Press, Inc., Suite 1308, 230 Fifth Avenue, New York, NY 10001-7704.

Distributed in the United States, its territories and possessions, Canada, Mexico, and Central and South America by Rizzoli International Publications, Inc.
Distributed in the United Kingdom, Eire, Europe, Israel, and the Middle East by Phaidon Press Limited.
Distributed in Japan by Yohan (Western Publications Distribution Agency).
Distributed in South Korea by Nippon Shuppan Hanbai.

Editor and Publisher, Hudson Hills Press: Paul Anbinder
Senior Editor, Hudson Hills Press: Virginia Wageman
Editor, Walker Art Center: Phil Freshman
Designer: Abby Goldstein
Indexer: Michelle Piranio
Composition: Trufont Typographers, Hicksville, New York
Manufactured in Japan by Toppan Printing Company

Library of Congress Cataloguing-in-Publication Data

Armstrong, Elizabeth.
    First Impressions : early prints by 46 contemporary artists Elizabeth Armstrong with Sheila McGuire.—1st ed.
        p. cm.
        Bibliography: p.
        Includes index.
        1. Prints, American—Exhibitions. 2. Prints—20th century—United States—Exhibitions. I. McGuire, Sheila, 1961– . II. Walker Art Center. III. Title.
    NE508.A68   1989   88-35551
    769.973′074′013—dc 19   CIP

ISBN: 1-55595-017-5 (alk. paper)

Contents

Acknowledgments

This exhibition grew out of conversations and correspondence during the past two years with many artists, printers, and publishers. Without their insights and cooperation, neither the exhibition nor this book could have taken shape. I am especially grateful to the artists whose achievements are documented here; their responses to my early queries regarding their "first impressions" were especially helpful. A number of printers and publishers also shared information with me as I embarked on the project. Among these, I particularly want to thank Brooke and Carolyn Alexander, Steven Andersen, Timothy Berry, Peter Blum, Pat Branstead, Kathan Brown, Robert Feldman, A. Lynn Forgach, Bill Goldston, Marian Goodman, Garry Kennedy, Jack and Ethel Lemon, Jeryl Parker, Arturo Schwarz, Sidney Singer, Kenneth Tyler, and the late Stanley William Hayter. Others who have been helpful in various ways include Diane Bucci, Joe Fawbush, Judith Goldberg, Julie Graham, Julia Sagraves, Kathleen Slavin, Esther Sparks, and Deborah Wye. I greatly appreciate the generosity of the many lenders, listed on page 143, who helped make the exhibition possible. Finally, for their encouragement and advice, I am grateful to Richard S. Field, Ruth E. Fine, Martin Friedman, Marge Goldwater, and Betsy Wright.

I am also pleased to acknowledge Champion International Corporation, whose generous support of *First Impressions* gave the project tremendous impetus from the beginning. The commitment of Marian Jill Sendor, Director, Field Location Creative Services at Champion, has been particularly important to the project as it has evolved.

Among the many former and current staff members of Walker Art Center who worked with me on *First Impressions*, I especially want to thank: Sheri Stearns and Timothy Peterson, who provided a wide range of administrative assistance; Glenn Halvorson, who carefully photographed a large portion of the works reproduced in this catalogue; and Jane Weisbin, who helped collect the works on loan and, as exhibition registrar, will oversee circulation of the exhibition. Mildred Friedman and Glenn Suokko, of the museum's Graphic Design Department, made useful suggestions about the layout of the book. My appreciation also goes to Phil Freshman for his probing and meticulous editing of the text. At Hudson Hills Press, I want to thank Paul Anbinder and Virginia Wageman for their scrupulous editorial and production guidance. Abby Goldstein deserves special credit for her sensitive design of this publication.

Finally, I am indebted to Sheila McGuire, who assisted me during every phase of catalogue preparation. She was a true collaborator, with whom I discussed myriad problems and possibilities. Her intelligence, knowledge, and enthusiasm contributed significantly to the success of this project. Her thoughtful contributions to this book speak for themselves.

Elizabeth Armstrong

Foreword

First Impressions explores the early graphic work of forty-six contemporary American artists who are widely recognized for their contributions to printmaking. Less well known, however, are the first prints and multiples by these painters and sculptors. This study examines their earliest publications, focusing on the first editions they produced under the auspices of a publisher or a professional printer.

When I began research for this book, I found that my subject matter provided a remarkably fertile ground for the study of an artist's work. That is because printmaking, perhaps more than any other art form, lays bare the everyday realities and problems of artistic creation. The images used by artists in their first publications tend to crystallize their current formal concerns and aesthetic ideas. Furthermore, their choice of print technique, their relationship with the printer, the role of the publisher, and a host of other factors ultimately affect the final image. These diverse elements are explored in each artist's entry in *First Impressions*.

I chose to present the entries in a chronological sequence governed by the date of each artist's first publication. This allows for a historical view of the evolution of art movements, styles, and techniques in relation to the emergence of specific publishers and print workshops. When an artist worked on several prints at once, which may have been published simultaneously, I have sometimes taken the liberty of reproducing more than one of these images. If an artist's first mature prints were self-published, these are also documented in the text.

In talking to artists about making prints, I have been struck by how they emphasize their first collaborations. Especially for those with little exposure to the medium, the initial experience in the print shop provided a singular challenge. While technical difficulties and restrictions imposed by the medium were at times frustrating, the process always had a stimulating effect on their work. Like actors' first takes, these germinal publications resonate with the energy brought to a new endeavor. Taken together, these early graphic works give an overview of stylistic and technical approaches that have transformed the medium in recent decades.

—E.A.

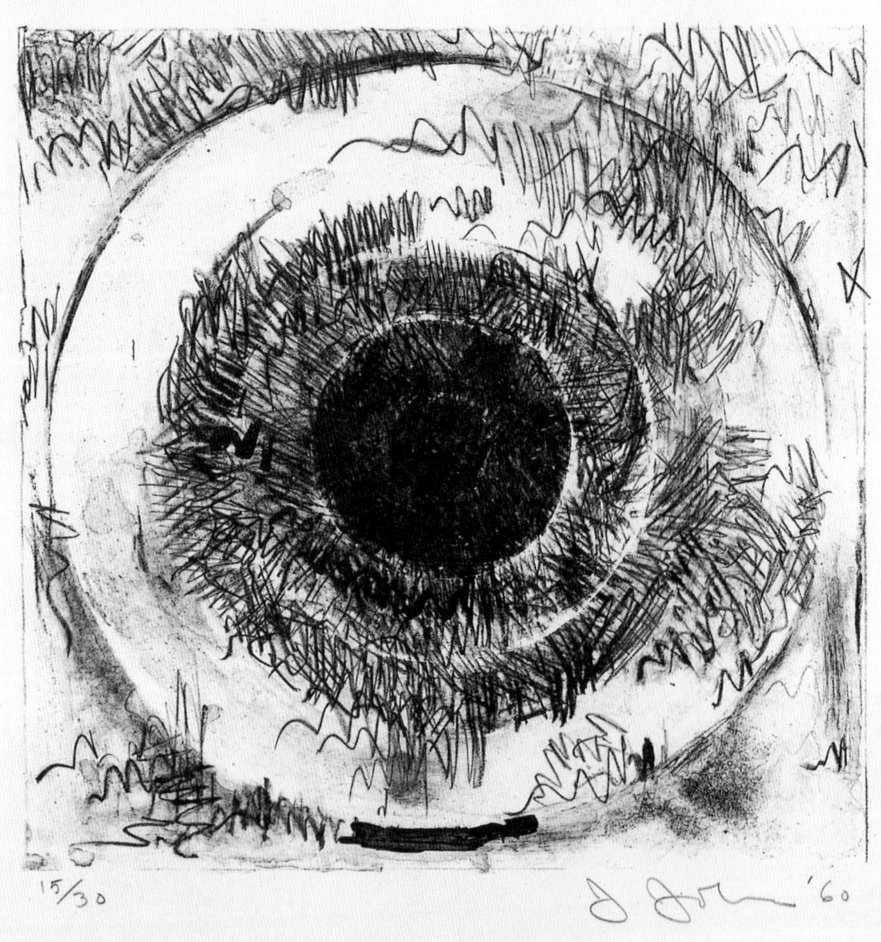

Jasper Johns *Target* 1960
lithograph (cat. no. 3)

Introduction

by Elizabeth Armstrong

"To create is divine, to reproduce is human."

—Man Ray[1]

In 1957 Larry Rivers and Frank O'Hara began work on the first lithography stone at Universal Limited Art Editions (ULAE), initiating a new era of publishing in American art. The story of the American print renaissance has been told before: how in the late 1950s and early 1960s Tatyana Grosman enticed young artists such as Jasper Johns, Robert Rauschenberg, and Jim Dine to ULAE, her East Coast workshop, leading the way for American painters and sculptors to make prints; how on the West Coast June Wayne established the Tamarind Lithography Workshop to revive the art of lithography, training master printers in the medium and enabling artists to work closely with skilled printers; and how a new generation of master printers, many trained at Tamarind,[2] set up print workshops across the country, providing the resources and services essential to the burgeoning artist-printmaker movement. The print renaissance received additional stimulus from a variety of energetic and purposeful publishers, whose ranks included master printers, art dealers, and private collectors. Print publishing was reinvigorated at a time when an increasingly affluent society began displaying a taste for the arts, contemporary art in particular. Consequently, as the critic Judith Goldman notes, "the American art market [in the 1960s] boomed like a frontier town."[3]

In Europe the fine arts and graphic arts had long coexisted, and, in the twentieth century, print editions by preeminent artists such as Pablo Picasso, Marc Chagall, and Joan Miró proliferated. No comparable artist-printmaker tradition existed in the United States. Before Stanley William Hayter temporarily moved his intaglio workshop, Atelier 17, from Paris to New York during the Second World War, many American painters had never attempted to make prints.[4] But it was not until the 1960s, when the United States began training its own master printers and offering artists the technical and collaborative resources of the printmaking workshop, that the medium began flourishing here. Indeed, it is the collaborative nature of contemporary printmaking—the ingenuity of artists, publishers, and printers and the relationships among them—that has contributed most significantly to the success of the printmaking revival and is at the heart of this study of artists' first prints.

At the time they embarked on their first publications, the majority of artists discussed in this book were in their thirties and beginning to receive critical attention. Considering the financial risks inherent in print publishing, it is hardly surprising that young or unknown artists are less frequently commissioned to make prints. In fact, the demands of working in a printmaking studio, particularly for the first time, call for a certain maturity on the part of the artist. As one artist-printmaker succinctly noted, "most people start to make prints about five years after they pull themselves together."[5]

Nonetheless, these artists were at a relatively early point in their careers, and publishers such as Tatyana Grosman saw this as an advantage. When she began editioning prints, "the artists were very young and very appreciative that someone was interested in them."[6] In Grosman's estimation, the reason there had been so few American artists making prints prior to the 1960s was that "there was nobody who was *after* them, who was interested in them."[7] But disinterest also stemmed from the commonly held notion, based on the history of printmaking, that the medium is a public one—a notion that did not correspond well with the predominant emphasis in the 1940s and 1950s on making art that was private and unique.[8] Furthermore, because there was not a strong tradition of fine-art printmaking in the United States, Americans typically thought of it as a secondary medium. In an article he wrote in 1963, Larry Rivers expressed the prevailing sentiment among his fellow American artists toward the medium: "If I wasn't thinking about a Picasso or a Matisse print I thought printmaking the dull occupation of pipe-smoking corduroy deep-type artisans."[9] In order to overcome these biases, printers and publishers had to pursue artists aggressively to get them to make prints.

In light of all this, it is hardly surprising that one of the artists courted by ULAE during its infancy, Robert Rauschenberg, initially responded to Grosman's overtures with his now famous remark that "the second half of the 20th century was no time to start writing on rocks."[10] His initiation to lithography, in 1962, came only after

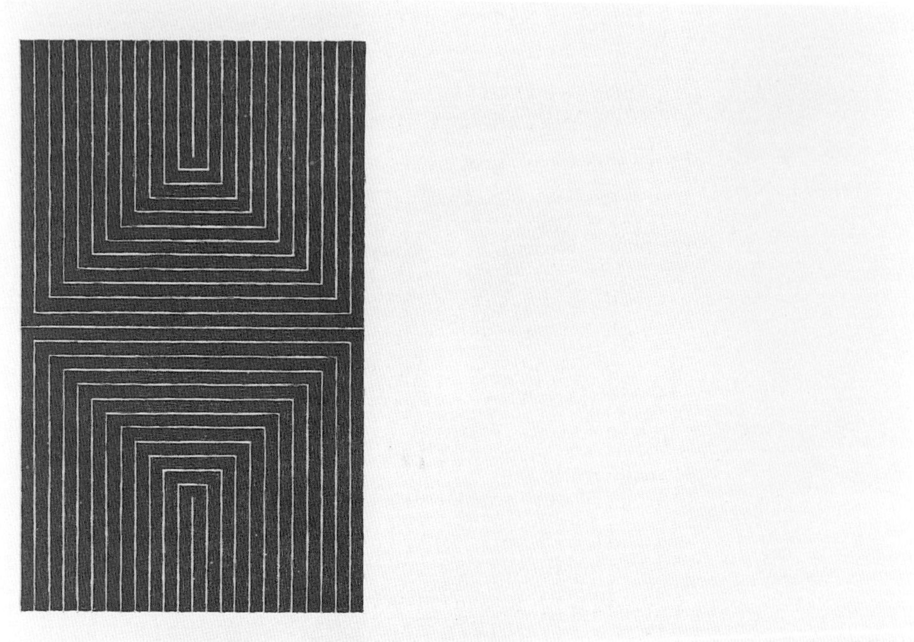

Frank Stella *Arundel Castle* 1967
lithograph (cat. no. 40)

repeated requests from Grosman, of whom it was said: "If Tanya wants somebody, . . . there's no escaping her. You have to come."[11] Another factor in Rauschenberg's conversion was the serious involvement in printmaking of his friend and neighbor Jasper Johns, who, a couple of years earlier, had also received Grosman's call. Unable to entice Johns out to Long Island long enough to make a print, she personally delivered the heavy lithography stones to his New York City studio; Rauschenberg, in fact, was enlisted to help carry the stones up the stairs.

The first prints of these two artists reflect both the imagery and the creative processes they characteristically employed. Rauschenberg worked freely, seemingly oblivious to the conventions of a medium in which images were traditionally derived by drawing with a grease ink or crayon on the stone. He combined hand-drawn imagery with photography and also incorporated the impressions of commonplace objects into his prints in much the same way he included sculpture in his paintings of that time. During his first year of experimentation, too, he found a primitive way to screenprint directly onto the lithography stones. Johns, on the other hand, immersed himself thoroughly and with customary meticulousness in the proofing process, exploring subtle nuances of the stones. By the time his first series of prints was completed, in 1963, he had pulled more than ninety-five proofs that enabled him to study and refine a wide variety of ways to control color, texture, and tone. Grosman observed that

Johns "investigates all the possibilities and chooses the richest one"; and master printer Kenneth Tyler, phrasing his enthusiasm about Johns' printmaking more dramatically, commented: "His stones yield the last ounce of blood lithography has to yield."[12]

Tyler's collaboration with Johns began in 1968 at Gemini G.E.L. (Graphic Editions Limited), the Los Angeles workshop he had established with partners Sidney B. Felsen and Stanley Grinstein two years earlier. Trained as a printer at Tamarind in the early 1960s, Tyler became active as a publisher at Gemini as well. Like Grosman before him, he had to use considerable wile to convince certain artists to make prints. Among the most obstinate, he recalls, was Frank Stella, who finally succumbed only in order to get Tyler "off his back."[13]

Not all painters and sculptors had to be coerced into making prints during the 1960s. Jim Dine, who had studied printmaking at the Boston Museum School and later at Ohio University, felt a strong affinity for the graphic arts. Moving to New York in 1959, he sought out a publisher and, by 1960, had begun making prints at Pratt Graphic Art Workshop—then one of the few professional fine-art print shops in the city.[14] Two years later Grosman would have little trouble luring Dine to ULAE. Another artist well versed in printmaking was Leon Golub, who, prior to working at Tamarind in 1965, had explored the medium in depth as a student at the School of the Art Institute of Chicago. Before emerging as a major Pop artist, Roy Lichtenstein had been making prints while teaching art at the college level and was awarded a Purchase Prize for one of his woodcuts at the 5th National Print Annual Exhibition at the Brooklyn Museum in 1951. Andy Warhol and Edward Ruscha, who both had experience in commercial graphic design, readily embraced the medium. Among the first artists to use silkscreen in fine-art printmaking, they liberally borrowed commercial styles, processes, and techniques for their graphic work.

The rejuvenation of printmaking in the 1960s owed much to the visual accessibility of work by such Pop artists as Lichtenstein, Warhol, and Ruscha and to the corresponding growth of a body of print collectors. As prices for unique artworks escalated, the demand for prints by these artists grew. Contemporary prints began replacing paintings on collectors' walls, instead of being stored in solander boxes as those acquired by an earlier generation of collectors had been. Prints were deemed so salable that they were used to raise money—though not always successfully—for a variety of causes. Ellsworth Kelly's first commissioned print (1964; p. 49) was included in a fund-raising portfolio sponsored by a museum, the Wadsworth Atheneum; and Robert Rauschenberg's first publication, *Abby's Bird* (1962; p. 43), was made for an ambitious project, backed by the Hilton chain, to decorate rooms in one of its new hotels.[15] The first publications of Frank Stella and Alex Katz sold out almost immediately, and Edward Ruscha, astounded by the marketability of his prints, commented that they "sell like pancakes."[16]

As the art-buying public became more interested in artwork made in editions, an adventurous group of independent publishers helped to give the mass-produced object a new aesthetic identity. Inspired by the example of László Moholy-Nagy and Edition MAT in Europe, which embraced the concept of sculpture made in editions (or "multiples"), Marian Goodman began publishing three-dimensional prints and other nontraditional editions. One of her first projects as director of Multiples, Inc., in New York City, was Claes Oldenburg's *Tea Bag* (1965), a trompe l'oeil tea bag made of vacuum-formed vinyl, Plexiglas, and silkscreen on felt. To produce such editions, Goodman contracted a variety of commercial shops skilled in such techniques as offset photolithography, silkscreen, and the fabrication of rubber, plastic, and other industrial materials.

Another important patron of innovative publications in the 1960s was Rosa Esman, who, through her Tanglewood Press, offered many Pop artists their first opportunity to produce multiples. Impressed by the pioneering efforts of ULAE, Esman had a true enthusiasm for prints and all works made in editions. She invited groups of artists to contribute to portfolios such as *7 Objects in a Box* (1965–1966), which featured key Pop practitioners Allan D'Arcangelo, Jim Dine, Roy Lichtenstein, Claes Oldenburg, George Segal, Andy Warhol, and Tom Wesselmann and utilized such industrial materials as cast aluminum, enamel, and vacuum-formed Plexiglas.

When Brooke Alexander began publishing in 1968, one of his first projects was also a multiple. He had been intrigued by Richard Artschwager's Whitney Museum installation that year of one hundred small oblong sculptures, which the artist dubbed "blps." Alexander invited him to edition a box of these objects. Having produced furniture during the 1950s and 1960s, Artschwager was comfortable with the notion of machine-manufactured objects; making the blps into an edition seemed a natural extension of his art. The project resulted in his first publication, *Locations* (1969; p. 65), which comprised blps made from Plexiglas, redwood, mirror glass, and rubberized horsehair that were housed in a Formica container.

The sponsoring of multiples generally demanded a willingness on the part of publishers to extend their means into uncharted areas and to risk their resources on a market that was not so viable as the one for prints. But even for prints the market was subject to sharp fluctuations. And, although by 1970 the print revival was in full swing, publishers at that time still found many artists unconvinced of the medium's relevance to their work.

Nevertheless, Robert Feldman, who founded Parasol Press in 1970, convinced a number of artists to make their first prints. One of his greatest challenges was the painter Chuck Close, who had studied printmaking at Yale but was disinclined to pursue it further. He felt particular skepticism about the dependency of print shops on machinery and technology, and about "the fact that printers know something that you don't know."[17] At Feldman's urging, however, Close agreed to make one print but only if it could be a "stretch for the print shop."[18] He intentionally chose to work in mezzotint, an archaic medium in which no American print shop was versed; his equal footing with the printers was thereby assured.

The resulting mezzotint, *Keith* (1972; p. 83), is a striking example of a print that not only extended the

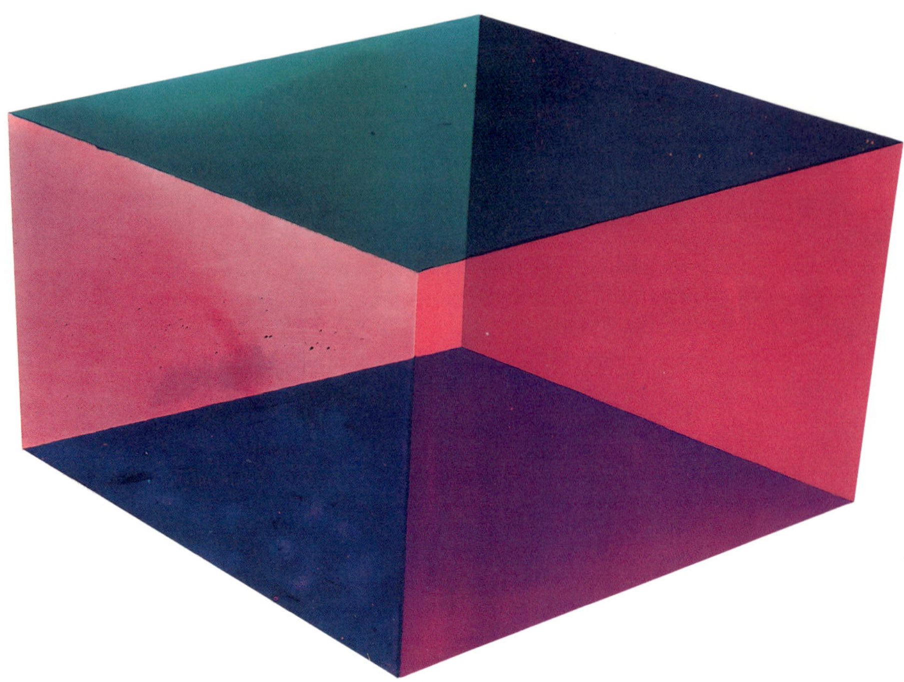

Ronald Davis *Cube II* 1971
photo-offset with laminated Mylar overlay,
mounted on plastic (cat. no. 49)

limits of the medium but also pulled the artist's work in a new direction. The grid Close used to transfer his image from photograph to etching plate remained embedded in the plate and appeared in the print; he began emphasizing it in subsequent drawings, paintings, and prints. While the success of *Keith* was due in large part to Close's vision, patience, and sheer technical skill, two other factors were crucial: the involvement of a flexible print shop, Crown Point Press, with an experienced and inventive staff headed by Kathan Brown; and the unbridled support of publisher Feldman. When technical difficulties seemed to threaten the successful production of *Keith*, Feldman told Brown: "You know my feeling about these things—you get the right artist and the right printer together and then you give them every possible financial support and leave them alone, right?"[19]

Independent publishers such as Feldman generally employed outside workshops to print their editions. During the 1970s, however, the printer-as-publisher combination grew increasingly popular. As already noted, Tyler became active as a publisher when he cofounded Gemini G.E.L. in 1966. The Nova Scotia College of Art and Design (NSCAD) opened its Lithography Workshop in 1969; Landfall Press in Chicago started publishing in 1970; and Crown Point Press, now located in San Francisco, has printed its own publications exclusively since 1979.

At Gemini G.E.L., Tyler's propensity for technical innovation and his attraction to an industrial aesthetic were significant in helping to modernize the graphic arts. Because of his considerable knowledge of industrial fabrication, he could bend these techniques to artists' needs. For example, in the early 1970s Tyler found a way of working with Ronald Davis on sheets of Mylar and plastic that captured the illusionistic depth of the artist's fiberglass pieces without duplicating them (see also p. 75).

While Tyler was busy fostering innovations with industrial materials and multimedia techniques, a development of a very different sort was taking place across the continent at the NSCAD Lithography Workshop. Its initiating objective was to spark the kind of lithographic renaissance in Canada that had begun at Tamarind; to this end the workshop spent its first year proving itself technically. However, it was soon working with artists whose prints "seemed to travesty the ideals of Tamarind."[20] Responding to Conceptual Art, one of the most vital movements of the early 1970s, the workshop began making prints in which lithography per se was tangential to the artists' ideas. Through its visiting-artists program, NSCAD became a stopover for Conceptual artists; the prints made during this period document their momentum.[21]

John Baldessari *I Will Not Make Any
More Boring Art* 1971
lithograph
edition: 50
22⁷/₁₆ × 30¹/₁₆
Printed and published by the Nova Scotia
College of Art and Design, Halifax
Collection The Museum of Modern Art,
New York, John B. Turner Fund

Since the primary aim of the workshop was educational—that is, it did not seek to produce commercially viable images[22]—NSCAD had no reservations about collaborating with artists such as John Baldessari and Vito Acconci, who had no printmaking experience. Baldessari's lithograph *I Will Not Make Any More Boring Art* (1971), which consists of that assertion written seventeen times, was directly related to an exhibition in which he invited NSCAD students to write "I will not make any more boring art" on the gallery walls as many times as they wished. Acconci's first print, *Kiss-Off* (1971; p. 73), bore text that documented a performance. "The first print," he wrote, "provided a way to get me out of the closure of my own body . . . to transfer myself to the outside. . . . I could transfer myself to stone, then to paper, then to the observer of the paper. The act of printmaking could serve as a mid-point, a medium, between 'me' and 'you' (the viewer)."[23] In making *Kiss-Off*, Acconci put on lipstick, transferred it from mouth to hand, then wiped his hand across the stone. Photographs of Acconci applying the lipstick, the red hand-rubbings, and the artist's handwritten description of the act were combined in the final lithograph. A year later Acconci returned to NSCAD and made *Touch Stone (for VL)*, another performance-related print in which he massaged a lithographic stone with "rubbing ink" as if it were a woman's body, while speaking his fantasies into a tape recorder.[24]

Jack Lemon, who in 1969 was the first master printer at NSCAD, left after a year to start his own shop, Landfall Press, in Chicago. There he invited a number of women to make prints, among them Nancy Graves, Pat Steir, and Lynda Benglis. Many of the group known as the Chicago Imagists also worked at Landfall, including Ed Paschke, Roger Brown, and Karl Wirsum, as did California artists Robert Arneson, Terry Allen, and William T. Wiley. In 1972 Wiley made his initial visit to Landfall while visiting Chicago for his first retrospective exhibition, then showing at the Art Institute. He had previously turned down an invitation to work at Gemini because he found its sprawling facility too busy; by 1973 the Los Angeles print shop employed twenty-two people and occupied twenty thousand square feet of space.[25] By contrast, he was attracted to Landfall's smaller, more subdued operation. They accommodated his odd desire to produce prints on chamois, a soft, pliant leather material he had used in his painting and sculpture. The variations between each print in the resulting editions of *Little Hide* and *Coast Reverse* (p. 88), caused by the uniqueness of the hides, were further emphasized by the hand-coloring Wiley added.

The "variant edition"—images that have been identically printed and then altered by some method to make them different from one another—was a direct response to the meticulously uniform editions in which American

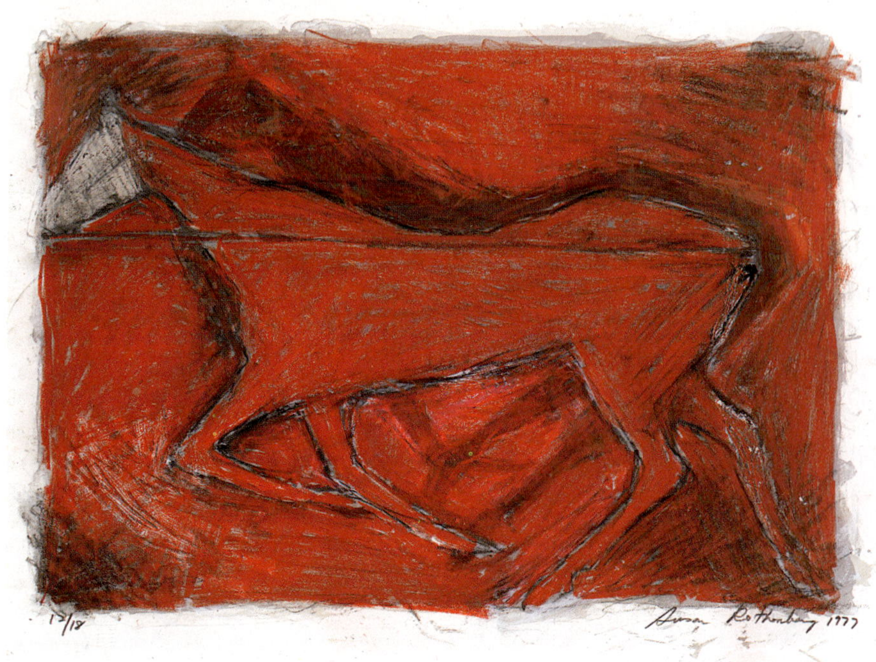

Susan Rothenberg *Untitled* 1977
hand-colored lithograph (cat. no. 81)

print shops excelled by the 1970s. Noting the successive popularity and mastery of lithography, silkscreen, and etching in the 1960s, Brooke Alexander sought an alternative mode; in 1973 he invited twenty-four artists to make hand-colored prints. By stressing the potential for personalizing each printed image, he attracted artists, such as Yvonne Jacquette, who had previously eschewed the medium. And, although it was not her original intention, Susan Rothenberg also began hand-coloring her first lithographs, made with Maurice Sanchez in 1977 (see also p. 99). Executed in pencil, gouache, crayon, and pastel, these richly textured images are closer to drawings than prints. By 1980 this ambiguous combination of drawing and printmaking was being freely explored by a wide range of artists and publishers.

Related to this interest in the individualizing of prints was a growing fascination with handmade paper. After years of serving simply as the substrate for prints, paper began to be freed and elevated from that role. One of the artists whose innovations with paper contributed to its new status was Alan Shields. In 1971 he began *Sun Moon Title Page* with the specific intention of creating a work that would be "a lot more personal than most of the prints being made at the time."[26] The making of this two-sided image involved dipping sheets of paper into dye, silkscreening the sheets, applying potato printing, weaving strips of paper through each print, and, finally, running the prints through a sewing machine filled with colored threads. Two years later Shields learned to make his own paper, an experience that led him to create numerous handmade-paper editions. When Tyler Graphics set up a paper mill on its premises in 1978, Shields was one of the first artists to take full advantage of it.[27]

While Shields gives his prints a tactile quality, other artists have used paper with the express purpose of making three-dimensional forms. The first publications of sculptor Lynda Benglis, for example, were large multiples made by casting paper pulp. To these large-scale, bulbous wall pieces, called Lagniappes (p. 105), the artist applied acrylic, glitter, polypropylene, and gold leaf. To some she even added plastic flounces that transformed their primitive, masklike forms into giant Mardi Gras party favors.

To produce the Lagniappes, Benglis collaborated for more than two years with A. Lynn Forgach, a printer and papermaker from Ohio who established Exeter Press in New York City specifically to finish this project. A growing number of printers have set up independent shops around the country, and individually tailored collaborations have become increasingly prevalent. Sometimes working for publishers and at other times initiating their own undertakings, these printers provide an accessibility and a sense of intimacy not always available at more established workshops. These smaller operations, which tend to specialize in one or two techniques, have also exerted a strong influence on contemporary printmaking.

Like many members of the younger generation of printers, Pat Branstead is an artist who began printing editions as a means of livelihood. She received training in printmaking in the early 1970s, first as a student of Kathan Brown at the San Francisco Art Institute and then as an apprentice at Crown Point Press—at that time situated across the bay in Oakland—a shop noted for its devotion to etching. One of her first tasks there was working on Chuck Close's *Keith*. Moving to New York in 1974, she founded Aeropress and quickly established a reputation as one of the best etching printers in the city. In 1978 she worked with Jennifer Bartlett on her first series of prints, Day and Night (pp. 106–107), and in 1979 she introduced Nicholas Africano to the medium (pp. 112–113). In the 1980s she has initiated projects with Les Levine, Joan Snyder, and Eric Fischl (p. 123).

Another influential printer is Hiroshi Kawanishi. His collaboration with Jasper Johns, which began in the early 1970s, helped transform the medium of silkscreen. Used for its ability to print hard edges and bright, unmodulated colors, screenprinting became, in Hiroshi's hands, a medium capable of producing images rich in surface nuance. It was his reputation that convinced Robert Moskowitz, a painter who depends on the most subtle variations of color and texture, to make his first prints. The shadowy, nearly six-and-one-half-foot-high image of a lighthouse in *Eddystone* (1983), for example, emerges from a shroud of nine shades of black, printed by Hiroshi in inks mixed with wax.

Aquatint has also undergone a metamorphosis in the 1980s. Jeryl Parker, who worked at Crown Point Press during the mid-1970s, opened Jeryl Parker Editions in New York City in 1981. His first solo project marked the initiation of artist David Salle into the medium. Backed by Parasol Press, Salle, Parker, and printer Brenda Zlamany approached the undertaking with the uninhibitedness that often makes a new endeavor successful. In an ambitious suite of eight oversized aquatints, related to Salle's concurrent white chalk drawings on sandpaper, they decided to use white on black. Working from projected images he made for the prints, Salle drew directly on the prepared plates with a soft litho crayon that functioned as a stopout, blocking the acid from etching the drawn areas. This technique served perfectly to create overlapping layers of contoured figure drawings that emerge and disappear like ghosts from their rich black background. Another young artist who has called on Parker's consum-

Robert Moskowitz *Eddystone* 1983
screenprint
edition: 23
77½ × 34½
Printed by Simca Print Artists, New York
Published by the artist and Simca Print Artists, New York
Courtesy First Bank System, Inc., Minneapolis

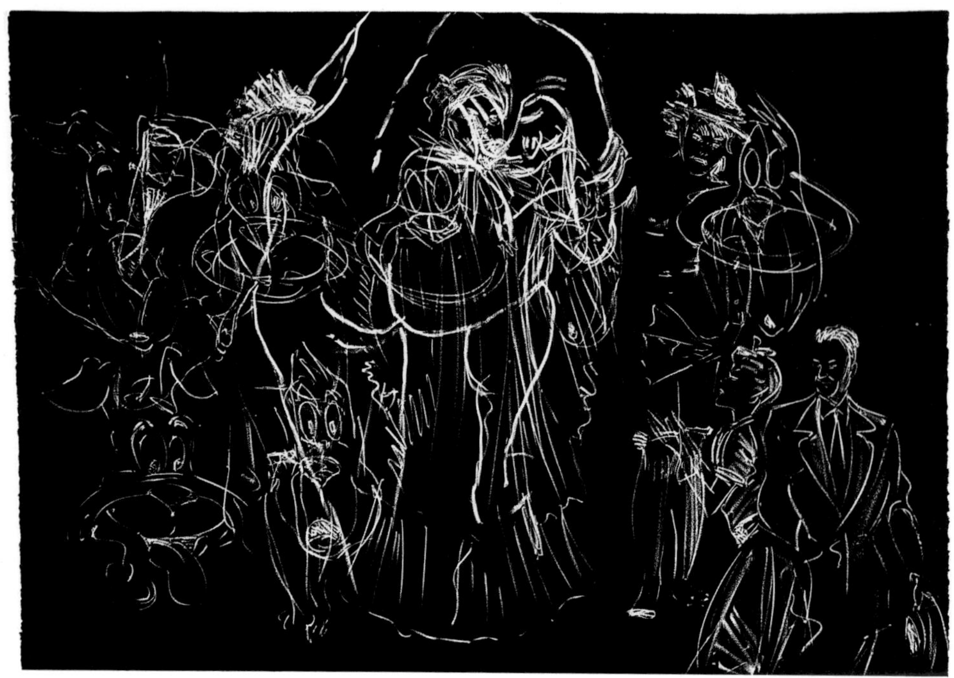

David Salle *Until Photographs Could*
Be Taken from Earth Satellites 1981
aquatint
edition: 10
29 × 41
Printed by Jeryl Parker Editions,
New York
Published by Parasol Press, Ltd.,
New York
Courtesy Print Collection, Miriam and
Ira D. Wallach Division of Art, Prints
and Photographs, The New York
Public Library, Lenox and Tilden
Foundations

mate skill with aquatint is Donald Sultan, who collaborated with the printer in the mid-1980s to make his
monumental and voluptuous images of black lemons.
Likewise, David True relied on the experience of Crown
Point's etching printers when he made his first prints in
1983 (p. 131). At the same time, feeling blissfully ignorant
of printmaking conventions, he manipulated the rosin in a
free gestural fashion rarely seen in aquatint.[28]

Woodblock printing is another technique that has seen
a resurgence. It had been little used for several decades
when, in the 1970s, ULAE, Tyler Graphics Ltd., and
Vermillion Editions of Minneapolis added it to their
repertoires. Landfall Press followed suit in the 1980s. In
this decade, too, Pat Branstead began making woodblock
prints with Susan Rothenberg and Louisa Chase; and
printer Chip Elwell specialized in woodcut almost exclusively, collaborating with young expressionists, such as
Gregory Amenoff and Richard Bosman (p. 119), who
were particularly drawn to it. A major exhibition of
German Expressionist paintings and prints at the
Guggenheim Museum, New York, in 1980, which included woodcuts, also had an influence on the popularity
of this enduring technique.

The 1980s have, in addition, seen a new generation of
artists coming to work at ULAE. Under the direction of Bill
Goldston since 1982, this venerable print shop has upheld
many of the principles that guided it in the 1960s,
emphasizing above all the importance of rapport between
artist and printer and continuing to provide the "luxury
of time and freedom to follow an idea to its best
conclusion."[29] Literally following in the footsteps of
Tatyana Grosman, who had died in 1982, Goldston
personally delivered a lithographic stone to artist Carroll
Dunham when he began making prints. Dunham's intention was simply to explore drawing on the stone, which
he did for six weeks in his studio. His first prints are pure
expressions of one-color lithography (p. 135).

In the 1980s the revolution in printmaking has come
full circle. The innovations of the workshops and the
abundance of independent printers, in the United States
and abroad, provide contemporary artists with the means
to make multimedia prints using the most advanced
technologies and on any scale desired, while at the same
time giving artists the opportunity to execute traditional
black-and-white prints in linocut, woodcut, or lithography. But perhaps the most important element of the
print renaissance has been the general change in attitude
toward the medium. The growing interest on the part of

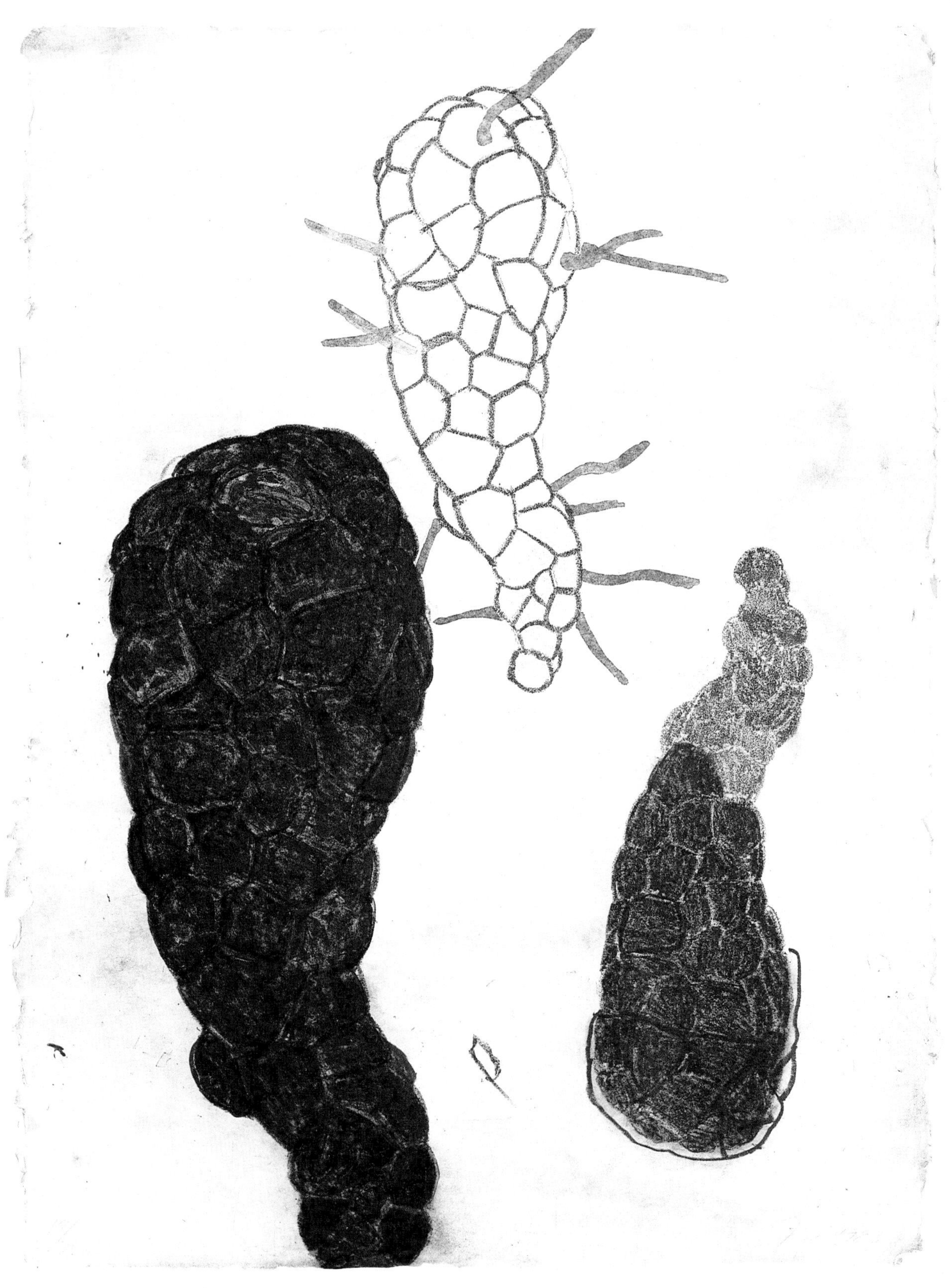

Terry Winters *Factors of Increase* 1983
lithograph (cat. no. 100)

the public, media, museums, dealers, and, above all, artists, has given printmaking new dynamism.

Publishers who had to cajole artists to make prints in the 1960s have little trouble convincing them today. When Terry Winters was first invited to produce lithographs at ULAE in 1982, he felt no hesitation about working in this foreign medium, citing the "encouraging precedent of the significant bodies of work in prints produced by [Johns and Rauschenberg]" and "the interesting relationship their printed works bore to their works in other media."[30] A growing number of young artists have already become accomplished printmakers and consider their graphic work an integral element of their art.

---

1. In a statement entitled "Originals Graphics Multiples," which appears as the frontispiece in *Man Ray: Opera Grafique*, vol. 1 (Milan: Studio Marconi, 1987). In the 1920s Man Ray joined Marcel Duchamp in his attack on the fetishism surrounding the uniqueness of works of art.

2. During the 1960s sixty-six printers completed the rigorous master-printer training program at Tamarind.

3. Judith Goldman, "Twenty-five Years of American Prints and Printmaking: 1956–1981," Pratt Graphic Art Workshop 25th-Anniversary Issue, *Print Review* 13 (1981), p. 8.

4. For example, Robert Motherwell made his first prints at Atelier 17 in 1943–1944. Although he did not make prints again until the 1960s, it should be noted that Hayter had a decisive influence on many artists who worked at Atelier 17 during the 1940s. Many, such as Gabor Peterdi and Mauricio Lasansky, went on to start printmaking programs at university art departments. For example, in 1945 Lasansky established the print department at the University of Iowa, and in 1949 Peterdi organized the graphic workshop at the Brooklyn Museum; he then went on to join the staff of Yale University's Graphic Workshop. For more information on Hayter's influence on American printmaking, see Joann Moser, *Atelier 17*, exh. cat. (Madison: Elvehjem Art Center, University of Wisconsin, 1977), pp. 17–19.

5. Alex Katz quoted in "New Prints of Worth: A Question of Taste," *The Print Collector's Newsletter* 10 (September–October 1979), p. 110.

6. Quoted in Stephanie Terenzio, *The Prints of Robert Motherwell*, with a catalogue raisonné by Dorothy Belknap (New York: Hudson Hills Press in association with the American Federation of Arts, 1984), p. 52.

7. Ibid., p. 55.

8. Most artists at the time probably shared Franz Kline's view that "printmaking concerns social attitudes, you know—politics and a public." See Thomas Hess, "Prints: Where History, Style and Money Meet," *Art News* 70 (January 1972), p. 29; and Diane Kelder, "The Graphic Revival," *Art in America* 61 (July–August 1973), pp. 110–113.

9. Larry Rivers, "Life among the Stones," *Location* 1 (Spring 1963), p. 93.

10. The full quotation appears in Edward A. Foster, *Robert Rauschenberg: Prints, 1948/1970*, exh. cat. (Minneapolis Institute of Arts, 1970), unpaginated.

11. Terenzio, op. cit., p. 53.

12. The Grosman and Tyler quotations appear in "Original Art, Hot Off the Presses," *Life* 68 (23 January 1970), p. 60.

13. Tyler in an interview with Sheila McGuire at Tyler Graphics Ltd., Mt. Kisco, New York, 21 March 1988.

14. Pratt was established in 1956 and, by 1960, was under the direction of Andrew Stasik, whom Dine had known at Ohio University.

15. For more information on this ambitious endeavor, see B. H. Friedman, "Art for the New York Hilton," *Craft Horizon* 23 (July–August 1963), pp. 8–13, 43–44.

16. Quoted in Howardena Pindell, "Words with Ruscha," *The Print Collector's Newsletter* 3 (January–February 1973), p. 125.

17. Quoted in Lisa Lyons and Robert Storrs, *Chuck Close* (New York: Rizzoli International Publications, 1987), p. 33.

18. Close in a conversation with the author, 13 June 1988.

19. Quoted in Brown's text for a special-edition portfolio documenting the making of Chuck Close's *Keith*.

20. Eric Cameron, "The Lithography Workshop," in *NSCAD: The Nova Scotia College of Art and Design* (Halifax: Press of the Nova Scotia College of Art and Design, 1982), p. 9.

21. Vito Acconci in correspondence with the author, 4 January 1988.

22. Visiting artists were invited to make prints at NSCAD as part of a program designed to provide students in the workshop with insights into the working processes of artists and the workings of the art world.

23. Supra, note 21.

24. Cameron, op. cit, p. 20.

25. Judith Goldman, "The Print Establishment," *Art in America* 61 (July–August 1973), p. 108.

26. Shields quoted in Ronny Cohen, *Alan Shields: Print Retrospective*, exh. cat. (Cleveland Center of Contemporary Art, 1986), pp. 10–11.

27. For a detailed examination of papermaking in contemporary prints, especially at Tyler Graphics Ltd., see the essays by Leonard B. Schlosser and Ruth E. Fine in *Tyler Graphics: The Extended Image* (Minneapolis: Walker Art Center and New York: Abbeville Press, 1987).

28. True discusses his first prints in an interview with Margaret Wrinkle at Crown Point Press in *View* 4 (Spring 1988).

29. Supra, note 25, p. 107.

30. Clifford Ackley, "'Double Standard': The Prints of Terry Winters," *The Print Collector's Newsletter* 18 (September–October 1987), p. 122.

First Impressions

Early Prints by Forty-six Contemporary Artists

When Tatyana Grosman founded Universal Limited Art Editions (ULAE) in West Islip, New York, in 1957, it had long been her dream to bring together artists, writers, and printers to produce *livres d'artistes*—high-quality, handmade, limited-edition books. *Stones* (1957–1959), a collaboration between Larry Rivers and Frank O'Hara, was her first edition to achieve that objective, and, as the first lithographs made by ULAE, it represents a landmark in contemporary American printmaking.

While Grosman knew beforehand that she wanted Rivers—whom she had met nearly seven years earlier—to be the artist involved with ULAE's first book, she had to decide on a writer. Her publisher friend Barney Rosset, who was then publishing a book of O'Hara's work, highly recommended the poet for the job. It is probably because Grosman, too, was impressed with his poems that she went to the painter's Southampton home to propose that he collaborate with O'Hara; as Rivers later wrote, "(dopey fate) Frank was my guest when she arrived."[1] Already friends, the two men readily agreed to the project. Before they knew it, Grosman delivered a pair of limestones (which had been used for years as a path in her front yard) to Rivers' studio. There they began work on this project, which would take almost two years to complete.

Though the friends had never collaborated, they had often referred to one another in their works. In 1955, for instance, O'Hara wrote the poem "On Seeing Larry Rivers' *Washington Crossing the Delaware* [1953] at the Museum of Modern Art."[2] Likewise, Rivers had made the poet the subject of several paintings, including a nude portrait, *O'Hara* (1954). According to Rivers, the biggest question prior to working jointly was, "How were two super-serious, monstrously developed egos to find in this situation a way of allowing a complete and undiluted exposition of their two talents?"[3] They knew that if O'Hara were simply to write a poem and Rivers simply to illustrate it, the result would not be satisfying. They thus decided to make *Stones* a full collaboration and proceeded to work side by side—O'Hara writing and Rivers drawing—whenever their hectic schedules permitted.

The two men came to the project with a good deal of familiarity with and respect for each other's art. Rivers was well read and well versed in music, and O'Hara, having worked as an assistant curator at the Museum of Modern Art, New York, since 1952, knew a great deal about contemporary art. In *Stones* they combined these backgrounds into what Rosset, in the book's colophon, dubbed a "tabloscript," defined as what is produced "when the artist and the poet[,] inspired by the same theme, draw and write on the same surface at the same time, fusing both arts to an inseparable unity."

Rivers has noted that his and O'Hara's ignorance and enthusiasm enabled them to jump into the project without thinking too much about the details and difficulties involved. In the beginning, drawing on the stones posed some problems. Rivers, who had never made a lithograph, found the crayon difficult to handle and the adjustment to thinking in reverse a barrier to producing satisfying images. Not being able to erase also frustrated him.[4] O'Hara, on the other hand, had to adjust to thinking about how his words would appear as part of an image; he had to learn how big to make the letters, how hard to press the crayon, and where to put the words within the overall picture.

Each time they met to work they chose a specific subject and title. The first was a stone about themselves, entitled *US* (1957–1959). Rivers decorated the letters *US* at the top to look something like the United States flag and then drew O'Hara, replete with broken nose and bumpy forehead. Looking in a mirror, he roughly scribbled his own face onto the stone. All this led O'Hara to write, "They call US the Farters of our Country" and "Poetry belongs to me, Larry, and painting to you." In this kind of collaboration, each artist could change the meaning of the other's work with his own response.

Many of the images Rivers and O'Hara produced together in *Stones* are personal and resist easy deciphering. Take, for example, *Rimbaud & Verlaine*. Were it not for the explanation of the image Rivers later wrote, one might not guess that it derived from a picture of the two poets that hung in the artist's studio. Lacking that explanation, it would also be hard to tell that O'Hara's text refers to an evening on which he and Rivers attended a ballet at City Center.[5]

Once their work on the individual stones was completed, Grosman had to find a printer. She convinced Robert Blackburn, one of New York's most experienced lithographers, to come and work for her press.[6] He knew right away that his first ULAE assignment would not be an

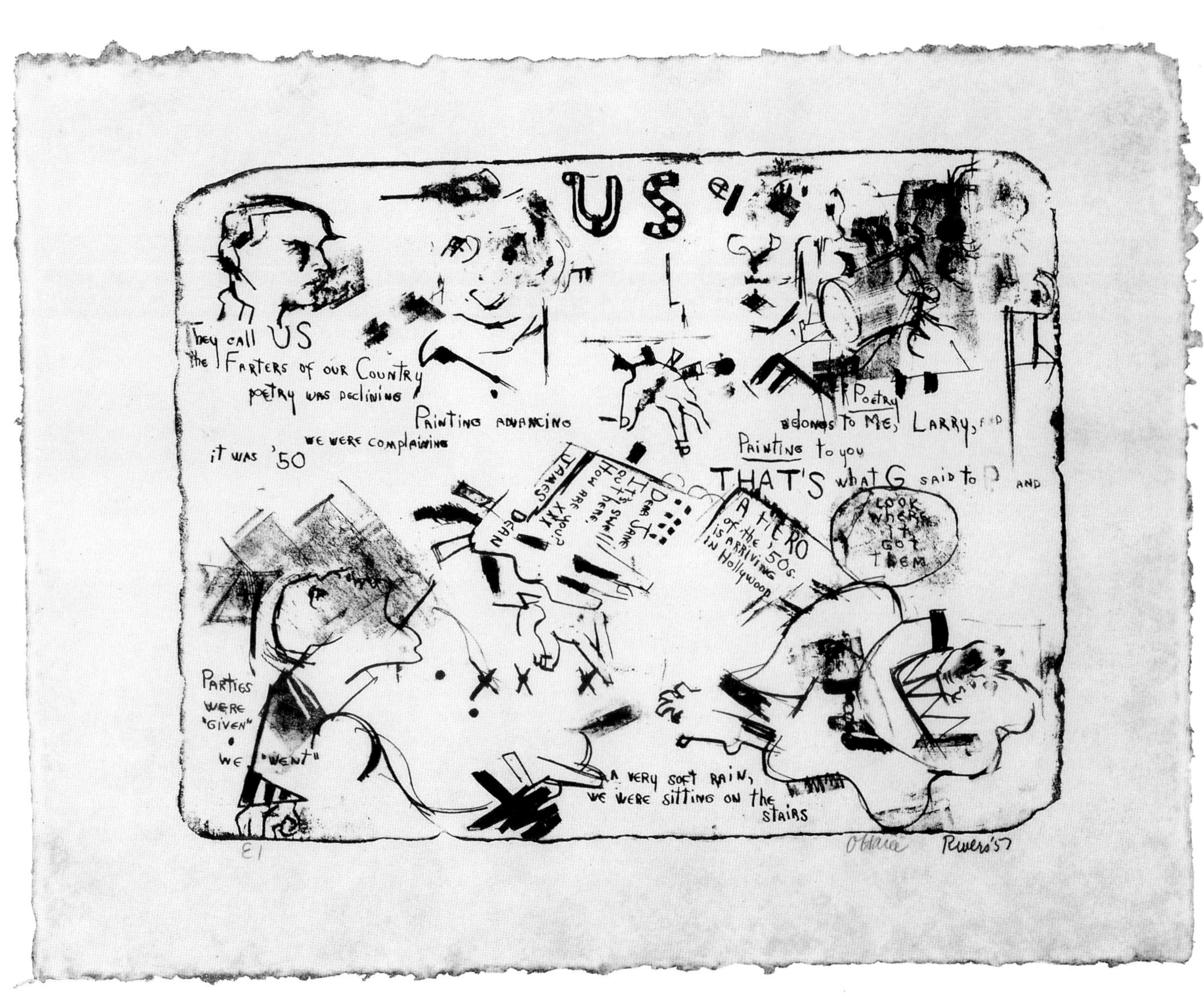

Larry Rivers and **Frank O'Hara** *US* 1957–1959
lithograph (cat. no. 2)

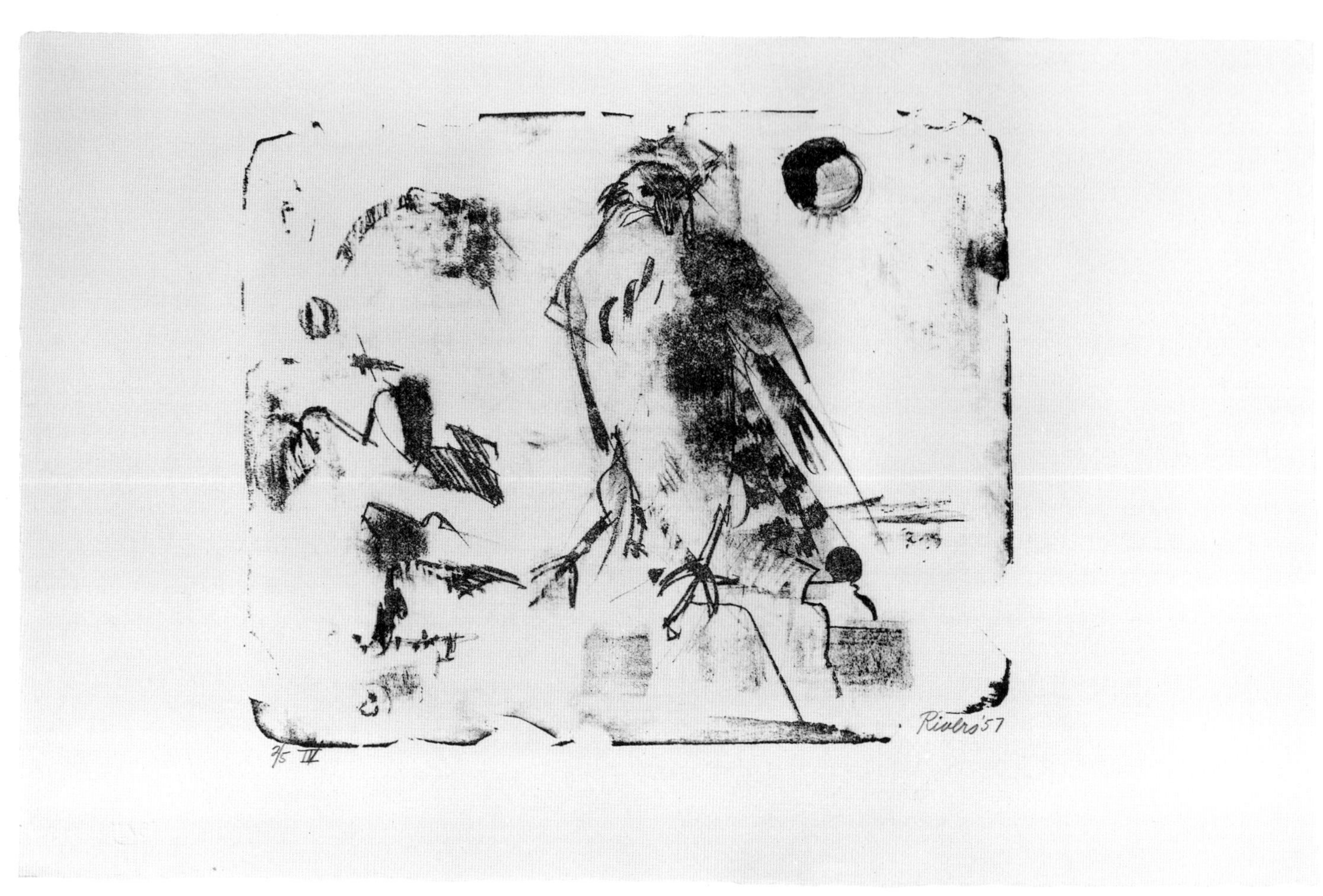

Larry Rivers *The Bird and the Circle*, State IV 1957
lithograph (cat. no. 1)

easy one. Lacking technical experience with lithography, neither Rivers, O'Hara, nor Grosman realized that the path stones lacked the well-grained surface necessary to create a successful print. Making the work hard, too, was Grosman's insistence that the entire stone be embossed on the paper to reveal its edges and thus emphasize the "stones" theme. A third technical challenge was posed by Grosman's antiquated Fuchs-Lang press—a type of hand-press that had not been used commercially since the 1920s—which was set up in her living room. Despite these obstacles, Blackburn found a way to execute the prints as requested.

Technical difficulties and the artists' busy schedules were not the only reasons why it took nearly two years to produce *Stones*. Another was Grosman's search for the appropriate paper. She ultimately hired papermaker Douglass Howell, who produced the handmade paper from pure linen rag at the rate of only a few sheets per day, owing to the difficulty of the task. She also commissioned him to design and make the clever linen-and-blue-denim cover for the book. Grosman wanted denim since she rarely saw Rivers and O'Hara wearing anything but blue jeans. Although the quality of the images in *Stones* varies, the book as a whole—with its informality, its unusual cover, and its special paper—helped set ULAE's innovative tone and establish it as one of the leading contemporary workshops in the United States.

During times when Rivers and O'Hara could not work jointly on *Stones*, Rivers produced several lithographs, including *The Bird and the Circle* (1957), ULAE's first single-print edition. Most of these lithographs deal with immediately personal subjects. *The Bird and the Circle*, for example, relates to the cages of exotic birds he kept in his home.[7] According to Grosman, it was Rivers' eagerness to explore the medium further during the interludes in his collaboration with O'Hara that "really got me started in single editions. . . . Until then, I had been thinking only of books."[8]

—S.M.

1. Larry Rivers, "Life among the Stones," *Location* 1 (Spring 1963), p. 92.

2. See Frank O'Hara, *The Collected Poems of Frank O'Hara*, ed. Donald Allen (New York: Alfred A. Knopf, 1972), pp. 233–234.

3. Rivers, op. cit., p. 92.

4. Ibid., p. 93.

5. Ibid., p. 94. Here the painter discusses the meaning of many of the images. Of *Rimbaud & Verlaine* he writes: "During an intermission we were making our way down the wide staircase from the cheap seats to the mezzanine when our mutual friend and my dealer John Meyers thinking he was being funny screamed out for general use 'there they are all covered in blood and semen.' This is a reference to something said about Rimbaud and Verlaine that Verlaine's wife hounded him with for his whole life."

6. In 1948 Blackburn established the Bob Blackburn Printing Workshop (after 1955 known as the Creative Graphics Studio) in New York City. From 1957 to 1962 he worked at ULAE. He returned to his own workshop in 1963. See Elizabeth Jones, "Robert Blackburn: An Investment in an Idea," *Tamarind Papers* 6 (Winter 1982–1983), pp. 10–14.

7. Esther Sparks, manuscript for *Universal Limited Art Editions: A History and Catalogue, the First Twenty-five Years* (New York: Harry N. Abrams Publishers in association with the Art Institute of Chicago, forthcoming 1989).

8. Quoted in Calvin Tompkins, "Profiles: The Moods of a Stone," *The New Yorker* 52 (7 June 1976), p. 60.

Jasper Johns

Although the story of Jasper Johns' introduction to printmaking has been recounted before, it bears repeating in a book about artists' first prints. Tatyana Grosman, having seen his work in the *Sixteen Americans* exhibition at the Museum of Modern Art, New York, in 1959, wrote Johns in South Carolina, urging him to visit her at ULAE. He agreed to come up.[1] After this meeting she delivered two weighty lithographic stones to the sidewalk below his second-story studio on Front Street in New York. Johns says he got Robert Rauschenberg and a neighborhood bum to help him carry the heavy limestone load up the two flights of stairs.

It seems likely that if Grosman had not taken the initiative, Johns would not have begun printmaking as early as he did. Once the process had begun, however, he was also indebted to master printer Robert Blackburn, who worked at ULAE between 1957 and 1962. Blackburn's expertise enabled Johns to tackle advanced lithographic problems even during his first printmaking year, as the Coat Hanger and Flag prints of 1960 attest. In addition to learning a new medium, the normally reclusive Johns had to adjust to the semipublic atmosphere of working with the printer and shop technicians. He also had to accept the fact that, in printmaking, nothing occurs quickly. As he later explained it: "Everything that happens out there happens awfully slowly, . . . when something doesn't come out just right, for example, Tanya [Grosman] gets upset and has to find out why. It may be that if the same process is repeated it will come out fine the second time, but she can't accept that—she has to *know*."[2] Apparently, he sometimes had to wait for weeks to see the results of his, Grosman's, and Blackburn's decisions.

That Johns' first published print (1960; p. 10) depicts a target is hardly surprising to anyone familiar with his imagery. Johns had made an icon of this subject as early as 1955 with such enigmatic works as *Target with Four Faces* and *Target with Plaster Casts*, both of which were executed in encaustic and collage. The characteristic of the target most attractive to Johns was its ordinariness; he considered it an object regularly seen but not really looked at. It thus provided him with an ideally neutral pictorial field on which to work. The print exhibits a masterful command of the lithographic crayon in its dense weave of strokes and squiggles, which render figure and ground inseparable. It is based on a conté crayon drawing, *Broken Target* (1958), in which layers of crayon strokes subtly shade and texture the target. Setting aside Johns' tendency to return to familiar themes in his art, the iconic target provided him with an easily adaptable image for a first printmaking experience since it did not require him to draw in reverse.

The Coat Hanger prints (1960) presented Johns with a different set of problems, the most difficult being how to translate his *Coat Hanger* painting (1959)—in which a real hanger was laid against the canvas—into a lithograph. In *Coat Hanger I* (cat. no. 4) he first drew the subject as though it were hanging on a nail, then obscured the illusion by embedding the object in a nest of strokes. In his next experiment with the theme, *Coat Hanger Variation* (cat. no. 6), he embossed a real hanger onto the sheet of paper, bringing this proof closer to his painting. He eventually decided against embossing because he felt that "when [the hanger] matched the drawing exactly, the embossing seemed too nearly invisible; and, when it didn't match, it seemed too visible and to have been imposed superfluously upon the print."[3] In *Coat Hanger II*, for which Johns believes he used the same stone as in *Coat Hanger I*, the image of the white hanger reemerges from the heavily worked gray background.

It should be noted here that Johns' very first lithographic markings were for a print of the Arabic numeral zero. Johns used this print, which was not published until 1963, to experiment with tusche and crayon on stone. From the beginning, he had in mind a series of prints, made from a single stone, whose subject would be the numerals zero through nine. When he came to produce the series, he indeed used the same stone throughout, successively erasing most of one image before drawing the next. Thus a vestige of the previous numeral is evident in each print, as seen in the existing trace of the *0* in *1*. As the art historian and critic Robert Rosenblum wrote in a text accompanying the *0–9* portfolios, "Above all, the inexhaustible richness of these lithographs lies in the step-by-step unfolding of this ten-part narrative drama, which

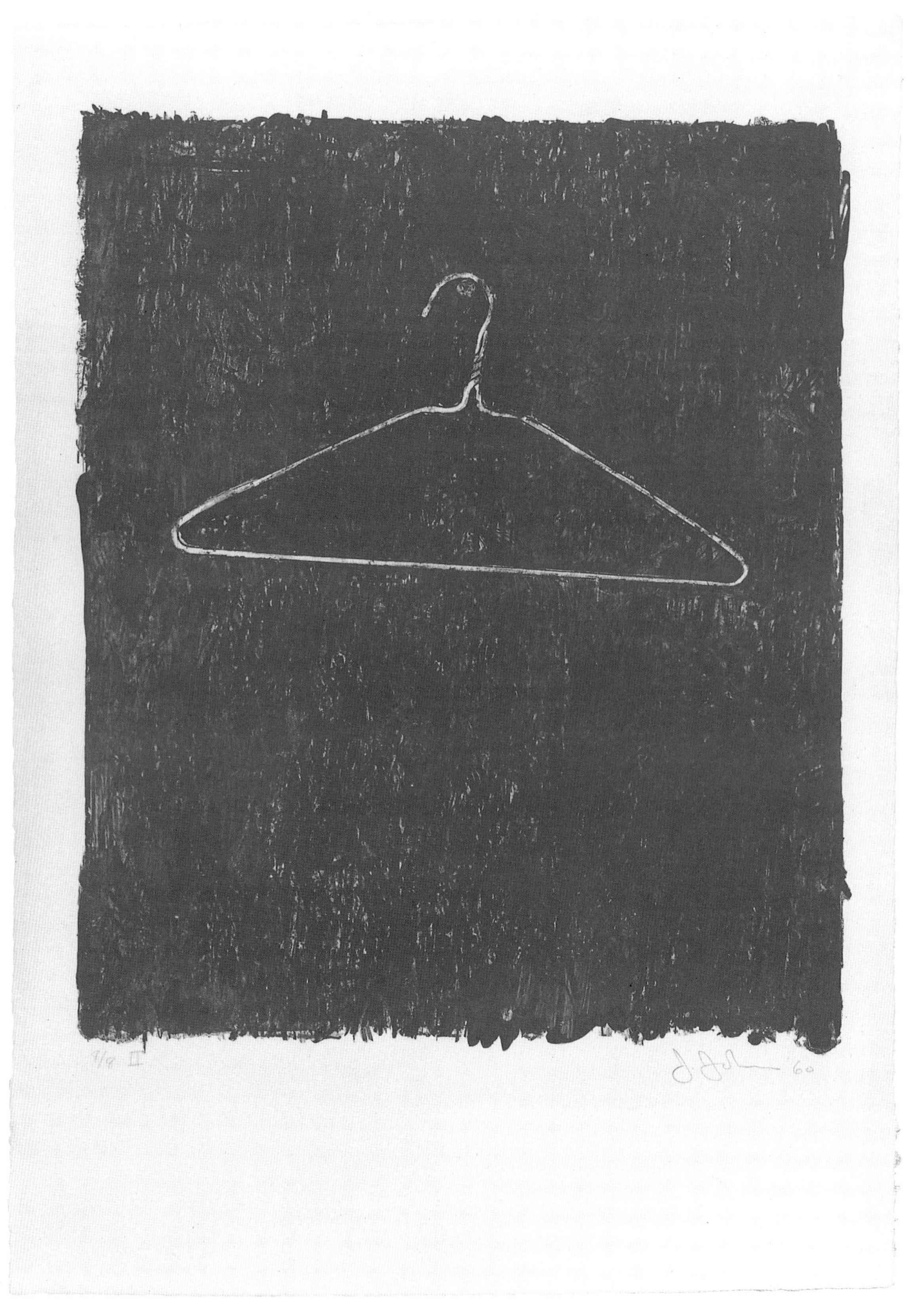

Jasper Johns *Coat Hanger II* 1960
lithograph (cat. no. 5)

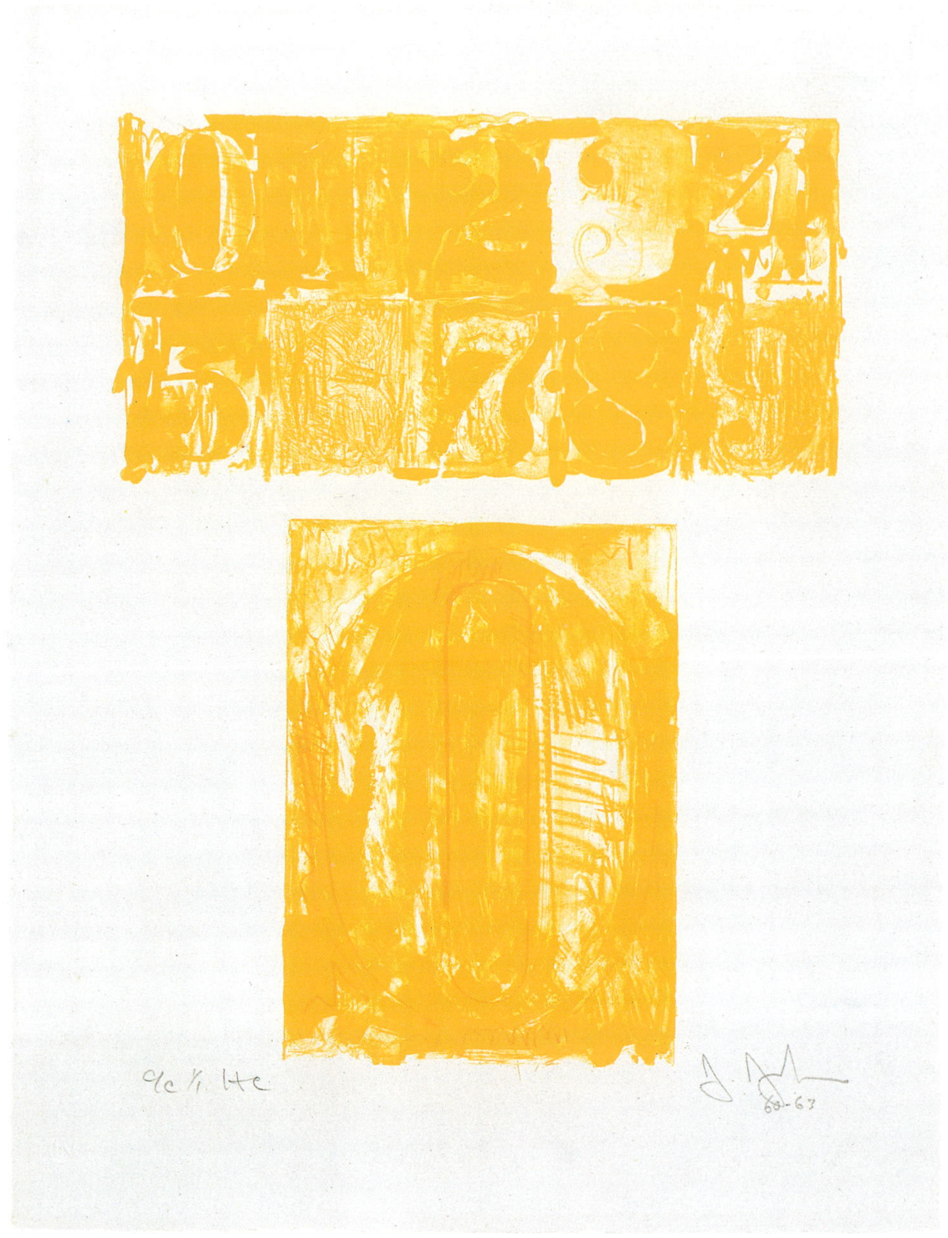

Jasper Johns *0* 1960–1963
lithograph (cat. no. 7)

becomes a metaphor for the organic disclosure of the artistic process itself." The numerals were printed in 1963, after a long search for the proper paper, by Zigmunds Priede, who succeeded Blackburn at ULAE. That year ULAE issued three series of the prints, all titled *0–9*: one in gray, one in black, and one in colors; each series was printed on a different colored paper.[4]

More than ninety-five trial images, which Johns meticulously compiled in two notebooks, document the extensive proofing that the *0–9* stone underwent before the prints were editioned. The proofs reveal the sense of challenge with which Johns approached lithography. Knowing nothing about the process, "he wanted to see how much he could complicate it."[5]

—S.M.

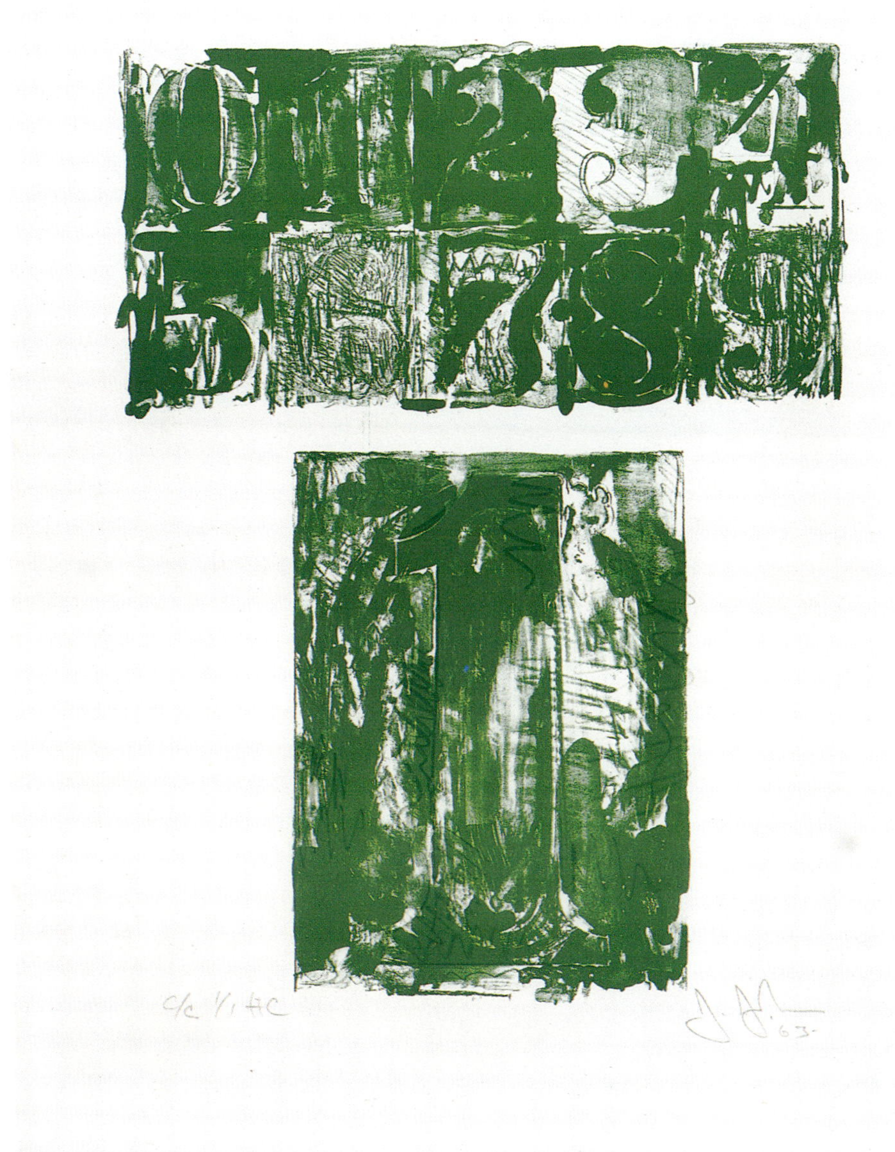

Jasper Johns *1* 1960–1963
lithograph (cat. no. 7)

1. Calvin Tompkins, "Profiles: The Moods of a Stone," *The New Yorker*
52 (7 June 1976), p. 62.

2. Quoted in ibid., pp. 65–66.

3. The artist in correspondence with Elizabeth Armstrong, 27 January
1988.

4. For illustrated listings of Johns' graphic work, see Richard S. Field,
Jasper Johns: Prints, 1960–1970, exh. cat. (New York: Praeger
Publishers and Philadelphia: Philadelphia Museum of Art, 1970);
Richard S. Field, *Jasper Johns: Prints, 1970–1977*, exh. cat.
(Middletown, Conn.: Wesleyan University, 1978); and Judith
Goldman, *Jasper Johns: Prints, 1977–1981*, exh. cat. (Boston: Thomas
Segal Gallery, 1981). See also Riva Castleman, *Jasper Johns. A Print
Retrospective*, exh. cat. (New York: Museum of Modern Art, 1986).

5. Tompkins, op. cit., p. 62.

Jim Dine

In 1960, a year after his arrival in New York City, Jim Dine published his first prints, six lithographs closely related to the drawings, paintings, and Happenings of this early period of his career. Having always enjoyed the medium, which he studied at the Boston Museum School and Ohio University, he was eager to make prints again and approached gallery director Martha Jackson for her support as publisher. Printmaker Andrew Stasik, a classmate of his from Ohio University, had recently joined the staff of the Pratt Graphic Art Workshop, so Dine naturally brought his project there. Working with printer Emiliano Sorini, he made *Car Crash I–V* and *End of the Crash*, which superficially appear to have been created in a spontaneous outburst of activity. Yet lithographs always take time, and these are masterfully controlled.

The crash to which the lithographs refer was an automobile accident in which a friend of the artist was killed.[1] Dine made a number of drawings and paintings that, like the prints, also appear to have been created in a frenzied state, communicating his emotional response to the death. Dine's preoccupation with this subject reached a fever pitch in *The Car Crash* Happening at the Reuben Gallery in New York in November 1960. During one part of the performance, Dine, who was dressed in a raincoat and shower cap that had been sprayed silver, uttered guttural noises and made drawings of cars. Recognizable at first, albeit with human features such as eyes and mouths, the cars became increasingly abstract the more rapidly he sketched them.[2]

The lithographs capture much of the cacophany of this Happening. Hyperkinetic lines race across the prints like car skids, suggesting uncontrollable speed. These markings come together with force in the black crosses, which could allude either to the Red Cross or to a cemetery. The palling whiteness of the sixth print, *End of the Crash*, provides a stark contrast to the noise and confusion of the previous images. The largest of the prints, it is also the first to employ color—in the form of the single red cross at the center. In addition to this simple image, the word *crash* appears again but printed more lightly and smaller than before, with three exclamation marks and a few stray scribbles. Otherwise, the blankness of this image is resounding.

As the art historian and critic John Russell points out in the first catalogue of Dine's graphic work, the Car Crash lithographs are unique among his prints in terms of both content and style.[3] The artist's debt to the Abstract Expressionists, clearly revealed in the expressive dynamism of these gestural images, has never entirely disappeared. But his subject matter has been largely replaced by more symbolic themes embodied in everyday objects from his immediate environment.

Dine's next series of prints, *These Are Ten Useful Objects Which No One Should Be Without When Traveling* (1961),[4] suggests the direction his mature work would take. These whimsical, hand-colored drypoints were made at Pratt shortly after the Car Crash lithographs, with printer Nono Reinhold. They picture a variety of objects—an apple, a doughnut, a tie—whose names are written directly beneath or atop the images. Dine often incorporated text into his paintings in the 1960s and continued to use words in his prints through the 1970s.

Several of the domestic motifs pictured in the Pratt drypoints would undergo further transformation in subsequent prints. In 1962, for instance, he began work at ULAE on a humorous series of etched ties, the first of many projects he would pursue there. As his graphic work became increasingly sophisticated, the objects he portrayed became vested with deeper personal meaning, conveying a wide range of emotions. Possessing an insatiable appetite for variety and experimentation, Dine has collaborated with a diversity of printers, including Chris Pater in London, Mitchell Friedman in Vermont, Aldo Crommelynck in Paris, Maurice Sanchez in New York, and Toby Michel in Los Angeles.

—E.A.

---

1. John Gordon, *Jim Dine*, exh. cat. (New York: Whitney Museum of American Art, 1970), unpaginated.

2. Michael Kirby, *Happenings* (New York: E. P. Dutton, 1965), p. 198.

3. In *Jim Dine: Complete Graphics* (Berlin: Galerie Mikro and London: Petersburg Press, 1970), unpaginated. Two catalogues raisonnés have subsequently been published: Thomas Krens, ed., *Jim Dine Prints: 1970–1977* (New York: Harper and Row in association with Williams College, 1977); and Ellen G. D'Oench and Jean E. Feinberg, *Jim Dine Prints: 1977–1985* (New York: Harper and Row, 1986).

4. These early prints are not documented in the Mikro-Petersburg catalogue, supra, note 3. Reproductions of the entire series do appear, however, in *Selected Prints II/Brooke Alexander, Inc.* (New York: Brooke Alexander, Inc., 1978), unpaginated.

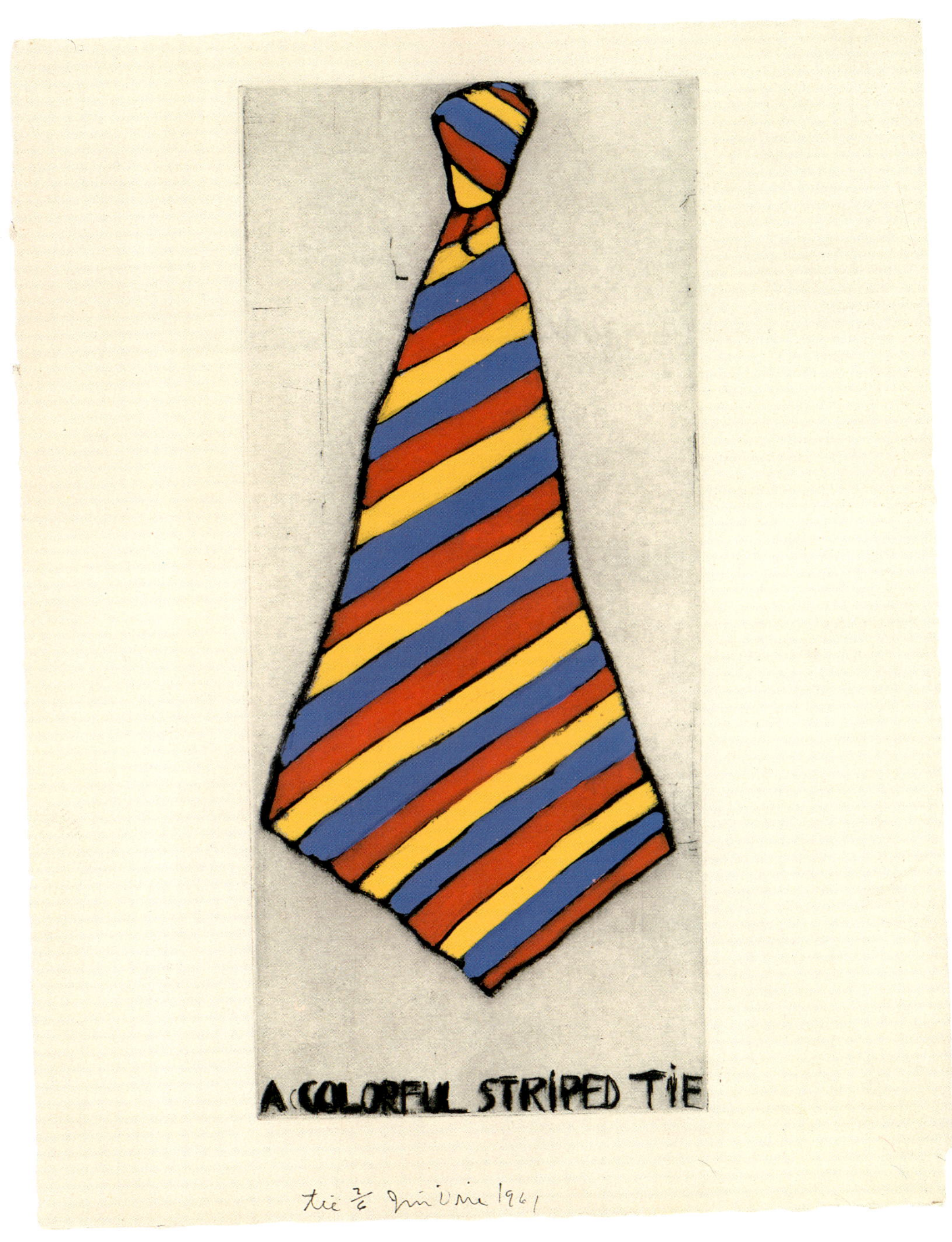

Jim Dine *Tie* 1961
drypoint (cat. no. 12)

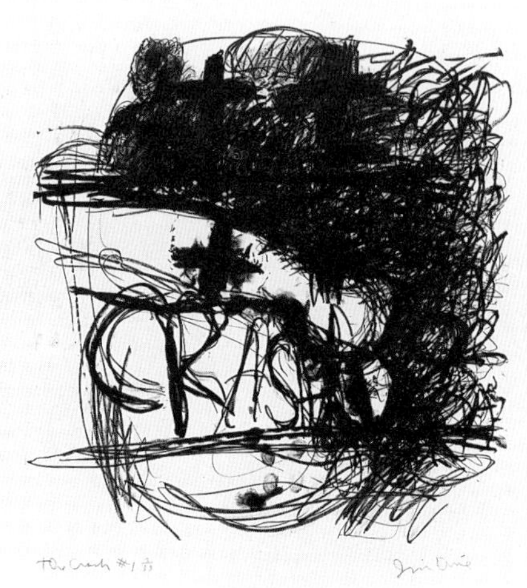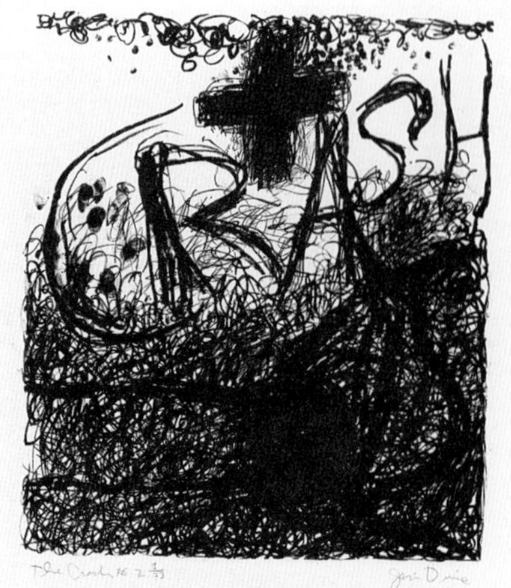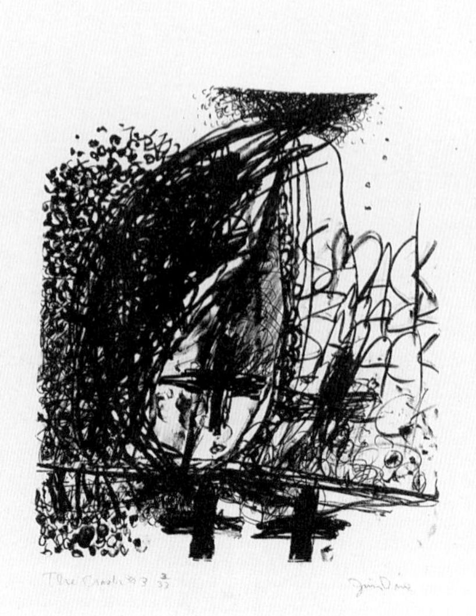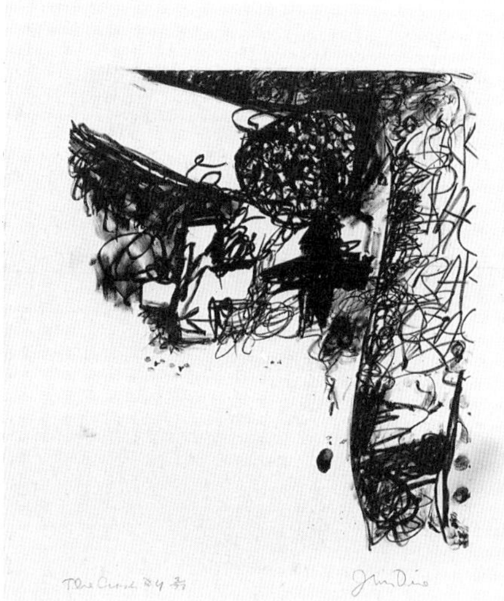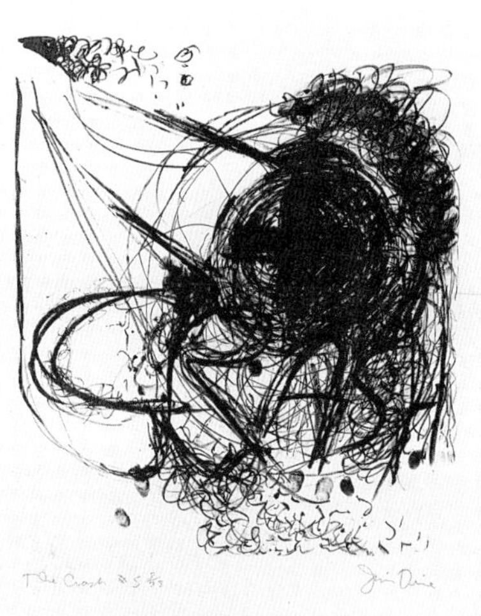

Jim Dine *Car Crash I–V* 1960
five lithographs (cat. no. 10)

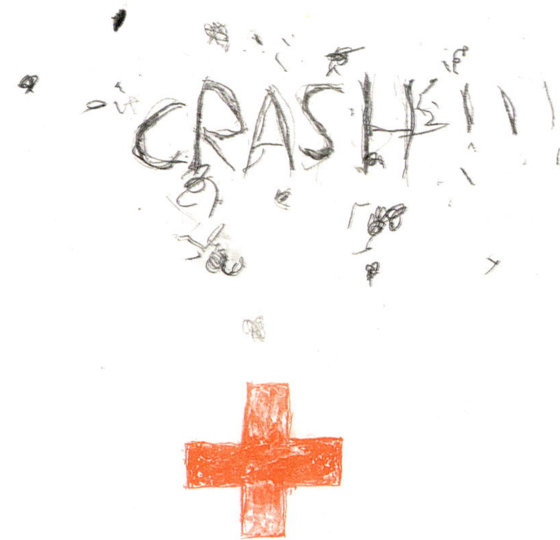

Jim Dine *End of the Crash* 1960
lithograph (cat. no. 11)

Claes Oldenburg

Claes Oldenburg moved to New York City from Chicago, where he had attended the School of the Art Institute, in 1956. Settling on the Lower East Side, he spent part of every day exploring the street life of his neighborhood, taking this environment as the theme of his art.[1] In 1960 he presented two exhibitions called *The Street*, which consisted of drawings and constructions made from wood fragments, newspaper, cardboard, garbage bags, and other discarded materials. Oldenburg's work at this time, as he described it, "takes on an 'ugliness' which is a mimicry of the scrawls and patterns of street graffiti. It celebrates irrationality, disconnection, violence and stunted expression—the damaged life forces of the city street."[2] A year later he wrote a statement that further clarified his position, declaring his belief in "an art that does something other than sit on its ass in a museum."[3]

Oldenburg made a point of working outside the traditional museum context. He began presenting Happenings in 1960, referring to these performances as a "poetry of everywhere," inhabited by people and props, that revolved around ordinary, everyday acts.[4] The Happenings functioned as workshops for exploring new forms and ideas. It was during this fertile period that Oldenburg made his first prints.[5]

Sometime during 1961 he was approached by Billy Klüver, who had participated in some of his Happenings, about making a print. Klüver, an engineer at Bell Telephone Laboratories and a free-lance curator, was assisting the Italian art dealer Arturo Schwarz with his ambitious publication *America Discovered*, a portfolio of prints by twenty American artists.[6] Schwarz was the first print publisher, in either Europe or America, to recognize the thematic similarities of a group of young Americans who dealt with consumer culture in their art. *America Discovered* was the fifth volume in an ambitious cycle entitled *The International Avant-Garde*, in which Schwarz attempted to give an overview of "what was happening all over the world in the field of the arts."[7]

Most of the artists in the *America Discovered* portfolio had not previously published prints. In Oldenburg's case, this was his first experience working directly on the printing plate. Lacking even rudimentary knowledge about the etching medium, he took the plate supplied by Klüver for this project to the Pratt Graphic Art Workshop, then one of the few fine-art print shops in New York City. Oldenburg decided to handle the etching plate like one of his cardboard pieces, cutting it into the shape of a sign he had seen on a movie marquee. He wanted to treat the print as a sculpture, and the plate itself must have looked like one of the scraps the artist found in forays around his neighborhood. The imprint of its irregular form, silhouetted against the blank background, emphasizes the work's feeling of dimensionality. The charred look and jagged edges of the printed image, *Orpheum Sign* (1961), with its jumbled placement of the letters O-R-P-H-E-U-M, closely related to Oldenburg's street drawings of this period, in which "the paper became a metaphor for the pavement, its walls (gutters and fences). I drew the materials found in the street."[8]

Oldenburg proofed the plate at Pratt and then sent it to Schwarz's printer, Georges Leblanc, in Paris. Sometime during this process, probably while in transit, the plate was badly scratched. Like a web of hairline fractures, the scratches are so small and so cover the plate that they almost look intentional. Oldenburg had printed his own edition of *Orpheum Sign* before the plate left Pratt, but it was the scratched version that ultimately appeared in the Schwarz portfolio.

—E.A.

---

1. See Gene Baro's introduction to *Claes Oldenburg: Drawings and Prints* (London and New York: Chelsea House, 1969), pp. 11–20.

2. Ibid., p. 15.

3. The complete version of this often-quoted statement first appeared in the exhibition catalogue *Environments, Situations, Spaces* (New York: Martha Jackson Gallery, 1961).

4. Ellen H. Johnson, *Claes Oldenburg* (Harmondsworth, England: Penguin, 1971), p. 20.

5. Between 1959 and 1961 Oldenburg made a number of monoprint posters for upcoming performances. (For one such example, see *Injun*, reproduced in Baro, op. cit., p. 85.) In 1960 he made a poster for the exhibition *New Media–New Forms I* at the Martha Jackson Gallery, which was used as an announcement to publicize the event (see Baro, op. cit., p. 70). Also that year he made several Ray Gun drawings on stencil paper that were mimeographed and distributed by the Judson Gallery. His first printmaking experience in which he worked directly on the plate, however, was with *Orpheum Sign*.

6. The other artists in the portfolio are: George Brecht, Allan D'Arcangelo, Jim Dine, Stephen Durkee, Lette Eisenhauer, Stanley Fisher, Sam Goodman, Red Grooms, Robert Indiana, Allan Kaprow, Roy Lichtenstein, Boris Lurie, James Rosenquist, George Segal, Richard Stankiewicz, Wayne Thiebaud, Andy Warhol, Robert Watts, and Robert Whitman.

7. Schwarz in correspondence with the author, 4 September 1987.

8. Quoted in Baro, op. cit., p. 15.

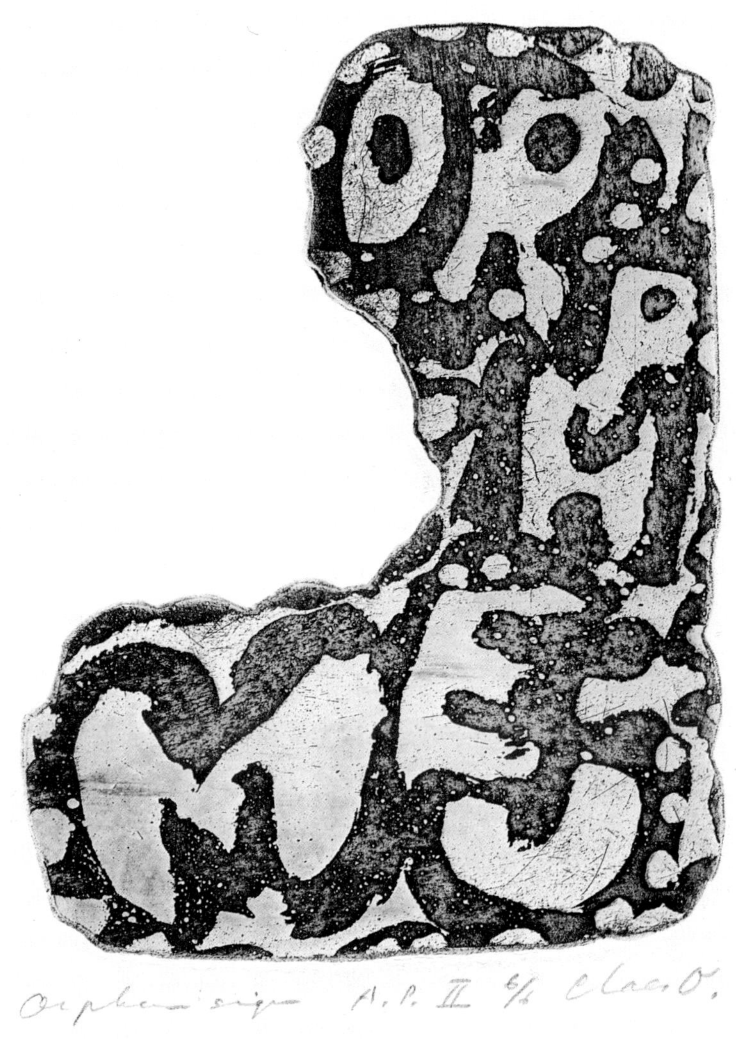

Claes Oldenburg *Orpheum Sign* 1961
etching, aquatint (cat. no. 13)

Roy Lichtenstein

In 1962 Roy Lichtenstein was invited to make an etching for *America Discovered*, a portfolio of prints by twenty American artists that would be published by Arturo Schwarz two years later. (See the Claes Oldenburg entry for a fuller description of this project.) The artists Schwarz selected struck him as being "the most representative of a certain American situation finally set free from Europe and authentically U.S."[1] It was his collaborator on the project, Billy Klüver, who suggested a number of names for the portfolio, including Lichtenstein's.

For most of the *America Discovered* artists, the portfolio represented one of their first experiences with printmaking. Lichtenstein, however, had made a number of prints on his own during the 1950s, working in etching, lithography, and especially woodcut. As early as 1951, in fact, he was awarded a Purchase Prize in the 5th National Print Annual Exhibition at the Brooklyn Museum for one of his earliest woodcuts, *To Battle* (1950).[2] Like this woodcut, his prints of the 1950s contain figurative images rendered in a whimsical, semiabstract style. Schwarz's invitation, though, provided Lichtenstein with his first opportunity to make a print in his signature Pop style.

He picked a fittingly Pop image—a light switch—for his *America Discovered* print, *On*. In choosing to elevate the banal to high art, the Pop artists had indeed "pulled a switch,"[3] and Lichtenstein, like many of the artists contributing to the Schwarz portfolio, focused on common objects in his art. The images of electric cords, soda fountains, and comic strip characters in his paintings of 1961 and 1962, derived from cartoons, newspaper ads, and even the Yellow Pages, astonished the prevailing avant-garde.

It was not only Lichtenstein's boldly appropriated subject matter that surprised critics but also his outright rejection of the predominant aesthetics of style. When compared with the gestural brushwork of the Abstract Expressionists, his deadpan objectivity struck some as nihilistic. *On*, with its startling simplicity, stood in direct contrast to the virtuoso manipulations of etching and lithography by major practitioners of the medium in the 1940s and 1950s. Also, in retrospect, *On* seems uncharacteristically "homemade" for a Lichtenstein print. Because the image was drawn directly onto the plate, the etching

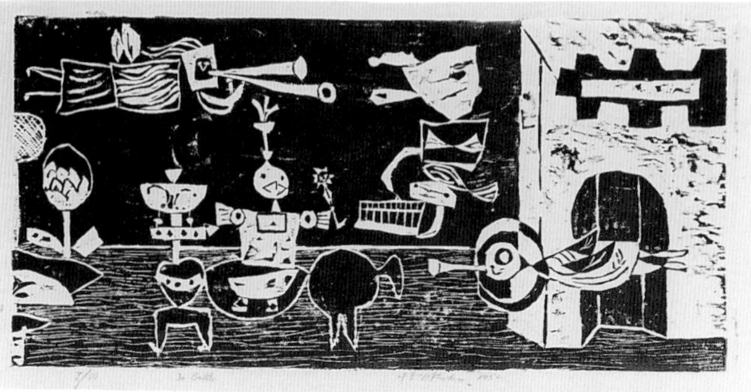

Roy Lichtenstein *To Battle* 1950
woodcut
edition: 10
11⅛ × 23⅜
The Brooklyn Museum, Museum Collection Fund

seems closer to a sketch than any of his other Pop prints. The artist was not really pleased with this effect, and in subsequent prints he employed lithography and screenprinting—media that generated the more mechanical look he sought.

Since 1962 Lichtenstein has made close to two hundred thirty prints. It was not until 1980, however, that he returned to intaglio. A series of eight etchings, made at Tyler Graphics Ltd. in 1980 and 1981, have a distinctly different feel from the hard-edged, intentionally commercial look of his prints of the 1960s and 1970s. The more recent etchings are also smaller and have a slightly irregular, handmade quality similar to the intimate, sketchlike feel of his first commissioned print.

—E.A.

1. Arturo Schwarz in correspondence with the author, 4 September 1987.

2. For more on this print, see James Watrous, *A Century of American Printmaking, 1880–1980* (Madison: University of Wisconsin Press, 1984), pp. 279–280.

3. Or so it seemed at the time to critics writing for such magazines as *Time, Newsweek,* and *Life.* See, for example, "Art" in *Time* 79 (11 May 1962), p. 52.

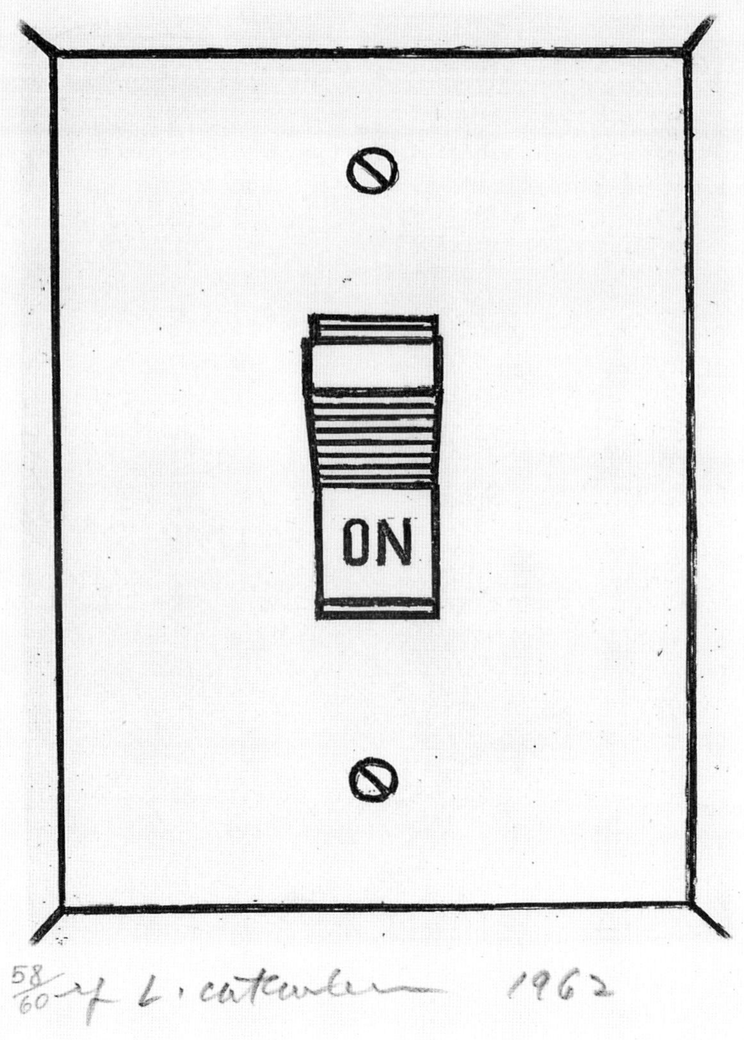

Roy Lichtenstein *On* 1962
etching (cat. no. 15)

James Rosenquist

In 1955, after several years of painting signs on grain elevators and gasoline tanks across the Upper Midwest, as well as outdoor advertisements in Minneapolis, James Rosenquist went to New York City to study at the Art Students League. During his early years there, he painted billboards during the day and worked on his own paintings at night. Capitalizing on his firsthand knowledge of commercial techniques, the young artist adeptly translated ordinary subjects, drawn from advertisements, newspapers, and magazines, into richly painted canvases. He frequently combined fragments of different images and made the relationship of those fragments the subject of his paintings. The enlarged scale and disjunctive treatment of such imagery in these paintings earned Rosenquist his first one-man exhibition at Richard Bellamy's Green Gallery in 1962 and the ambiguous label "Pop" artist.

That year Billy Klüver invited him to make a print for Arturo Schwarz's *America Discovered* portfolio. (See p. 34 for a description of this project.) Around this time he was passing through Minneapolis and stopped by the art department at the University of Minnesota, where he had once studied. Using their print facilities and a discarded photo-plate he had picked up at a local newspaper plant, he pulled the first proof for *Certificate* (1962), his contribution to the Schwarz portfolio. The work is a small photoengraving with etching that bears an intriguing relationship to Rosenquist's large paintings. Its fragmented quality and inclusion of random photographic elements evince his interest in how we see ordinary images when they are removed from their original context. The square photographic plate located on the right side of the sheet is dominated by the arms of a man leaning over a document of some kind. A nest of deeply etched hatchings surrounds this image, and a blanket of printed marks—nicks, scratches, and dots—subtly textures the rest of the sheet. By deliberately cropping the photograph and turning it upside down, he abstracts it and strips it of any symbolic meaning or narrative implication. Marcia Tucker's observation that Rosenquist "diverts our expectations of illusion by using the perceptual abstraction of a photograph to enforce the painted actuality of the canvas"[1] can readily be applied to this print.

In his introduction to the *America Discovered* portfolio, Klüver writes of Rosenquist's work in general that "the unrelatedness and the large scale of the images give us the incentive to discover the paintings."[2] With *Certificate*, it is the purely abstract surface and the intimate scale—so uncharacteristic of Rosenquist—that capture one's attention. It was only a matter of time before he started making prints whose scale was more closely related to that of the paintings. In 1965, on the advice of Jasper Johns, Rosenquist went to Long Island to make lithographs with Tatyana Grosman at ULAE. Despite his inexperience with lithography, he learned quickly and, within a year, produced four multicolored prints, each considerably larger than *Certificate*, that use airbrush and stencil to evoke the commercial look of his source material. Since then he has made a number of large-scale prints, including the twenty-two-foot-long *Horse Blinders* (1972), a four-part lithograph printed at Styria Studios in New York City.

—S.M.

---

1. Marcia Tucker, *James Rosenquist*, exh. cat. (New York: Whitney Museum of American Art, 1972). This publication includes a catalogue, prepared by Elke M. Solomon, of Rosenquist's graphics through 1972.

2. Billy Klüver, introduction to *The International Avant-Garde: America Discovered*, vol. 5 (Milan: Galleria Schwarz, 1964).

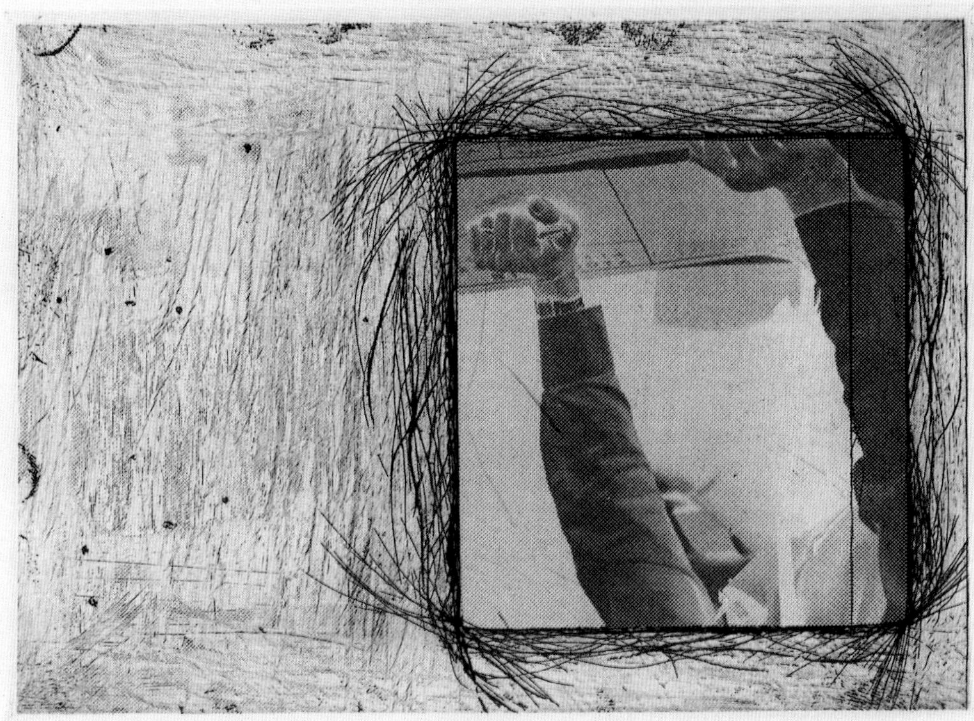

James Rosenquist *Certificate* 1962
photoengraving, etching (cat. no. 16)

Andy Warhol

born Pittsburgh, Pennsylvania   1928–1987

Andy Warhol's prints were vital in establishing his artistic identity and would prove to be a key element in his large oeuvre. In 1962 he began silkscreening images on top of acrylic backgrounds, finding this technique easier and more effective than painting by hand. "It was so simple—quick and chancy," he later wrote. "I was thrilled with it."[1] Further, silkscreening enabled the artist to relinquish his designs to assistants, who would execute the paintings for him. His many prints and paintings helped legitimize silkscreen and expanded the artistic possibilities of the process.

Warhol had become familiar with printing and publishing processes during the 1950s through his work as a commercial artist.[2] During this period he produced a series of self-published, sometimes self-printed, books on such sundry subjects as cats, cooking, and shoes. A burning desire to be famous, however, soon led him to abandon the blotted-line drawing technique and fanciful imagery that characterized this early work.

In 1960 he began transforming mass-produced images of American consumer goods into the painted icons that earned him the Pop artist label. He was particularly attracted to banal newspaper advertisements, which he reproduced in large-scale, black-and-white acrylic paintings such as *$199 Television* (1960) and *Storm Door* (1961). In concentrating on such products and images, he came closer than any other artist to epitomizing the advertisement-based aesthetic that was essential to Pop Art. His commitment to this aesthetic was exemplified by his decision to use silkscreen on his canvases because he liked the "assembly-line" effect.[3]

In light of all this, it is ironic that Warhol's first published print was not a silkscreen. Along with nineteen other artists, he was approached by Billy Klüver to contribute a print to Arturo Schwarz's *America Discovered* portfolio. (See p. 34 for a description of this project.) *Cooking Pot* (1962) is the only engraving Warhol ever made. It faithfully reproduces part of a newspaper advertisement for an enamel cooking pot, complete with the benday dots used in commercial printing to add shade and tint to images. It is possible that this image of the shiny bargain utensil led to his extraordinary silkscreen paintings of soup cans, made during the same year. Warhol signed his first edition with an embossed stamp of his signature, explaining, "I feel an artist's signature is part of style, and I don't believe in style."[4]

Warhol's first editioned screenprint, *$1.57 Giant Size* (1963),[5] was published by Klüver in conjunction with *The Popular Image Exhibition* of American artists, which he organized with Alice Denney, assistant director of the Washington Gallery of Modern Art, in 1963. Klüver and the artist printed *$1.57 Giant Size* on coated stock in four different colors in an edition of seventy-five. Unsigned, unnumbered copies were also made available. The screenprint served as the cover for a recording of interviews with the artists who participated in the exhibition.[6]

During the rest of his career, Warhol continued to appropriate mass-media imagery for both his paintings and his prints. When asked what distinguished his works in the two media, he once said, "I suppose you could call the paintings prints, but the material used for the paintings was canvas. The prints, if they were silkscreened by us, were always done on paper." He concluded, "Anyone can do them."[7]

—S.M.

---

1. Andy Warhol and Pat Hackett, *POPism: The Warhol 60's* (New York: Harcourt Brace Jovanovich, 1980), p. 22.

2. Warhol's career as a commercial artist is widely documented. See, for example, Carter Ratcliff, *Andy Warhol* (New York: Abbeville Press, 1983).

3. The artist quoted in Warhol and Hackett, op. cit., p. 22.

4. Quoted in Gerard Melanga, "A Conversation with Andy Warhol," *The Print Collector's Newsletter* 1 (January–February 1971), p. 127.

5. Art historian Roberta Bernstein notes that "among Warhol's earliest prints, including his first done in silkscreen, are small editions of five to eight prints on paper or plexiglas." Roberta Bernstein, "Warhol as Printmaker," in Frayda Feldman and Jörg Schellmann, eds., *Andy Warhol Prints: A Catalogue Raisonné* (New York: Abbeville Press, 1985), p. 15. Because these early works were hand-printed and never published, they are not included in the catalogue raisonné. For another overview of Warhol's graphic work through 1980, see Hermann Wünsche, *Andy Warhol: Das Graphische Werk, 1962–1980* (Bonn: Bonner Universitäts-Buchdruckerei, 1981). Although Warhol cooperated on both catalogues raisonnés, the information in them is not always consistent.

6. *The Popular Image Exhibition* was on view at the Washington Gallery of Modern Art, Washington, D.C., from April to June 1963. Those interviewed on the recording are: George Brecht, Jim Dine, Jasper Johns, Roy Lichtenstein, Claes Oldenburg, Robert Rauschenberg, James Rosenquist, Andy Warhol, Robert Watts, John Wesley, and Tom Wesselmann.

7. Melanga, op. cit., p. 126.

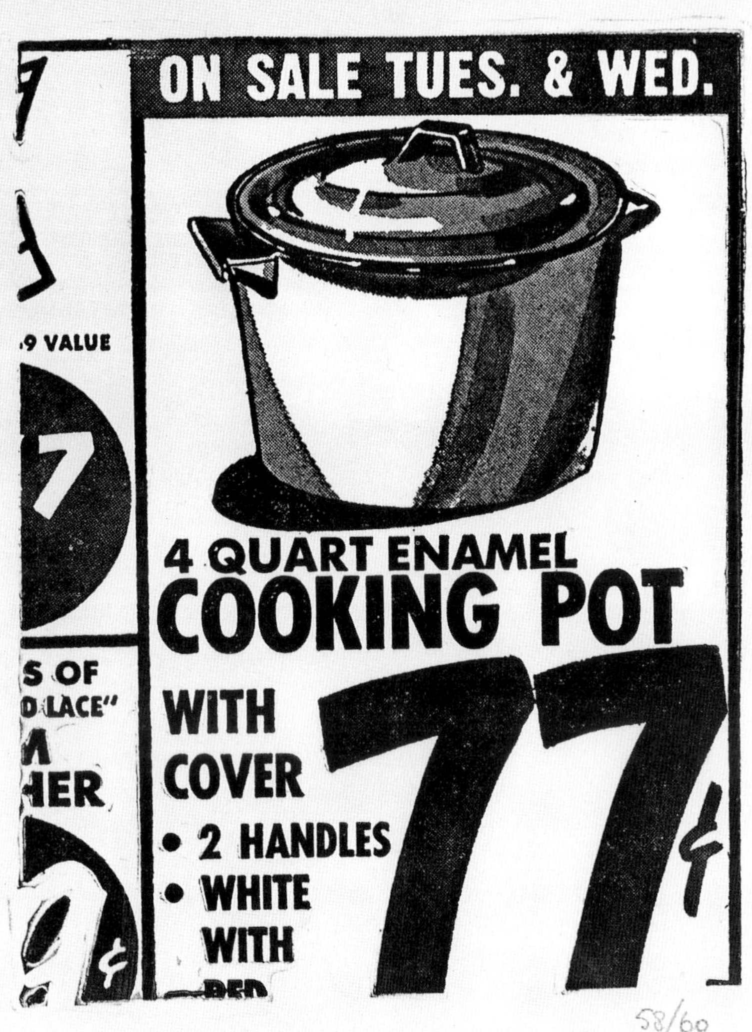

58/60

Andy Warhol *Cooking Pot* 1962
photoengraving (cat. no. 17)

Robert Rauschenberg

One of Robert Rauschenberg's earliest experiments with printmaking was a tire print he made in 1951 with the help of his friend John Cage. He cajoled the composer into driving his Model A Ford through a puddle of paint and onto a length of paper stretched out along a street. "He did a beautiful job," Rauschenberg later recalled, "but I consider it my print."[1] The large monoprint gave a foretaste of what was to become a preoccupation with seeking innovative ways to transfer images from life directly into works of art, no matter what the medium.[2]

Rauschenberg did not venture into print editioning until 1962, when he gave in to Tatyana Grosman's repeated requests that he work at ULAE. Although Grosman had already lured young artists of reputation, including Larry Rivers and Jasper Johns, to her lithography workshop on Long Island, she had been hesitant at first about inviting Rauschenberg. As she once explained it, "I really wanted to invite Rauschenberg first, but I was a little afraid that I might not be strong enough, that he would be too disruptive."[3] When she finally got up the nerve to call, she did so persistently. "Tanya called me so often," he later recalled, "that I figured the only way I could stop her was to go out there."[4]

Upon acceptance of her offer, Grosman delivered stones to Rauschenberg's studio. Shortly thereafter he embarked on his first print made at ULAE, *Abby's Bird*, published as part of a project commissioned for a new Hilton Hotel in New York.[5] The title refers to Abby Friedman, a friend of Rauschenberg and the wife of writer B. H. Friedman.[6] For the print Rauschenberg combined drawn and photographic imagery culled from everyday life, in much the same way that he used found objects in his freestanding constructions and "combine," or assemblage, paintings. The image of a red bird stands out from the other forms in the lithograph, which are printed in blue and black and include a door, a window, a policeman, and a football player. Dotted contours illusionistically pull the bird forward—a reminder of the artist's combine paintings of the 1950s in which stuffed birds were adhered to the surface.

Another project he had started for ULAE was to have been a collaboration with Jim Dine and Jean Tinguely. Although the print was never completed, his lithographic stone, which bore the tracing of a Coke bottle, served him for his second ULAE publication, *Merger* (1962). Earlier this American trademark had appeared in his freestanding combine *Coca Cola Plan* (1958) and in his combine painting *Curfew* (1958), two works that epitomize the artist's insistence on seeing ordinary commercial products as cultural icons. But perhaps more significant in *Merger* than the Coke bottle was the inclusion of an image of the astronaut John Glenn (who that year had become a national hero as the first American to orbit the earth), taken from the printer's mat for a newspaper ad. Rauschenberg had salvaged this image, along with an assortment of discarded printer's plates and mats, from the composing room of *The New York Times*.

The use of these plates, which he impressed directly onto his stones at ULAE, was just one part of his ongoing exploration of both the limitations and undiscovered possibilities of lithography. In his next print, *Urban* (1962; cat. no. 20), for example, Rauschenberg transferred the impression of a leaf to the stone. The complex collage of imagery here comments on America's fascination with outer space, President John F. Kennedy, and baseball. It was the first print in which he made extensive use of the printer's plates and mats, inventively turning them sideways and upside down. He marked and obscured each picture by rubbing or liberally drawing over it with tusche or by collaging it under another, unrelated image. Rauschenberg's mingling of recognizable images in *Urban* relates the print to his combine and collage paintings of the late 1950s and early 1960s.

During 1962 Rauschenberg accompanied curator Henry Geldzahler on a visit to Andy Warhol's studio.[7] Seeing how Warhol was using silkscreen in his paintings, Rauschenberg began to employ this medium as well. Taking his naturally inventive approach to printmaking, he began to experiment with screenprinting in his lithographs—pressing tusche directly through photoscreens onto the stones. He also used screenprinting in his paintings; because it replaced the three-dimensional objects he had been using, the appearance of this technique marked a significant change in his work.

—S.M.

Robert Rauschenberg *Abby's Bird* 1962
lithograph (cat. no. 18)

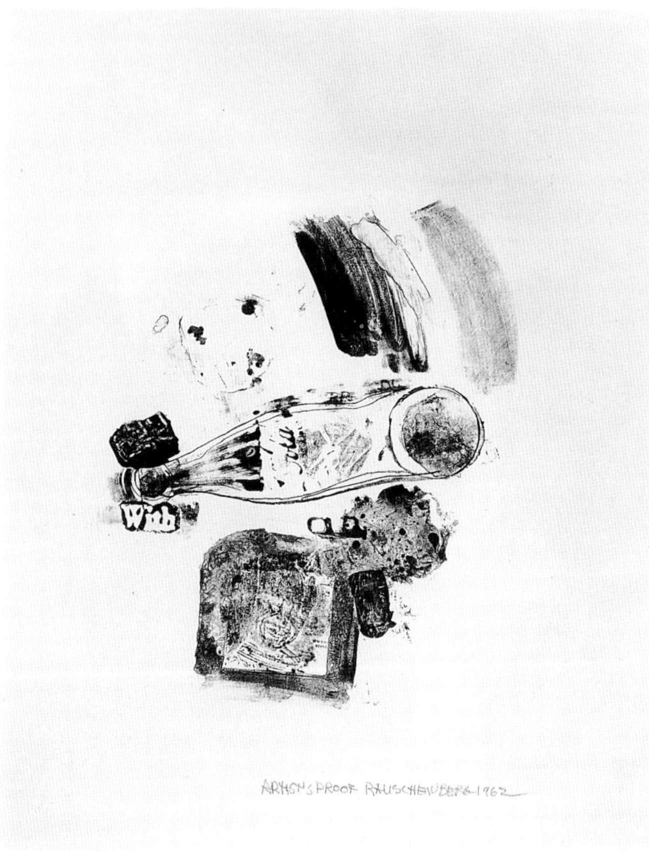

Robert Rauschenberg *Merger* 1962
lithograph (cat. no. 19)

1. Quoted in Dorothy G. Seekler, "The Artist Speaks: Robert Rauschenberg," *Art in America* 54 (May–June 1966), p. 81.

2. Around 1948, while studying with Josef Albers at Black Mountain College in North Carolina, Rauschenberg had produced a series of woodcuts. He also produced printed pictures on blueprint paper by exposing objects laid on the paper to direct light. These unpublished prints are included in two sources on his graphic work. See Edward A. Foster, *Robert Rauschenberg: Prints, 1948/1970,* exh. cat. (Minneapolis Institute of Arts, 1970); and Lawrence Alloway, *Rauschenberg: Graphic Art,* exh. cat. (Philadelphia: Institute of Contemporary Art, University of Pennsylvania, 1970).

3. Quoted in Calvin Tompkins, "Profiles: The Moods of a Stone," *The New Yorker* 52 (7 June 1976), p. 62.

4. Ibid., p. 66.

5. In 1961 Ruder and Finn, a public relations firm working for the hotel chain, had asked Grosman to commission artists to make original prints to be hung in the rooms of a Hilton being built at Rockefeller Center. (This information is taken, with permission, from Esther Sparks' manuscript for *Universal Limited Art Editions: A History and Catalogue, the First Twenty-five Years* [New York: Harry N. Abrams Publishers in association with the Art Institute of Chicago, forthcoming 1989]).

6. In his book *School of New York: Some Younger Artists* (New York: Grove Press, 1959) and in several articles, Friedman supported the new generation of American artists, which included Rauschenberg. Friedman was also vice president of the Uris Buildings Corporation, a partner in the Hilton construction project, and served on the five-man art-acquisition committee for the Hilton art program. For information on this program, see B. H. Friedman, "Art for the New York Hilton," *Craft Horizon* 23 (July–August 1963), pp. 8–13, 43–44.

7. See Reba and Dave Williams, "The Later History of the Screenprint," *Print Quarterly* 4 (December 1987), p. 398. For Warhol's account of this visit, see Andy Warhol and Pat Hackett, *POPism: The Warhol 60's* (New York: Harcourt Brace Jovanovich, 1980), pp. 22–23.

Edward Ruscha born Omaha, Nebraska   1937

Like many other Pop artists, Edward Ruscha had a background in commercial graphic design. After graduating from Chouinard Art Institute in Los Angeles in 1960, he worked at an advertising agency, set type for a printer of art catalogues, and did layout design for the magazine *Artforum*, then based in southern California. These early work experiences stimulated Ruscha's interest in combining image and text, and, in 1962, he began work on what would develop into a series of self-published offset books.

Ruscha started the series with an unpretentious paperback entitled *Twentysix Gasoline Stations*. Composed of twenty-six photographs he took of service stations along Route 66, it records the drive between Oklahoma—where he grew up—and California and provides early evidence of his abiding fascination with vernacular architecture. The text, like a list poem, consists simply of the name and location of each station: *Standard*, Amarillo, Texas; *Beeline Gas*, Holbrook, Arizona; *Texaco*, Jackrabbit, Arizona; *Union*, Needles, California; and so on. On the cover he used only the title, reflecting his great appreciation of typography. It was a format he would employ throughout his book series, which, in the 1960s, included *Various Small Fires* (1964), *Some Los Angeles Apartments* (1965), *Royal Road Test* (1967), *Thirtyfour Parking Lots in Los Angeles* (1967), and *Nine Swimming Pools and a Broken Glass* (1968). He was to make use of many of these in a 1970 series of prints entitled *Book Covers*.

Ruscha's paperback editions, which were unsigned, precipitated a new art form, and he has since been credited with "showing that the book could be a primary vehicle for art."[1] In contrast to the lavish tradition of limited-edition illustrated books, his publications, printed cheaply and in large runs, constituted an underground enterprise.[2] In part due to Ruscha's sustained involvement, such books became a valid art form, available in bookstores and galleries; by the late 1960s, a significant number of artists had incorporated books into their art-making activity.

Ruscha's interest in words, which continues in his current work, is evident not only in his books of the 1960s but also in his paintings from that decade. In these works he combined commercial imagery, such as advertised food products and corporate logos, with typography—blown up into emblematic, tongue-in-cheek landscapes. The importance of words in his imagery is also evident in several unpublished lithographs that he made in 1962, including *3327 Division (Soap)* and *3327*

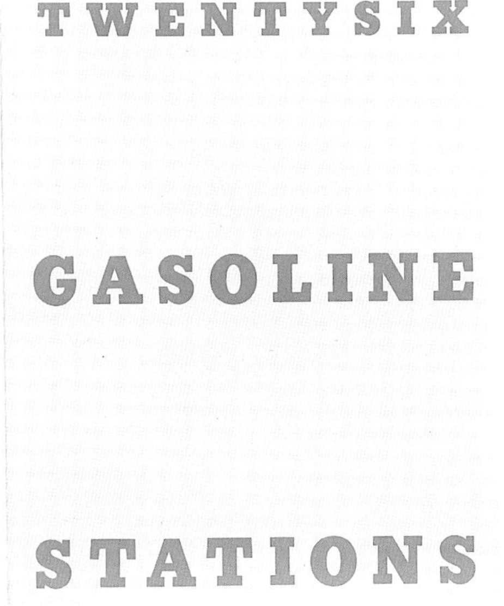

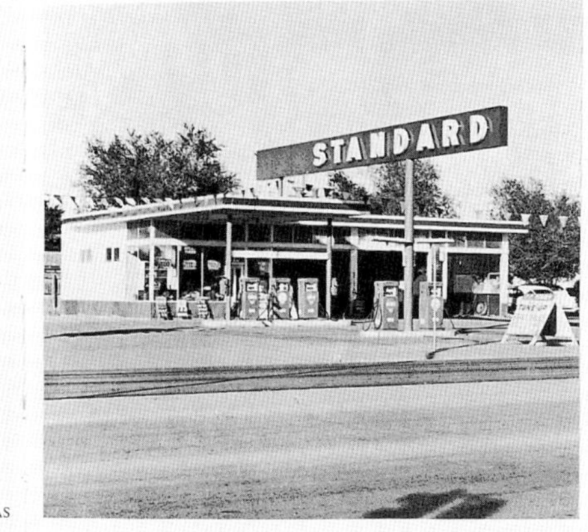

Edward Ruscha *Twentysix Gasoline Stations* 1962
book of twenty-six offset photographs (cat. no. 21)

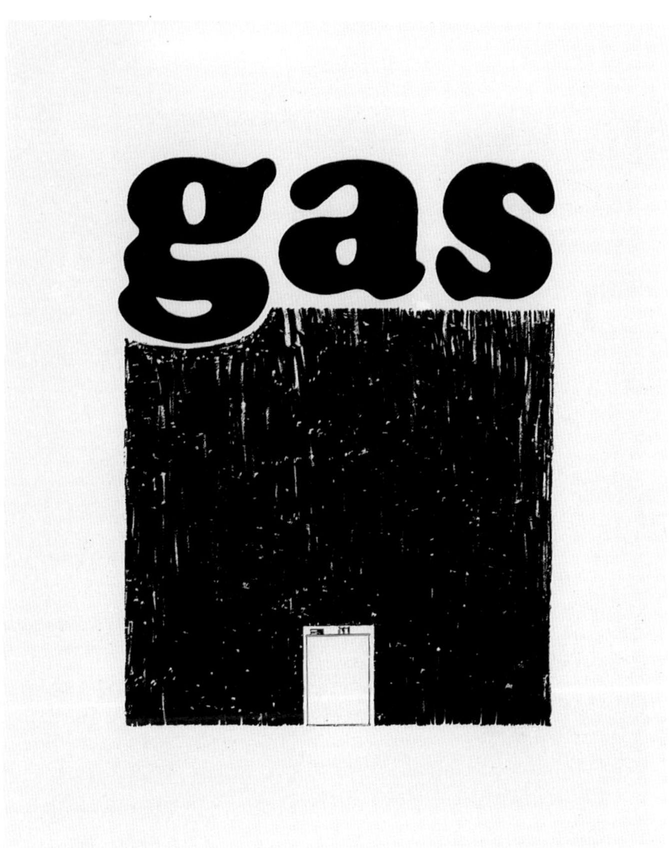

Edward Ruscha *Gas* 1962
lithograph (cat. no. 22)

Division ('39 Ford). The printed montages in these two
lithographs, in which Ruscha inserted such familiar
images as the Lux soap wrapper, the Sunmaid Raisin Girl,
and a 1939 Ford (which he owned then and still has), are
similar to his collagelike compositions of the early 1960s.
In a third print, *Gas*, the three letters of the title loom
over the rest of the image, dwarfing the drawing of a gas
can below, which is surrounded by a curtain of black
ink. Ruscha made these prints with Joe Funk at Kanthos
Press, a tiny Los Angeles shop next door to Tamarind
Lithography Workshop that did custom printing but did
not publish.

The first print on which Ruscha collaborated with a
publisher was *Standard Station* (1966). Art collector
Audrey Sabol, who commissioned the print, was a
newcomer to the publishing business whose introduction
to Ruscha's work was through *Twentysix Gasoline
Stations*.[3] The small book, she says, "floored me. . . . It's
hard to explain the impact of such a work, especially after
Abstract Expressionism."[4] Indeed, its straightforward
simplicity was quite original. When Sabol made a visit to
Ruscha's studio, she saw his painting *Standard Station,
Amarillo, Texas* (1963) and suggested he make it into a
print. Interestingly enough, images from *Twentysix
Gasoline Stations* served as source material for both
Ruscha's *Standard Station* painting and the related print.

Sabol left the execution of the print up to Ruscha,
who wisely chose to use screenprint in adapting the
image. The medium's ability to convey bright, unmodulated colors and sharp focus was well suited to the artist's
simplified geometric forms and clean lines; also, he had
studied screenprinting in school. Instead of depicting the
attenuated gasoline station at night, as he did in the
painting, Ruscha placed it against an apocalyptic (or
smog-ridden) sky of blues and oranges. This was achieved
through the use of a "split fountain," a technique of
blending ink to create a rainbow effect. Originally created
for commercial printing—the split fountain had been used
in commercial lithographic and screenprinting shops for
many years—this was one of the first examples of its
adaptation to fine-art printing. As the art historian Riva
Castleman has pointed out, the garish rainbow effect used
by Ruscha in this print was so often imitated that, by the
late 1960s, it had become a cliché of fine-art printmaking.[5]

—E.A.

1. Clive Phillpot, "Some American Artists and Their Books," in *Artists'
Books: A Critical Anthology and Sourcebook*, ed. Joan Lyons (Layton,
Utah: Gibbs M. Smith, Peregrine Smith Books and Rochester, N.Y.:
Visual Studies Workshop Press, 1985), p. 97.

2. In 1963 *Twentysix Gasoline Stations* sold for around four dollars. Its
first run was 400, and it was subsequently reprinted in editions of 500
(1967) and 3,000 (1969).

3. Sabol, an art collector from Villanova, Pennsylvania, commissioned a
number of innovative multiples and prints over the next eight years from
a variety of artists, including Roy Lichtenstein and Marisol.

4. Sabol in a conversation with the author, 26 April 1988.

5. See Riva Castleman, *American Impressions* (New York: Alfred A.
Knopf, 1985), p. 72.

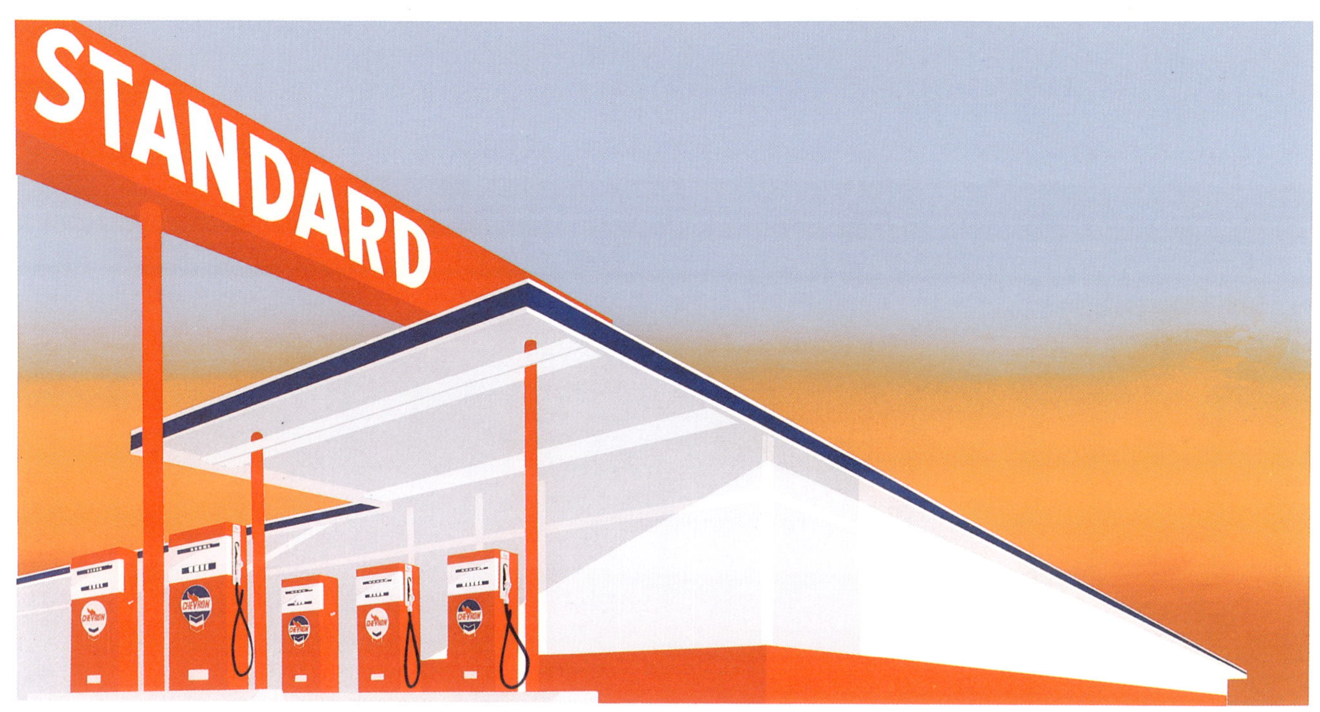

Edward Ruscha *Standard Station* 1966
screenprint (cat. no. 23)

Ellsworth Kelly

While living in Paris during the 1950s, Ellsworth Kelly developed a unique nonobjective painting style, which in a decade came to serve as a paradigm of Post-Painterly Abstraction in America. His flat, hard-edged forms are abstractions of things he has seen, such as shadows, architectural details, and, especially, plants. He translates fragments of nature into simplified shapes—the dominant subject of his art. As Kelly distills his visual sources, he strips away all volume, texture, and natural color until a pure configuration is obtained. To this configuration he often adds one or two highly saturated colors.

In 1963 Samuel Wagstaff, Jr., then curator at the Wadsworth Atheneum in Hartford, Connecticut, invited his friend Kelly to contribute a print to a portfolio entitled *Ten Works by Ten Painters*.[1] Although Kelly had experimented with lithography while studying at the Ecole des Beaux-Arts in Paris, this invitation provided him with his first opportunity to edition professionally.[2] The resulting bold screenprint, *Red/Blue* (1964), is quintessential Kelly. An oblong red shape juts from the lower-left corner into a sea of solid blue, only to be abruptly stopped by the right edge. The round red curve abutting the straight edge creates a lateral tension and eliminates any perception of depth.

Red/Blue is deceptively simple in appearance. In fact, it derived from numerous pencil-and-ink drawings and collages on which Kelly had also based the large-scale painting *Red Blue* (1964).[3] For the screenprint, he submitted a collage that was made into two screens from hand-cut stencils at Scirocco Screenprinters, under the supervision of Ives-Sillman, Inc., a New Haven publishing firm. In addition to the red-and-blue collage, he submitted a variation on the same motif in yellow and blue, as in the painting *Yellow Blue* (1963). After proofing, however, Kelly rejected this color scheme in favor of the more assertive arrangement.

Earlier in the year he had approached Tatyana Grosman about the possibility of making prints at ULAE. He presented his idea for a series of prints that would show color variations on some of the basic forms he had used in his paintings of the previous decade. Preconceived and leaving little room for improvisation, this proposal did not sit well with Grosman, whose notion was that a lithograph ought to be the unique product of an artist's spontaneous dealings with the stone.[4] Because of this incompatibility, Kelly initiated a collaboration with Maeght Editeur, a Parisian firm with which he had worked several times on posters and magazine illustrations.[5]

Printed by Marcel Durassier at Imprimerie Maeght, in the Paris suburb of Levallois-Perret, the *Suite of Twenty-seven Color Lithographs* (1964–1965) became the first of Kelly's many serial printmaking projects. As he had planned, these colorful abstract images reintroduce earlier forms, studied in sequential relationship to one another.

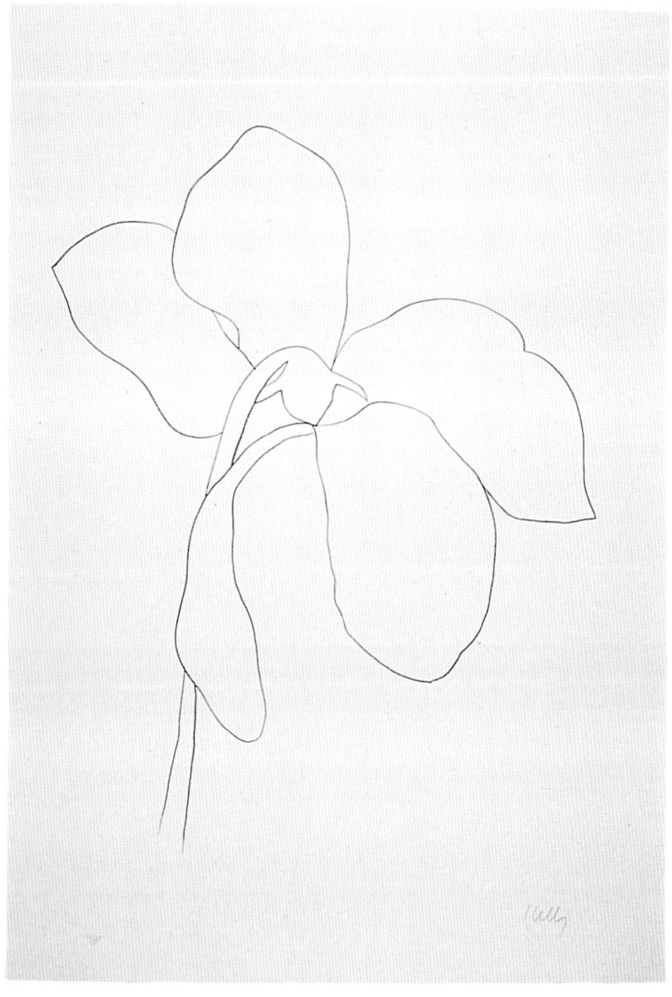

Ellsworth Kelly *Cyclamen III* 1964–1965
transfer lithograph (cat. no. 27)

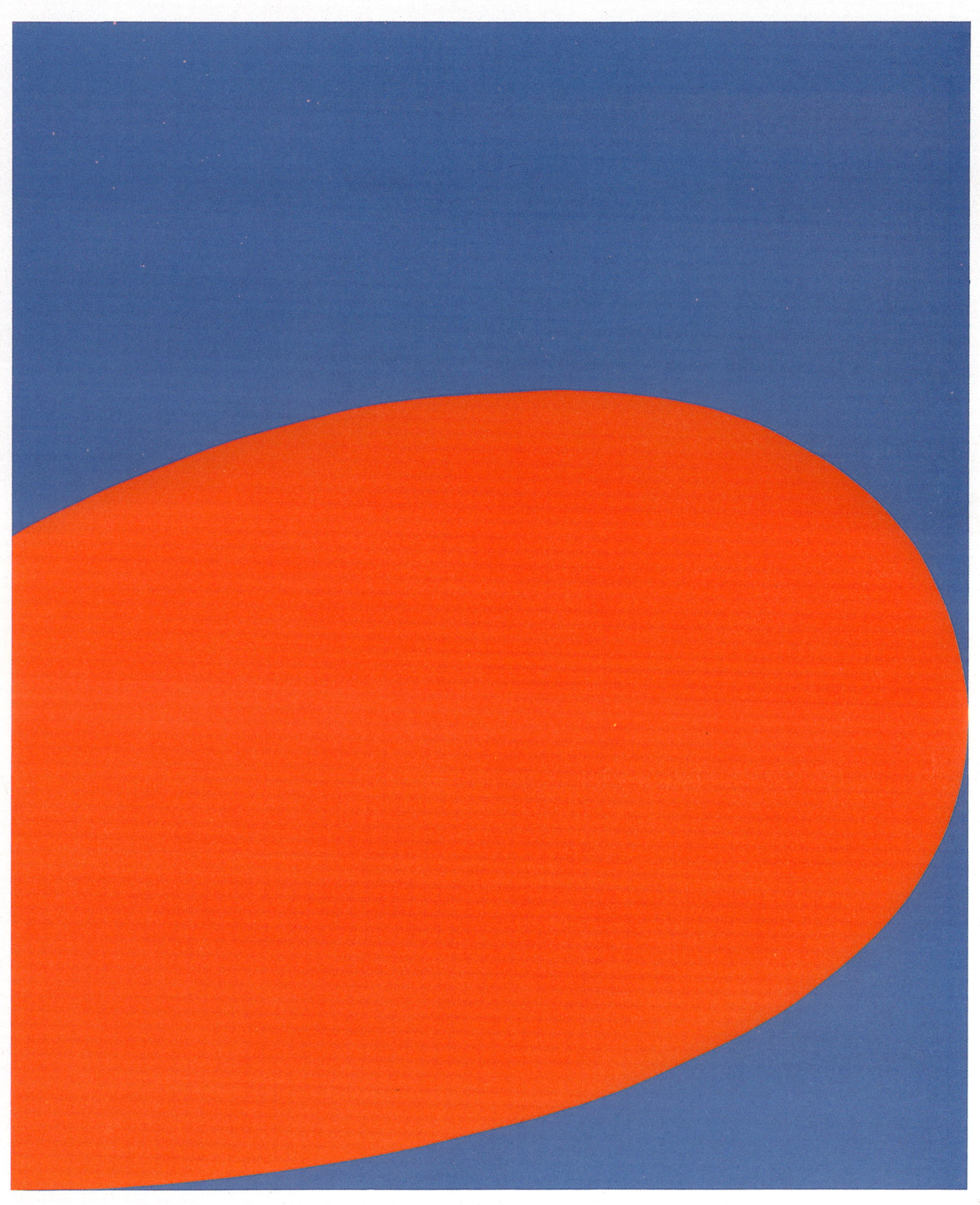

Ellsworth Kelly *Red/Blue* 1964
screenprint (cat. no. 24)

At this time he also began work on the *Suite of Plant Lithographs* (1964–1966). The first twelve images in this series of twenty-eight transfer lithographs were printed at Imprimerie Maeght by early 1965; the next sixteen, printed at Imprimerie Arte in Paris, were not ready for release until 1966.[6] The elegant lines and minimal forms of the *Plant Lithographs* reveal Kelly's reliance on natural sources as the inspiration for his bold abstractions.

—S.M.

1. The other artists included in this portfolio, published in 1964, are: Stuart Davis, Robert Indiana, Roy Lichtenstein, Robert Motherwell, George Ortman, Larry Poons, Ad Reinhardt, Frank Stella, and Andy Warhol.

2. In 1949, while at the Ecole des Beaux-Arts, Kelly made *Untitled,* using the school's printing facilities. The small, sixteen-print edition comprises various states. For a complete chronology of Kelly's printmaking activity, see Richard H. Axsom, *The Prints of Ellsworth Kelly: A Catalogue Raisonné, 1949–1985* (New York: Hudson Hills Press in association with the American Federation of Arts, 1987); and Diane Waldman, *Ellsworth Kelly: Drawings, Collages, Prints* (Greenwich, Conn.: New York Graphic Society, 1971).

3. Kelly develops his ideas for projects in numerous drawings and collages, which he keeps and often returns to for inspiration on other projects. See Diane Upright, *Ellsworth Kelly: Works on Paper* (New York: Harry N. Abrams Publishers in association with the Fort Worth Art Museum, 1987).

4. Axsom, op. cit., p. 18.

5. Prior to this project Kelly had exhibited at Galerie Maeght in Paris. The posters and magazine illustrations, on which he worked with Aimé and Marguerite Maeght, are illustrated in the appendix of Axsom, op. cit., pp. 173–186.

6. Ibid., p. 54.

Alex Katz

During the 1950s, when abstraction was the dominant theme in American art, Alex Katz insisted on painting representational subjects drawn from firsthand observation. In large paintings, and later in collages and painted-wood cutouts, he made highly stylized depictions of his friends and family, marked by broad areas of vivid color that reduced his sitters to their most prominent features. By minimizing modeling and gestural brushwork, he emphasized both the visual and the emotional aspects of color. Although primarily a portrait painter, Katz also produced numerous landscape pictures that similarly relied on bold shapes and patterns.

In 1965 artist and printmaker Steve Poleskie, then affiliated with Chiron Press in New York City, invited Katz to make a screenprint there for inclusion in a portfolio of work by emerging artists. Prior to this Katz had had some exposure to printmaking. In 1947 and 1948, while attending classes at Cooper Union in New York, he made two drypoint engravings under the instruction of printer Robert Blackburn. Between 1951 and 1955 Katz independently made one woodcut and eight linoleum prints from stencils, which he says were "about using concrete color. They weren't really about printmaking."[1] The cut-out forms of his collages developed out of these early experiments with printmaking.

Although Katz made no more prints for nearly ten years, he did keep an eye on what other artists were doing in the medium. He acknowledges the importance of Andy Warhol's and Jasper Johns' contributions, noting of the latter, "He's a person you had to think about if you thought about making prints seriously."[2] By the mid-1960s, with much printmaking going on around him, Katz decided that he would make prints as a means of clarifying his images in other media. He was interested in the replicability of prints, in the idea that a single image could be made available to a wider public without compromising its vitality. "Reproductions, the four color kind you buy in museum shops," he later explained, "have nothing to do with the real thing. They don't give you any of the energy of the real thing. So I was trying to figure a way to make a reproduction that felt like the real thing but was in another medium."[3]

He based the first screenprint,[4] *Luna Park* (1965), published by the Fischbach Gallery in New York, on a painting of the same name made in 1960. Its size almost

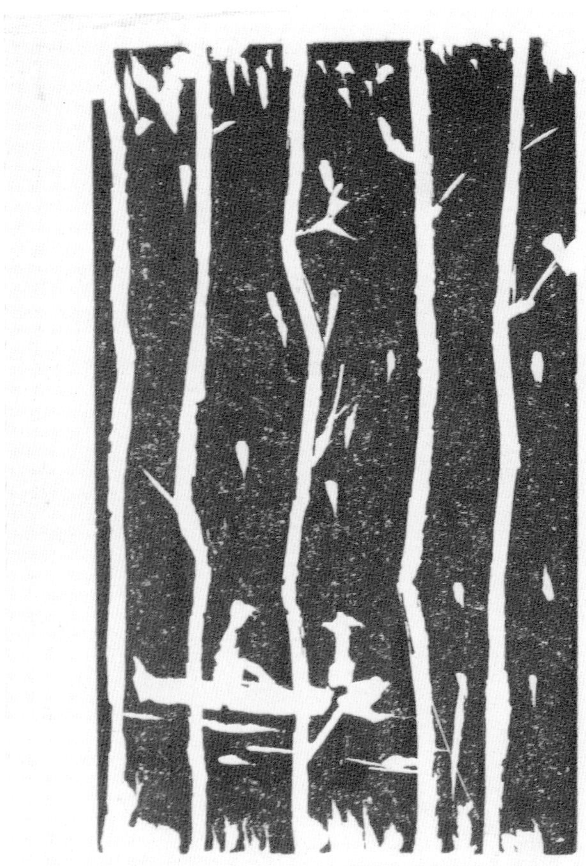

Alex Katz *Maine Landscape* 1951
linoleum cut
edition: approx. 200
4⅞ × 2⅞
Collection the artist

exactly replicates that of the painting, being but an inch narrower. The simple image of the moon behind two trees reflected on a body of water, which shows the influence of Edvard Munch's painting *The Voice* (1893), lent itself to reduction. He considered it a challenge to reduce the painting's nearly three hundred tones to five or six.

The major difference between the *Luna Park* painting and its corresponding screenprint is the lack in the latter of tonal modulation. Expansive areas of flat opaque color, inherent in screenprinting, draw attention to the geometry of the composition. Only the edges of the forms give evidence of the artist's hand. Katz attempted to achieve this autographic quality by hand-painting with tusche on

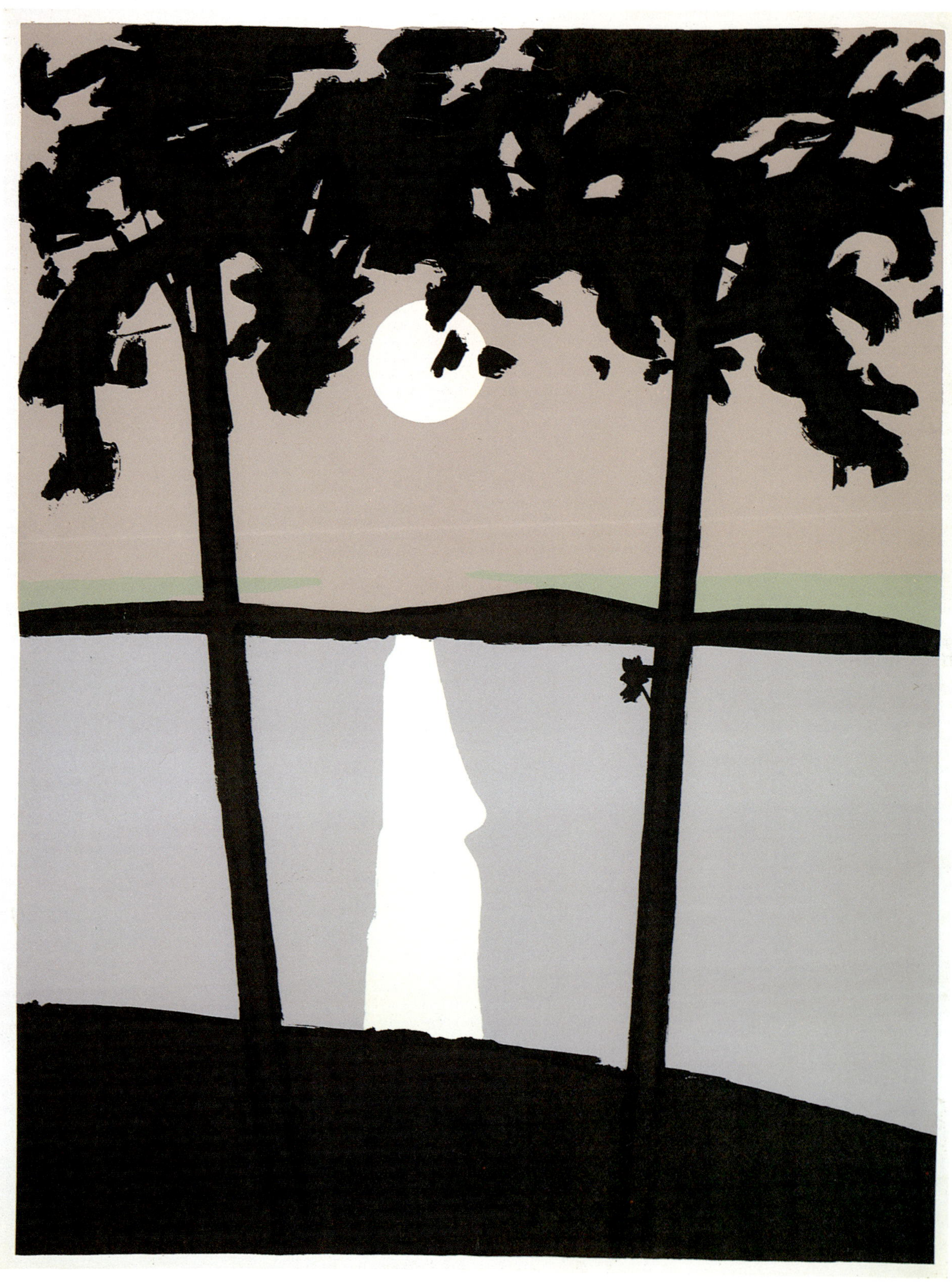

Alex Katz *Luna Park* 1965
screenprint (cat. no. 28)

each of six screens.[5] He was also deeply involved in mixing the colors for the print. He subsequently recalled that at one point, when he insisted on blending thirty grays in order to get just the right one, he grew concerned that he might be wasting Poleskie's time and money. But he found that "Steve was just delighted that an artist really cared that much. He was very enthused."[6] Eight years later he returned to Chiron to improve *Luna Park*, which he still felt did not accurately capture the color of the painting.[7]

Katz decided early that he would do something different every time he made a print. To this end, he has tried his hand at nearly every print medium, including lithography, offset lithography, drypoint, soft-ground etching, and woodcut. Many eminent printers have collaborated with him over the past two decades—Aldo Crommelynck, Hiroshi Kawanishi, and Chip Elwell among them. Experience has led Katz to maintain that his prints are intended as the final syntheses of his paintings.[8]

—S.M.

1. The artist in an interview with Barry Walker, in Barry Walker, *Alex Katz: A Print Retrospective*, exh. cat. (New York: Brooklyn Museum and Skira, Inc., 1987), p. 12.

2. Ibid., p. 14.

3. Ibid., p. 13.

4. Prior to *Luna Park*, Katz had worked on another print with Steve Poleskie, which he refers to as "a botch." See the artist in a discussion with Jacqueline Brody and others, in "New Prints of Worth: A Question of Taste," *The Print Collector's Newsletter* 10 (September–October 1979), p. 115.

5. The artist in correspondence with Elizabeth Armstrong, 4 January 1988.

6. The artist in an interview with Carter Ratcliff, in Nicholas P. Maravell, *Alex Katz: The Complete Prints* (New York: Alpine Fine Arts Collection, Ltd., 1983), p. 11.

7. *Luna Park II* (1973) was printed by Larry Rosen at Chiron Press and copublished by Brooke Alexander, Inc., New York, and Marlborough Graphics, Inc., New York. For an illustration, see Maravell, op. cit., cat. no. 67, n.p.

8. Katz-Walker interview, op. cit., p. 17.

Bruce Conner

By the early 1960s Bruce Conner had established his reputation as an assemblage artist with his disturbing collages formed from shredded stockings, women's undergarments, and junk jewelry, among other materials. At the same time he added another dimension to his oeuvre with a string of underground films. During the mid-1960s he made a large body of drawings, primarily with felt-tip pens, that reflected a variety of sources, including the concentric patterns found in nature, folk art, and wood engravings. In some of his drawings, he also wove intricate designs of lines and dots that bear a resemblance to fingerprint markings. Many of his first published prints were related closely, if not directly, to these drawings.

Conner's first intensive contact with the graphic media came in a rather stormy residency at June Wayne's Tamarind Lithography Workshop in Los Angeles in 1965. It is inappropriate to fix upon any one of the fourteen lithographs he made there, since they are only telling when taken as a group. For he experimented with a broad range of approaches to produce a variety of abstract compositions and semiabstract images of such subjects as rainstorms, jellyfish, and flowers. *Mandala*, the first lithograph he began at Tamarind and the fourth he completed there, is much more controlled than the others. In it, a labyrinthine complex of marks, printed in black and transparent orange, forms a calculated image of a circle divided into sections, each bearing symmetrical configurations of smaller circles.

The first two finished lithographs, both untitled, represent the polarities in the artist's approaches to the medium; one is a labored and tightly locked maze of marks, the other a spontaneous splashed-and-dripped entity. The fifth lithograph, *Rain* (cat. no. 31), eloquently records Conner's perceptions of Los Angeles, where it rained practically nonstop during his stay. He described the process of creating this print as a satisfying progression of additions:

> I started on the stone by taking tusche and water and solvent and standing up above the stone and just raining down. Then I started drawing over it with a pen, very intricate designs all over the thing and then working with a crayon on top of that, working with the pen on top of that and then finally everything became very, very dark. . . . My physical involvement with the rain was being acted out on the stone and then it became this landscape of clouds and rain.[1]

Though by no means ordinary, these lithographs fulfilled Tamarind's mission to produce technically perfected prints. But then there were the *other* prints. Little did June Wayne, who had invited Conner to Tamarind, guess that he would come in and challenge some of the workshop's basic precepts. When he arrived, Wayne was in Europe; she had left her associate Cal Goodman in charge. After the artist had been there only two weeks, Goodman became concerned about the aesthetic validity of several lithographs on which Conner was working and particularly about his refusal to sign his prints. Owing to what was then his artistic philosophy, Conner had not signed any of his work for over three years and had no intention of signing the Tamarind prints. Goodman argued that the works would be worth nothing but the cost of their materials without the artist's signature. In response to this traditional viewpoint, Conner proceeded to "sign" all of his prints with his thumbprint, which he felt was more autographic and certainly less forgeable than a signature. According to Conner, this annoyed Goodman even more. He remembers that "they were mortally offended that I was signing these things with my thumbprints—they considered it an assault, that I was doing this purposely to intimidate them."[2]

Goodman was further provoked by the artist's insistence that he be allowed to make a lithograph of that very same thumbprint on the largest plate he could locate at Tamarind. This violated an unwritten law that fingerprints should never appear on a print since they would render it less than perfect. Conner, at once disgruntled and amused by Tamarind's resistance to his ideas, considered the situation quite differently: "I felt I should be totally involved in their documentation process, so I did one where I inked my thumb and pressed it onto the largest plate they had so that the print of the thumbprint is reversed from the one that is down on the bottom. And you can compare reality to art." Goodman stopped production on *Thumb Print*, although it was printed after June Wayne's return.[3] Two other works that Goodman held up, but which Wayne also eventually approved, were *This Space Reserved for June Wayne* (cat. no. 32) and *Cancellation* (cat. no. 33). The second was made from a stone Conner first canceled with a big X but then decided to go ahead with, at the suggestion of printer Kenneth Tyler.

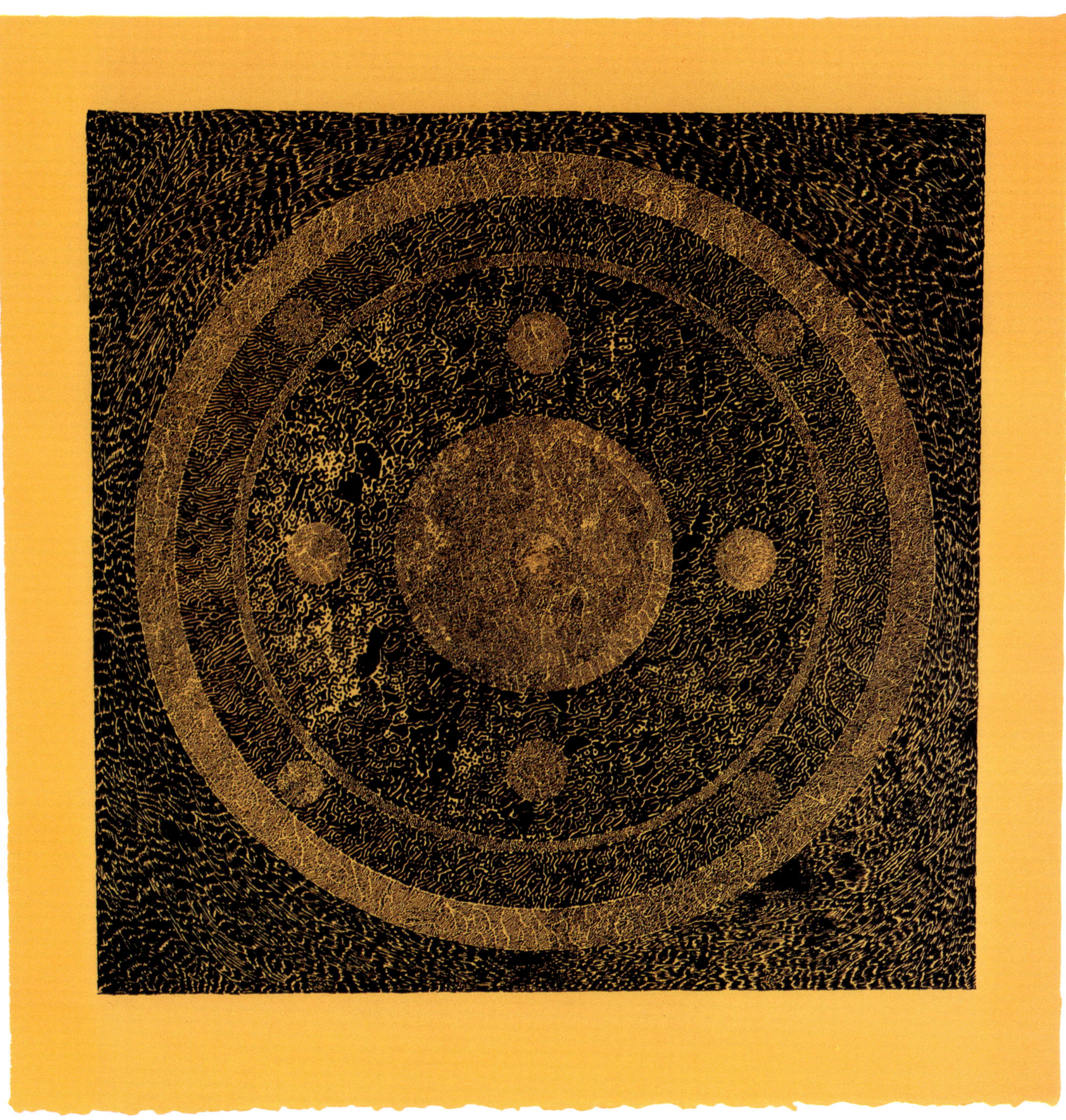

Bruce Conner *Mandala* 1965
lithograph (cat. no. 30)

Bruce Conner *Thumb Print* 1965
lithograph (cat. no. 29)

The project Conner felt most strongly about while at Tamarind was never realized, namely, a print of his birth certificate, replete with baby footprints; he saw this as a logical printmaking exercise.[4] Referring to the footprints, he says, "I thought that this would be the proper place for me to bring it around and to have my first prints made into art." Unwilling to produce a print that did not show the hand of the artist, Wayne suggested that Conner could print it if he added color to the image or drew over it. He opted not to "falsify" it in this way and left without executing the idea.

Although not entirely satisfactory, Conner's Tamarind residency was productive and certainly memorable. Thinking back to the thumbprint incident, Tyler recalls it not as a personal affront to Wayne or to Tamarind but rather as a "challenge to the whole printmaking system."[5]

—S.M.

1. Quoted in Mary Fuller, "You're Looking for Bruce Conner, the Artist, or What Is This Crap You're Trying to Put Over Here?" *Currant* 2 (May–July 1976), p. 11.

2. The artist in a conversation with Elizabeth Armstrong and the author, 23 October 1987. All subsequent Conner quotations here are also taken from this conversation.

3. When asked to submit his fingerprints to California State University, San Jose, where he had accepted a teaching position in 1973, Conner refused to do so without charging a fee. Based on the monetary value of his Tamarind thumbprint, he estimated that ten fingerprints were worth two thousand dollars. With the cooperation of the Palo Alto, California, police department, he ultimately published his fingerprints in an edition of twenty with Galerie Smith-Andersen. These prints, along with related documents and photographs, were placed in steel boxes and published as the *Art Steel Print Box* in 1974. See Fuller, op. cit., pp. 58–59; and Galerie Smith-Andersen, *Bruce Conner Prints*, exh. cat. (Palo Alto: Galerie Smith-Andersen, 1974), which includes a brief essay by Peter Selz, "The Artist as Dactylographer." This essay also appeared in *Art in America* 62 (July–August 1974), pp. 98–99.

4. Conner says of this project, "I wanted to print my birth certificate because there was more documentation at Tamarind than there was for my birth. And if I ever had to prove my birth, I could have twenty copies out there and they would be documented and notarized and stamped." Supra, note 2.

5. Tyler in a conversation with the author, 21 March 1988.

Leon Golub

Recognized today as one of America's foremost political artists, Leon Golub has consistently made power and vulnerability the primary subjects of his work. Until recently his commitment to figurative imagery—specifically to the raw and regressive side of the human condition—separated Golub from the mainstream of the art world.

Printmaking was an integral part of Golub's art long before he went to Tamarind Lithography Workshop in Los Angeles on a fellowship in 1965. In fact, the rough texture of the scorched, flayed, and tortured figures that haunt his canvases owes much to the prints he made before 1950. In 1946 or 1947 he made his first two prints, *Charnel House* and *Carnival*, both of which are lithographs, at the Southside Art Center in Chicago.[1] In 1949 and 1950, while a student at the School of the Art Institute of Chicago, he produced numerous lithographs and etchings.[2] Golub describes the etchings as "'expressionistic'—they change tremendously in process—etched and re-etched many times—[the] surfaces become highly corroded." Significantly, he adds, "the corrosive surface and corrosive psychologies deeply influenced the painting process—and vice-versa." Until 1961, when he began using acrylic paint, he achieved his coarse surfaces by applying successive layers of lacquer paint to his canvases, which he then vigorously scraped and gouged. In 1953 and 1954 he made over fifteen more lithographs whose subjects were iconic totem images that had their roots in pre-Columbian artifacts.[3] He printed these at the Chicago Graphic Workshop, a cooperative venture run by artists from 1952 to 1955.[4]

Prior to his two-month residency at Tamarind, Golub had done all of his own printing; thus collaborating with printers was new to him. He worked with artisan-printer Clifford Smith and a team of printer-trainees to create sixteen individual works and a portfolio of eight lithographs entitled *Agon*. All of the prints deal with themes of conflict, be they personal or universal. His brutal portrayals of the power in men and beasts (and men-as-beasts) developed from his intensive studies of antique statuary, particularly that of Greece and Rome. Though derived from these classical symbols of strength, Golub's orators and warriors lack the proportions, sensuousness, and confidence of their models; they appear physically powerful but psychologically vulnerable.

The splattered, scratched, and scuffed surfaces of many of the lithographs Golub made at Tamarind underscore the figures' physical and mental states. *Wounded Warrior*, from the *Agon* portfolio, is printed in bright red, blue, and fleshlike pink. One arm of the crawling fallen man is blue, while his other arm and his underside are blood red. A large slash of red pierces him under the forward arm. The fleshy hue of his back and face, in contrast to the huge animallike paw-hands, reminds one of his human frailty. Conflict and weakness are most poignantly represented in Golub's Tamarind lithographs of sphinxes, creatures possessing animal powers yet visibly prone to human suffering. The artist uses color in *Running Blue Sphinx* (cat. no. 37) to accentuate this disparity; its purple human head is visually, as well as symbolically, separate from its blue animal body.

Golub's work at Tamarind closely coincided with the beginning of his involvement with Artists and Writers Protest, a group organized to oppose the Vietnam War. He contributed a lithograph entitled *Killed Youth* to the portfolio *Artists and Writers Protest against the War in Vietnam* (1967), which included prints by fifteen other artists, Louise Nevelson and Ad Reinhardt among them. Golub, who points out that he has "always liked the 'graphic' or 'broadsheet' aspect of printmaking," has since contributed prints to benefit other antiwar groups,[5] including Artists Call against U.S. Intervention in Central America.

—S.M.

---

1. The artist in a conversation with Elizabeth Armstrong, 25 October 1988.

2. In correspondence of 9 December 1987 to Elizabeth Armstrong, Golub wrote that the first editions of the etchings made in 1949 were not produced until 1987, when an assistant of his printed them in New York City. Unless otherwise noted, all subsequent Golub quotations here are also taken from this source.

3. See Donald Kuspit, *Leon Golub: Existential/Activist Painter* (New Brunswick, N.J.: Rutgers University Press, 1985), p. 112, for an illustration of *Totemic Crucifixion* (1956).

4. Supra, note 1.

5. See Deborah Wye, *Committed to Print*, exh. cat. (New York: Museum of Modern Art, 1988), p. 73.

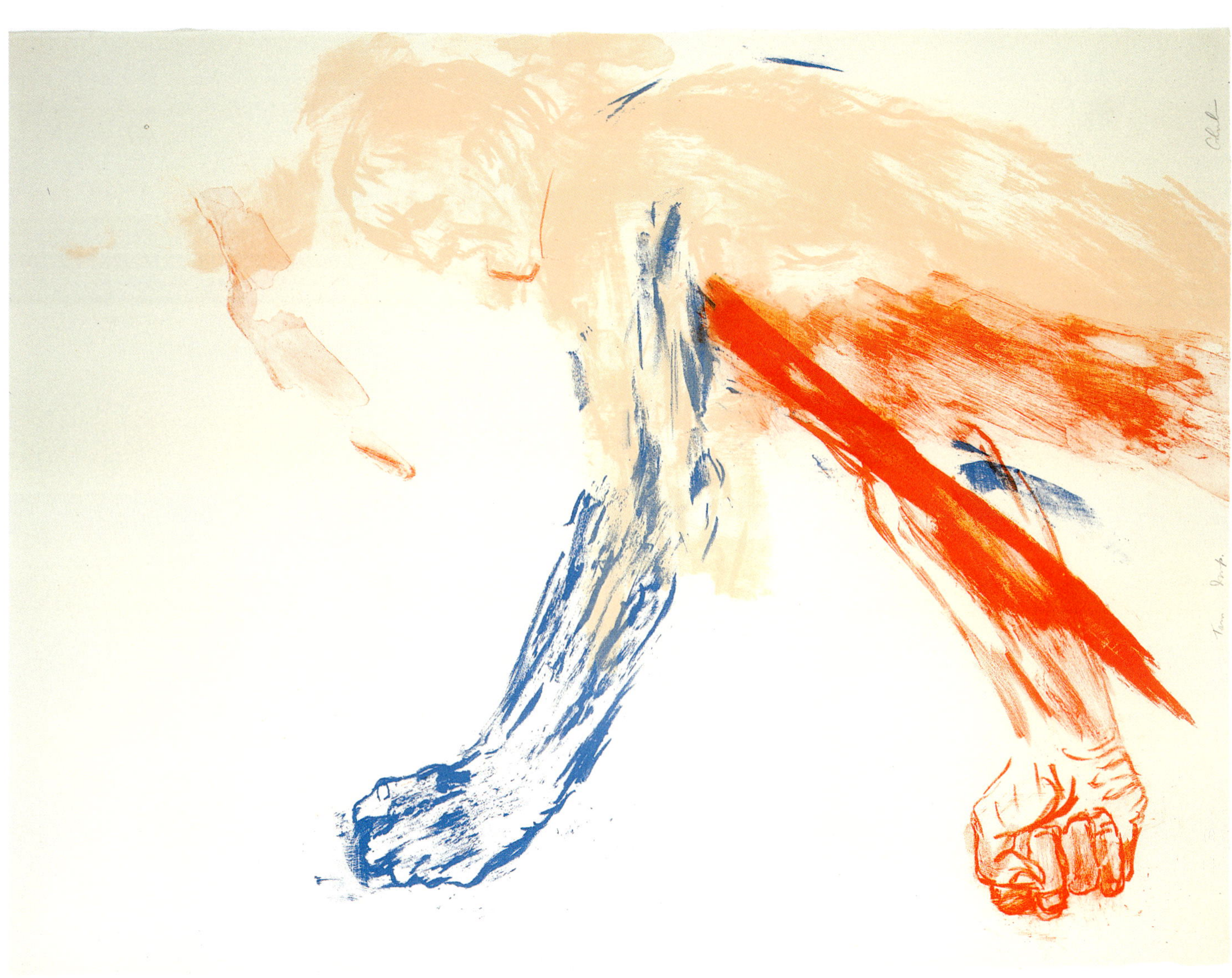

Leon Golub *Wounded Warrior* 1965
lithograph (cat. no. 36)

Frank Stella

In 1967 Frank Stella arrived in southern California to begin a stint as artist-in-residence at the University of California, Irvine. But because he would not sign the university's controversial loyalty oath, required by the state, he could not assume the position; he found himself on the West Coast with time on his hands. Kenneth Tyler, anxious to have the painter make prints at Gemini G.E.L., immediately began trying to coax him into the workshop. Stella was not interested.[1]

Tyler refused to take no for an answer. He constantly called and paid regular visits to the artist's home but invariably left without an agreement. Finally, Stella gave in. Tyler remembers the event with a gleam in his eye: "One day he said to me when I was out there, 'I draw with a magic marker—I wouldn't know what to do with a lithographic crayon.' So, I came back the next time with a magic marker filled with tusche. We seduced him!"[2]

As his first series of prints, *Star of Persia I* and *Star of Persia II* (cat. no. 39), demonstrates, Stella quickly adjusted to the nuances of lithography.[3] Based on an unrealized design for the artist's Notched-V painting series of 1964–1965, each lithograph represents a six-chevron configuration, with each segment printed in a different color. Stella wanted to use an ink that came close to replicating the metallic sheen of the paint in his recent works. Fortunately for him and the printers, the craftsmen at Gemini had been actively involved in the development of metallic inks. In addition, they were able to meet his request that the works be printed on graph paper, his preferred surface for drawings at that time. The shiny inks and streamlined vectors complement the title of the prints, which is taken from the name of a nineteenth-century British clipper ship.

More challenges revealed themselves during the proofing of *Star of Persia*. Flat silver lines running beneath and between all of the color areas—an integral part of Stella's design—required the utmost precision in registering the various printing plates. The colored inks had to be printed over a metallic silver base, subtly used to tone and raise the color areas. Further, it was necessary to align precisely the geometric design with the grid of the English vellum graph paper. According to Gemini's job sheet for Stella's prints, more than one hundred hours of shop time went into platemaking and proofing before the editions could be printed.[4]

A third version of the six-chevron figure was printed in metallic silver as the *Irving Blum Memorial Edition*

portfolio. Stella produced two other series of prints at Gemini in 1967, *Black Series I* (p. 12) and *Black Series II* (cat. no. 41), which repeat on a smaller scale the designs for his notorious Black paintings of 1958–1960. The first series focuses exclusively on the rectilinear-pattern compositions and is printed in a metallic black-gray ink on paper specially buff-colored by an offset press. The more dynamic diamond patterns of *Black Series II* called for blacker ink and whiter paper to heighten their optical effects. Stella's plan to compile and distribute these prints in loose-leaf binders accounts for their relatively small scale and for the keying of the images to the left margin of each sheet.[5]

The success of Stella's first prints and the close working relationship he developed with Tyler encouraged them both to pursue increasingly challenging projects. They have since collaborated on dozens of projects, both at Gemini G.E.L. and at Tyler Graphics Ltd., highlighted by the monumental Circuits series of 1981–1984 and the Swan Engravings series of 1982–1985.

—S.M.

1. See Richard H. Axsom, *The Prints of Frank Stella: A Catalogue Raisonné, 1967–1982* (New York: Hudson Hills Press in association with the University of Michigan Museum of Art, Ann Arbor, 1983), p. 13.

2. Tyler in an interview with the author, 21 March 1988.

3. Prior to his work at Gemini, Stella had marginally participated in two printmaking projects. In 1964 he submitted a gouache based on a painting that was adapted for the screenprint *Untitled (Rabat)*, included in the portfolio *Ten Works by Ten Painters*, published that year by the Wadsworth Atheneum. He also submitted a gouache for the screenprint *Fortin de las Flores* (First Version), included in the portfolio *Ten from Leo Castelli*, published by Tanglewood Press in 1967. Axsom has included these prints in the appendix to his catalogue raisonné (supra, note 1, pp. 170–171), noting, "Since his actual supervision and manipulation of the printing processes consisted essentially of approving colors before editioning, these screenprints are less autographic than those of his graphic *oeuvre* proper" (p. 170).

4. Ruth E. Fine, *Gemini G.E.L.: Art and Collaboration* (Washington, D.C.: National Gallery of Art and New York: Abbeville Press, 1984), p. 7.

5. The two series, released in notebook format, were the first installments of a larger project; the artist envisioned executing a complete set of portfolios based on his Stripe paintings of 1958–1965. The prints were to be mounted in acetate sleeves and compiled in binders. Gemini released several editions in this format but eventually stopped, since most of the sets were being dismantled by collectors who wanted to frame and display their prints.

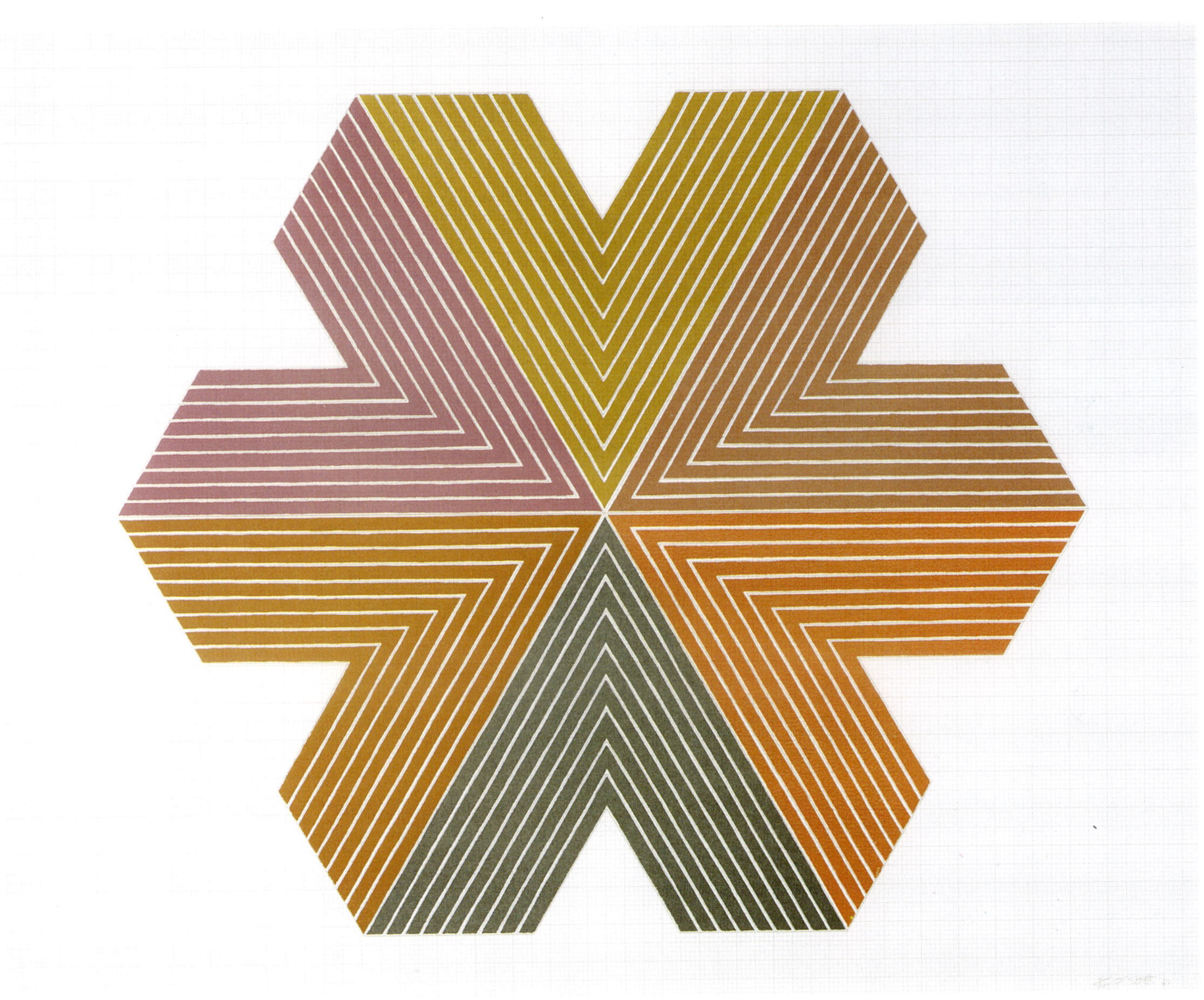

Frank Stella *Star of Persia I* 1967
lithograph (cat. no. 38)

Alan Shields

Printmaker William Weege once described Alan Shields' prints as "things with printmaking techniques."[1] Indeed, with their stitches, holes, embossing, applied grids, and even glitter additions, they transcend conventional definitions; simply calling them prints would be doing them an injustice.

Shields arrived on the New York art scene during the late 1960s, a time when he was beginning to make painted and subtly adorned objects. Neither paintings nor sculptures, they combined richly paint-stained and -splattered patterns, often on unstretched canvases, with beading, stitching, weaving, and patching. While these works were dependent on linear compositions and grid patterns for their underlying structure, they nonetheless represented a highly personal response to the strict formalism that informed much abstract art of the 1960s.

Rosa Esman, the founder of Tanglewood Press, invited Shields to make a print in 1968 for a forthcoming portfolio, *New York 10/69*. Like most of the other artists in the portfolio,[2] he was still relatively unknown, having exhibited only a couple of times at the Paula Cooper Gallery in New York. Despite his lack of experience with printmaking, he accepted Esman's invitation because "it seemed to be a good chance to try something new graphically and get exposure."[3] He based his first print on a recent watercolor in order to learn about the possibilities of reproducing the effects of that medium, which was also relatively new to him at the time. The printers at Maurel Studios photographically copied and color-separated the watercolor to produce the printing screens. In addition, pochoir (hand-coloring through stencils) was used to reproduce more accurately the subtle coloration of the original work.

The resulting print, *c,b.a.r.l.a.a.(old)y.(odd)o.* (1969),[4] though beautifully colored, in the artist's estimation still lacked a personal quality. Except for helping to choose the colors and the paper, he had not participated in the making of the print. Unaccustomed to such minimal involvement, Shields devised an innovative way to personalize the prints and distinguish them from others in the portfolio; he passed the printed sheets in stacks of ten through his sewing machine to perforate the edges and inside grids. The perforations form a symmetrical cross pattern around the central square, which contains a colorful octagon, itself made up of a grid of smaller triangles and squares. Only the perforation along the

bottom edge of the image is intended to be folded back. According to Shields, the square watercolor was printed on a standard rectangular sheet of paper to allow space underneath the image for his signature and the edition number. By perforating the edge of the image, he made it possible to fold back the bottom portion easily and thus achieve the perfect shape he wanted.[5]

Despite this personal touch, Shields' distance from the production of *c,b.a.r.l.a.a.(old)y.(odd)o.* discouraged him from making prints again until 1971, when he began collaborating with William Weege at the Jones Road Print Shop and Stable in Barneveld, Wisconsin. Weege, who had headed the printmaking workshop at the Venice Biennale in 1970, encouraged the artist's natural inclination to experiment with new ways of fabricating prints. Their first jointly produced work was *Sun Moon Titie Page* (1971), a unique two-sided print that incorporated hand-stamping, interwoven strips of dyed paper, and collage elements stitched on by sewing machine.

The success of this collaboration led Shields to immerse himself in printmaking. He continued working with Weege on numerous projects, including two books, *Tails of Brave Ulysses* (1972) and *The Incestuous Kids* (1973), which innovatively combine sewing, dyeing, flocking, embossing, and glitter additions with the conventional graphic processes of lithography, screenprinting, and etching. In 1978 he accepted an invitation from Kenneth Tyler to work at Tyler Graphics Ltd., where he has since made more than forty mixed-media editions. Today Shields continues to redefine the limits of printmaking in his "things with printmaking techniques."

—S.M.

1. Quoted in Diane Kelder, "Things with Printmaking Techniques," *Art in America* 61 (May–June 1973), p. 88.

2. Besides Shields, the artists included in this portfolio are: Alan Cote, David Diao, Ronnie Landfield, Lee Lozano, Brice Marden, William Pettet, Kenneth Showell, Lawrence Stafford, and Peter Young.

3. The artist in correspondence with Elizabeth Armstrong, 10 January 1988. Here Shields explains that his previous printmaking experience was limited to some experiments with hand-stamped woodblocks he had made in his basement one summer while still in college.

4. Shields says he assigned mysterious initials as titles to his works so that viewers would not know exactly what they were seeing. The artist in a conversation with the author, 6 May 1988.

5. Ibid.

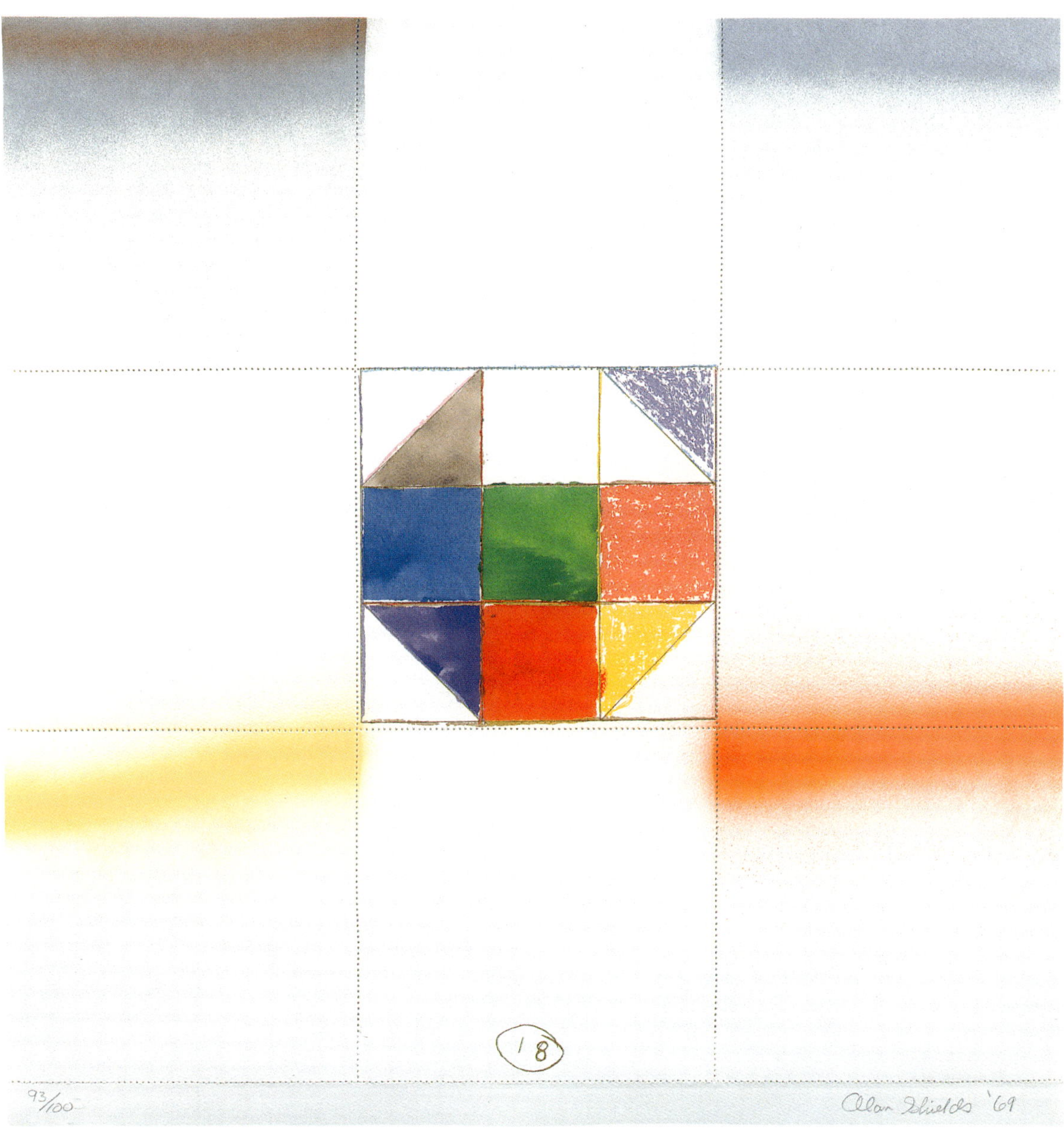

Alan Shields *c,b.a.r.l.a.a.(old)y.(odd)o.* 1969
screenprint with stencil, watercolor (cat. no. 42)

Richard Artschwager

born Washington, D.C.   1923

Since the early 1960s Richard Artschwager's art has taken the form of hard-edged, geometric furniture. His abstracted objects have been given a clean, functional appearance—reflecting the artist's early career as a professional furniture-maker—yet they are in fact non-functional. Although their formal, impersonal character reflects a certain affinity with Pop Art and Minimalism, Artschwager's constructions have a funky, cockeyed quality all their own. While contradicting the notion that furniture should be usable, they also attack conventional notions about how art ought to function.

Artschwager's smallest works, called "blps," are his most idiosyncratic queries into the nature of art. Neither sculpture nor painting, these elongated, oval-shaped objects have a strange, non-art look. The artist, who considers them akin to graffiti, first installed them, in the mid-1960s, at construction sites, in vacant lots, and on outdoor walls around Manhattan. In 1968 he brought them inside as the exclusive focus of his first European one-man show, held at the Konrad Fischer Gallery in Düsseldorf. Later that year they appeared as multiple sculptures spread over three floors in the Whitney Museum of American Art's *1968 Annual Exhibition: Contemporary American Sculpture*. Placed in one hundred locations, they drew attention to the Whitney's new building, designed by Marcel Breuer, and extended the boundaries of the exhibition both physically and conceptually.

Intrigued by the blps he saw at the Whitney, the young print publisher Brooke Alexander approached Artschwager about making an edition that reflected this essential aspect of his work. Others had invited Artschwager to make prints before, invitations he declined; this was his first offer to make a multiple. Having designed and produced furniture for nearly twenty years, Artschwager was at home with the notion of mass-produced objects; making the blps into an edition seemed a logical next step.

This project was also Alexander's first experience with producing a multiple, and, like Artschwager, he was fascinated by the notion of employing industrial materials to make art. Entitled *Locations* (1969), the multiple consists of five blps of varying size, shape, and character.

They are just small enough to fit into their fifteen-inch-high sculpture-container and are made from such diverse materials as Plexiglas, redwood, mirror glass, Formica, and rubberized horsehair. All but one are flat and designed to hang directly on the wall; the squatter, wooden blp, which is fully rounded, can be suspended from the ceiling.

The five blps fit snugly into their blue Formica box, with a sixth blp screenprinted on the Plexiglas cover. Except for Plexiglas, Artschwager had employed all of these materials before. Formica, a synthetic laminate, had held special appeal for Artschwager since the early 1960s. With characteristic iconoclasm, he described it as "the great ugly material, the horror of the age, which I came to like suddenly because I was sick of looking at all this beautiful wood."[1] Rubberized hair was a more recent discovery. Attracted to its "perfect imprecision,"[2] the artist felt that the pliant, rubber-coated horsehair provided a perversely tactile antidote to the hard edges of the other materials used in *Locations*.

When enclosed in their container, the *Locations* multiples suggest a high-tech version of a Joseph Cornell box—stuffed with mysterious, unidentifiable objects. Unlike Cornell's hermetic environments, however, the Plexiglas cover of Artschwager's box can be slid open and the pieces handled and arranged at will. As an object with no distinct function, *Locations* invites the viewer to rearrange its contents, to place the art outside the box— thereby defining its form and surrounding space. As Artschwager describes them, these portable blps actually need "both the where and the what."[3] Indeed, their character depends on their given location.

—E.A.

1. Quoted in Jan McDevitt, "The Object: Still Life," *Craft Horizons* 25 (September–October 1965), p. 54.

2. Richard Armstrong, *Artschwager, Richard*, exh. cat. (New York: Norton and Whitney Museum of American Art, 1988), p. 44.

3. The artist in correspondence with the author, 18 December 1987.

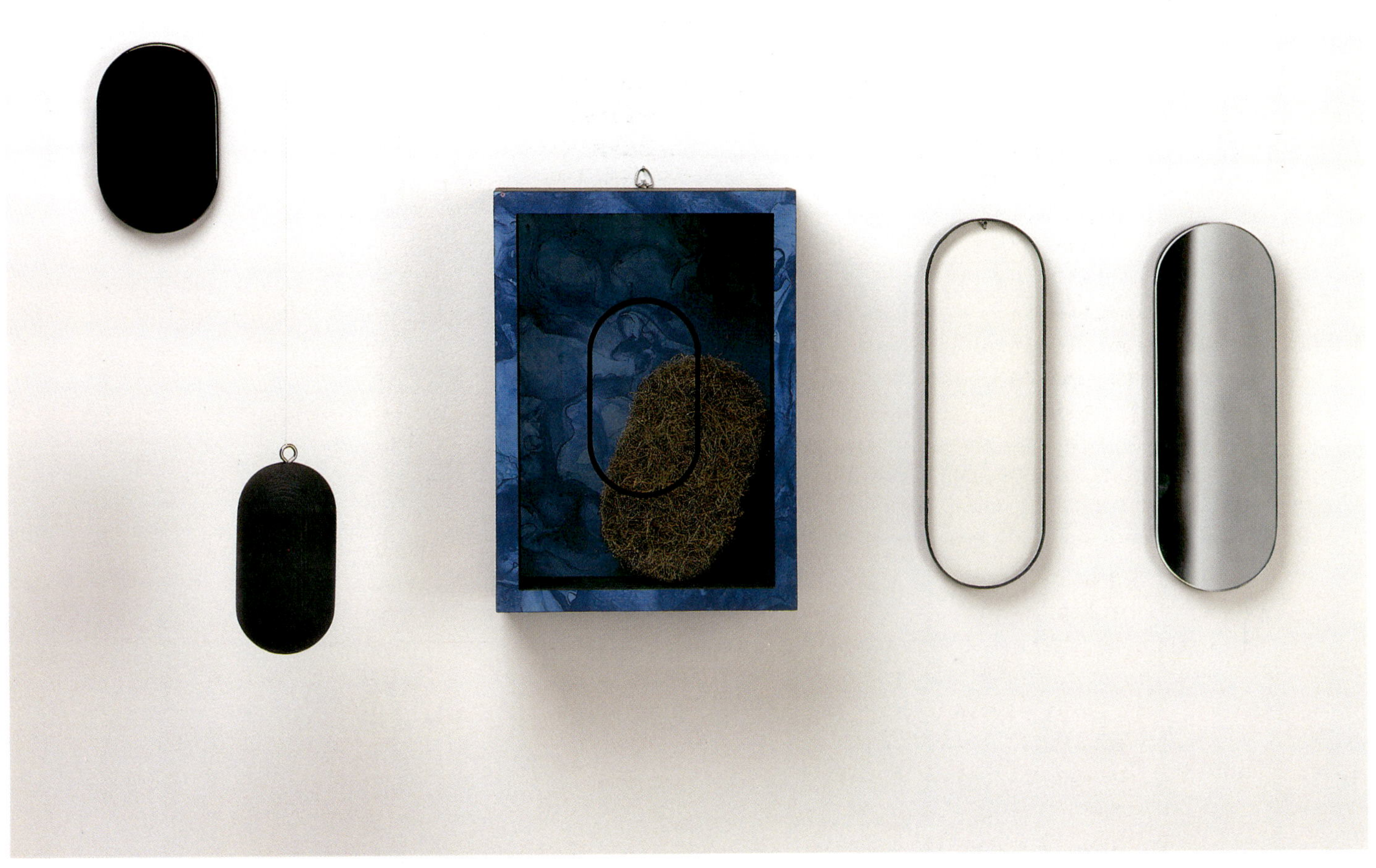

Richard Artschwager *Locations* 1969
six objects in Plexiglas, redwood, mirror glass, Formica, and rubberized horsehair (cat. no. 43)

Bruce Nauman

Bruce Nauman's is one of the most idiosyncratic, private voices in twentieth-century art. At the time he produced his first prints, *Studies for Holograms* (1970), he was also making installations, sculptures, holograms, drawings, and books[1] that employed such diverse materials as fiberglass, rubber, neon, photographs, film, videotape, audiotape, and his own body.[2] While Nauman's sensibility in these heterogeneous modes and media is difficult to grasp, much of his work from this period is connected by his underlying concern with experiencing the human body in unexpected ways.

After graduating from art school at the University of California, Davis, in 1966, Nauman spent much time in his San Francisco studio immersed in various forms of self-observation. There he began documenting on film such commonplace activities as walking, skipping, and stamping on the floor. Employing his body as an artwork, he made photographs such as *Portrait of the Artist as a Fountain* (1966–1967), in which he treated himself as a "readymade," using his mouth as a waterspout. This work, which has often been viewed as an exemplar of Conceptual and Body art of the 1960s, is also seen as an homage to Marcel Duchamp, who likewise used his body as a work of art and championed the artistic idea over the art object.

Duchampian wit and irony are indeed evident in several artist's books that Nauman made in the late 1960s. While still living in the Bay Area, he produced *CLEARSKY* (1967–1968), which comprises eight pages printed in different shades of blue; the book's title provides the key to its imagery. Shortly after moving to the Los Angeles area, Nauman made another book, *LAAIR* (1970), in which he paid ironic tribute to his new environment. It uses the same format as *CLEARSKY*, but its pages are colored in gradations of yellow, brown, and black, reflecting the city's notorious smog.[3]

Nauman's first extensive printmaking project was *Studies for Holograms*. This suite of five screenprints drew from a body of material he had explored in the late 1960s. In a series of videotapes made in 1968 and 1969, he used the camera as a mirror, watching himself in the monitor.[4] As part of these activities, he began making formal arrangements with his face, several of which he had featured in an earlier drawing, *Mouths* (1967). "The idea about making faces," Nauman told an interviewer some years later, "had to do with thinking of the body as

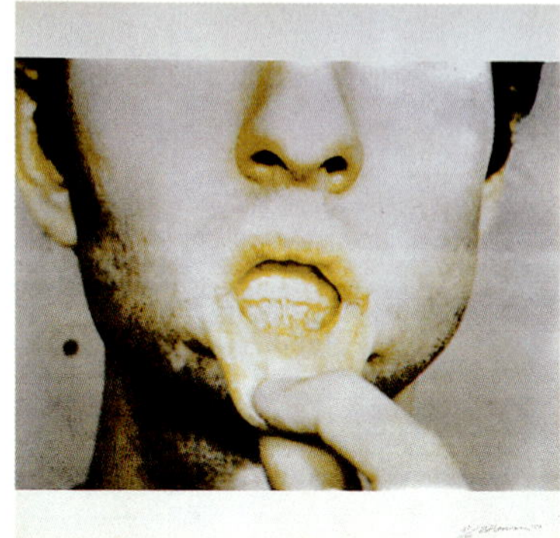

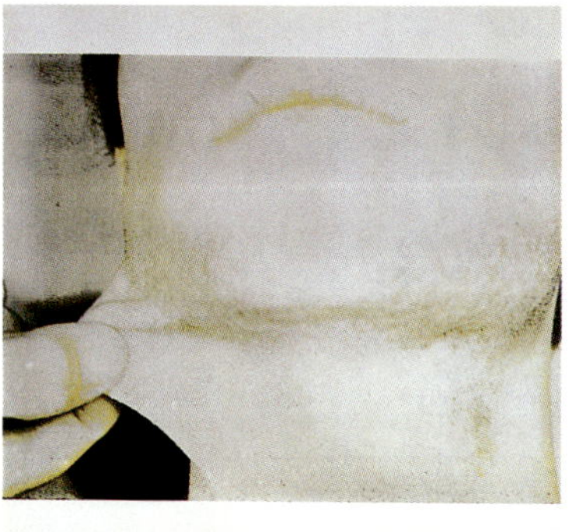

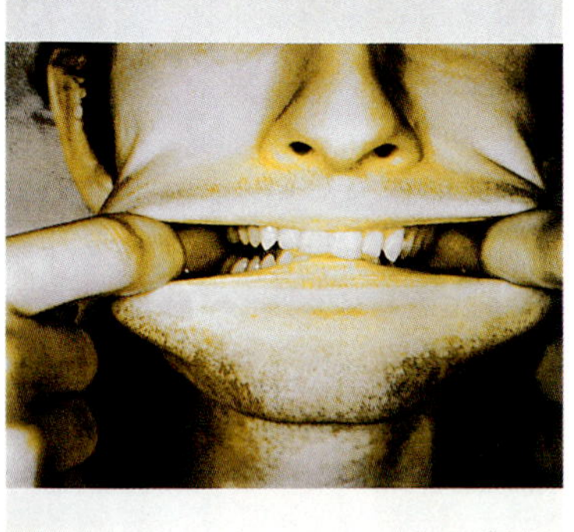

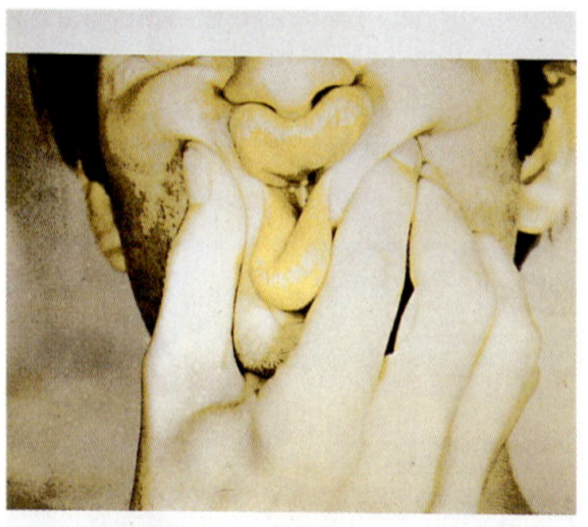

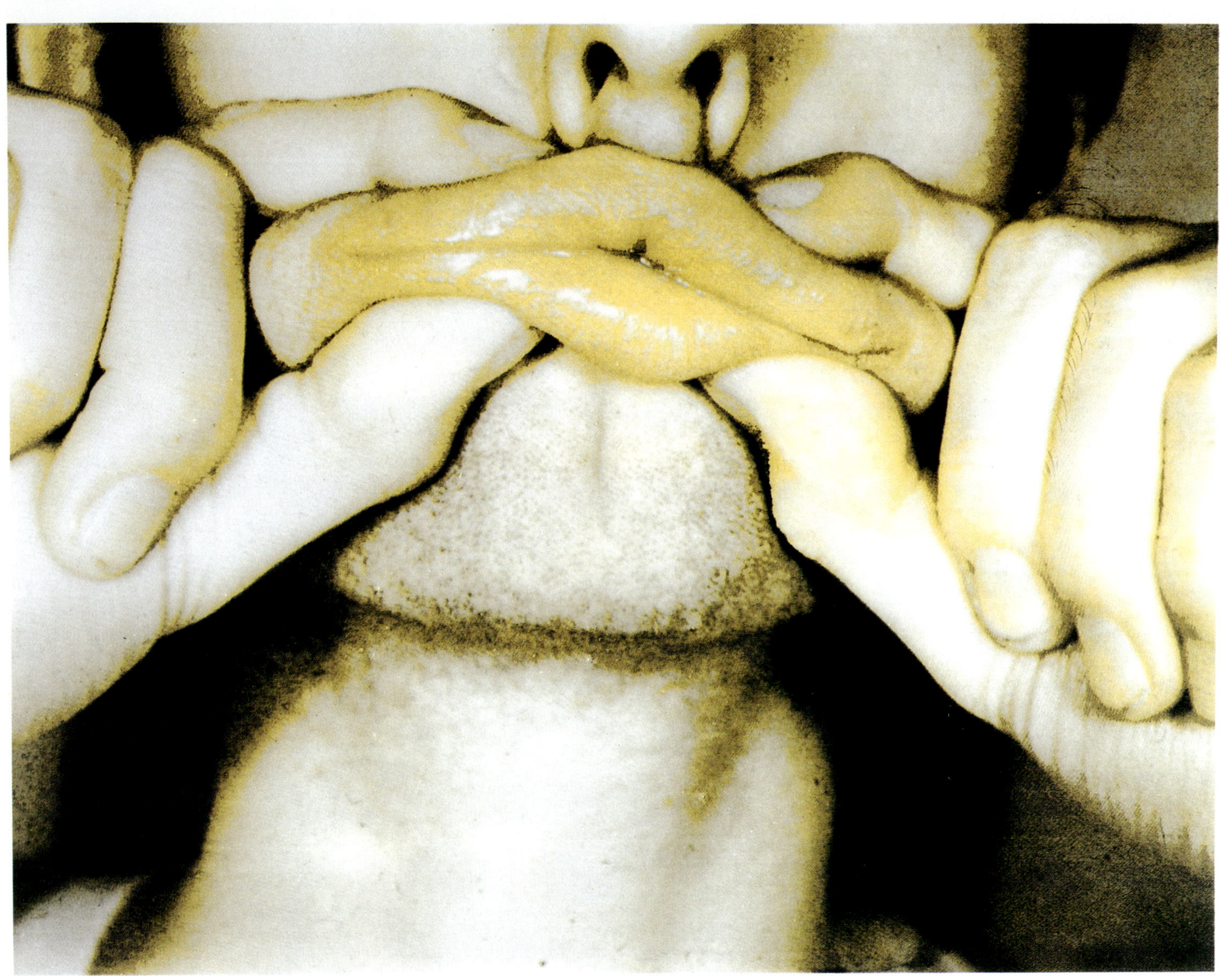

Bruce Nauman *Studies for Holograms* 1970
five screenprints (cat. no. 44)

something you can manipulate. I had done some perfor-mance pieces—rigorous pieces dealing with standing, leaning, bending—and as they were performed, some of them seemed to carry a large emotional impact. I was very interested in that. If you perform a bunch of arbitrary operations, some people will make very strong connections with them, and others won't."[5] In 1968 he had several of these photographs made into holograms, *First Hologram Series (Making Faces)*. Because of the general public fascination with the hologram technique at the time, he felt he had to make such contorted faces in order for the subject matter to counteract the novelty of the medium.[6]

In the long tradition of self-portraiture, Nauman's *Studies for Holograms* have an affinity with the Viennese artist Franz Xaver Messerschmidt's haunting *Self-Portraits Grimacing* (1776–1783).[7] In those disturbing works, sculpted in marble and lead, Messerschmidt portrayed himself with tensed muscles and tightly closed mouth, as if his head were under tremendous pressure. In *Studies for Holograms*, Nauman squeezed and pulled at his lips—making faces instead of grimaces. Because the eyes are cropped from these images, we focus on the mouth, which Nauman distorts to reveal teeth and the insides of the lips and lower gums. In one image the mouth goes slack while he pulls at the skin on his neck. These extreme gestures, like the artist's body manipula-tions in general, suggest a kind of self-exposure. Yet, at the same time, Nauman conceals himself behind the fragmented faces in *Studies for Holograms*, transforming private acts into confrontational images.

—E.A.

1. His books from this early period include *Pictures of Sculptures in a Room* (1965–1966), *CLEARSKY* (1967–1968), *Burning Small Fires* (1968; documents the burning of Edward Ruscha's 1964 book *Various Small Fires*), and *LAAIR* (1970).

2. For a general overview of his work from this period, see Jane Livingston and Marcia Tucker, *Bruce Nauman: Works from 1965 to 1972*, exh. cat. (Los Angeles County Museum of Art, 1972).

3. Both *CLEARSKY* and *LAAIR* were published by Multiples, Inc., New York. Two other publications from this early period are sound pieces: *Footsteps*, a strip of recording tape wound around a folded Op Art card (with instructions for playing the tape as a perpetual sound loop), in *SMS 5* (1968), a portfolio published by the Letter Edged in Black Press, New York; and *Record*, a sound track from various Nauman films and videotapes in a jacket silkscreened with photographs of the artist from his videotape *Stamping*, in *7 Objects/69* (1969), a portfolio of multimedia objects published by Tanglewood Press, New York.

4. From the transcript of an unpublished Nauman interview conducted by free-lance writer and print publisher Christopher Cordes in July 1977.

5. Ibid., p. 16.

6. See Willoughby Sharp, "Nauman Interview," *Arts Magazine* 44 (March 1970), pp. 22–27.

7. See Allesandra Comini, *The Fantastic Art of Vienna* (New York: Ballantine Books, 1978), pp. 5–6.

Sol LeWitt

In 1966 Sol LeWitt wrote that "the serial artist does not attempt to produce a beautiful or mysterious object but functions merely as a clerk cataloging the results of the premise."[1] No artist has been more consistent than LeWitt in creating conceptual systems and realizing them in a wide variety of media. In 1970, after a decade of executing some of these systems in complex steel-and-aluminum structures and documenting others in books, he made his first screenprints, *Composite Series (Set of 5)*, as a means of realizing his current ideas more efficiently.

Early in his career LeWitt recognized the value of publications as a vehicle for disseminating his ideas.[2] In 1966 his first pamphlet, *Serial Project No. 1, 1966*, was published with other artists' works—including films and records—in an *Aspen Magazine* portfolio. In it he describes the theoretical premise governing one of his multipart sculptures; schematic drawings systematically illustrate the text. He writes that his aim is not to instruct but rather to give information to the reader-viewer, adding that "whether the viewer understands this information is incidental to the artist."[3]

In 1968 Marian Goodman, director of Multiples, Inc., in New York, commissioned LeWitt to make a small steel-and-aluminum multiple based on his large serial installations of 1965–1968. The piece functions somewhat as a reproduction would for a painter in that it makes an idea available to a larger public on a more intimate, portable scale. Essentially, the work is an open-sided cube in the center of a nine-section grid. In 1969 LeWitt contributed an offset photograph, *Schematic Drawing for Muybridge II, 1964*, to another Multiples publication, the portfolio *Artists and Photographs* (1970). The photograph, which reproduces a work he had made in 1964 but is neither signed nor numbered, was distributed in an edition of 1,000. Depicted across its center is a row of ten boxes; a circle in the middle of each square reveals a portion of a photograph of the nude body of a woman who moves, sequentially, closer to the viewer until only her stomach remains visible.

These publishing ventures enabled LeWitt to appreciate the advantages of reproduction. When he was invited to make prints at Sarah Lawrence Art Press in New York City, he did not hesitate to accept. Prior to this contact with printmaking, he regularly illustrated his systems in meticulous, time-consuming drawings. He openly acknowledges that "the print technique was used instead of doing the piece as a drawing because it served the same

end with less work."[4] The frankness of this remark downplays the significance of graphic media in LeWitt's oeuvre.[5]

Composite Series (Set of 5), like many of his works in other media, is in effect a visual reiteration of a set of written instructions. The series begins with a square divided into four equal horizontal bands of color (from top to bottom): black, yellow, blue, and red. Each colored band contains lines drawn in one of four directions, horizontally, vertically, and diagonally from left to right and right to left. As he progresses, he systematically superimposes the colored bands of lines according to his predetermined formula to arrive at various configurations of lines in different colors and, eventually, at a uniform sheet composed of a dense mesh of lines of all colors in all directions. The fifth print in the series provides a kind of key to unraveling its overall logic, as it illustrates each of the stages that precedes it.

According to LeWitt, his participation in the project consisted in drawing a single sheet of ruled lines—rather than making an individual drawing for each image—which the printer John Campione then "used in different directions with different colors" to make the screens. The idea of having Campione execute the prints themselves was compatible with the artist's working methods in other media, where assistants made his pieces according to his specific instructions. The mechanical nature of commercial silkscreening suited him well; not only did it save time, but it also rendered his lines with a greater degree of consistency. Upon close examination, however, the prints inevitably reveal some evidence of the original hand-drawing.

Within the year LeWitt and Campione made a number of other related silkscreens, including two prints in 1970 entitled *Horizontal Composite*—one in color, one in black—and another *Composite Series (Set of 5)* (1971), which closely relates to the first series. His conceptual approach to printmaking reached its logical extension later in 1971, when he mailed instructions for a series of prints for students to implement at the Nova Scotia College of Art and Design in Halifax. Since the early 1970s he has created a great number of silkscreens, etchings, and lithographs, which, until several years ago, used the color scheme of red, yellow, blue, and black established in the earliest screenprints.

—S.M.

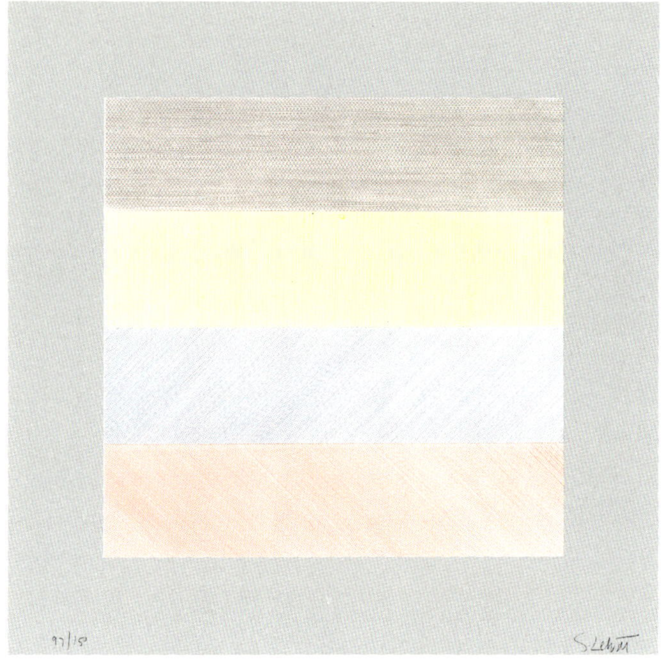 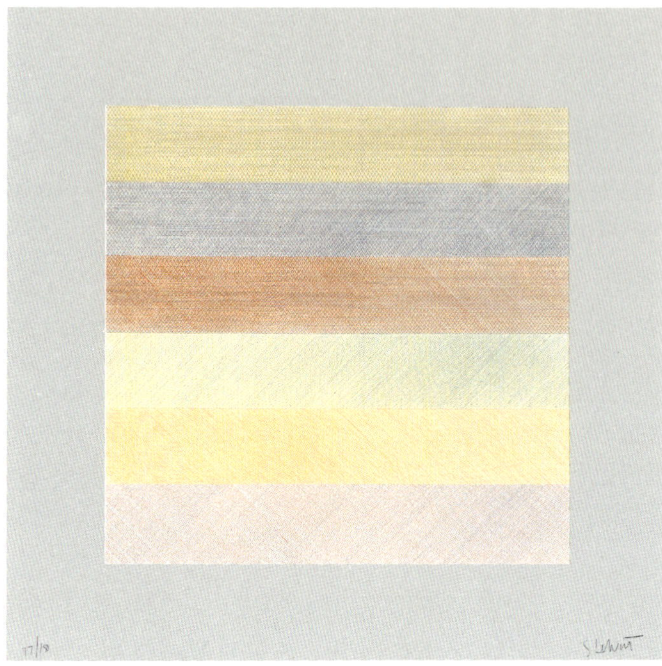

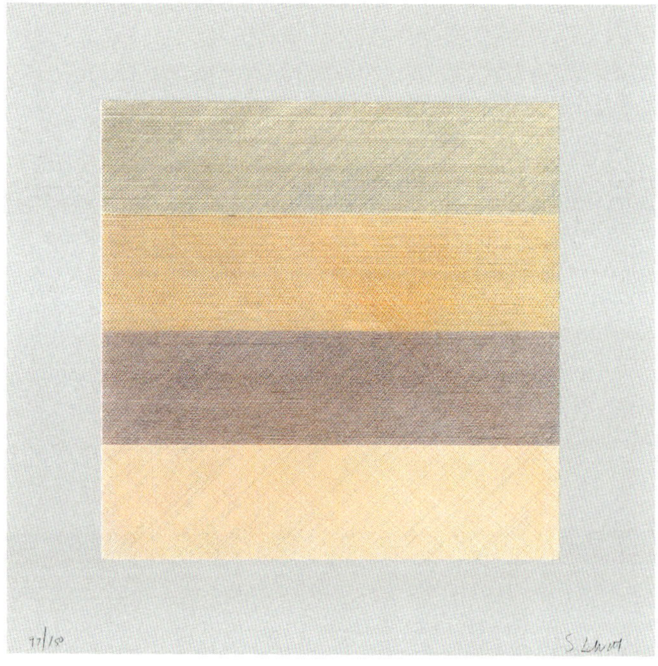 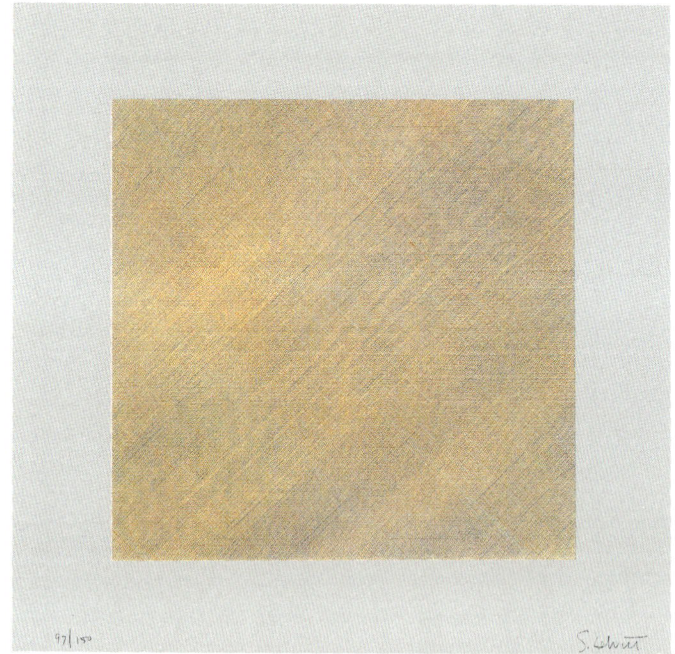

1. Sol LeWitt, *Serial Project No. 1, 1966, Aspen Magazine*, nos. 5 and 6, sect. 17 (1966), unpaginated.

2. LeWitt made some prints in college and later worked as a graphic artist in the I. M. Pei architectural firm, where he designed brochures and letterheads.

3. LeWitt, op. cit.

4. The artist in correspondence with Elizabeth Armstrong, 26 January 1988. All subsequent LeWitt quotations here are also taken from this source.

5. For a complete listing of LeWitt's prints and books published through 1986, see Tate Gallery, *Sol LeWitt: Prints, 1970–86*, exh. cat. (London: Tate Gallery, 1986). This catalogue includes a discussion of the artist's prints in an essay by Jeremy Lewison, "Sol LeWitt—Systems and Prints," pp. 9–15. For additional illustrations of the prints, see *Sol LeWitt: Graphik, 1970–1975*, exh. cat. (Basel: Kunsthalle and Bern: Verlag Kornfeld und Cie, 1975); and Betty Bright, *Pick up the Book, Turn the Page and Enter the System: Books by Sol LeWitt* (Minneapolis: Minnesota Center for Book Arts, 1988).

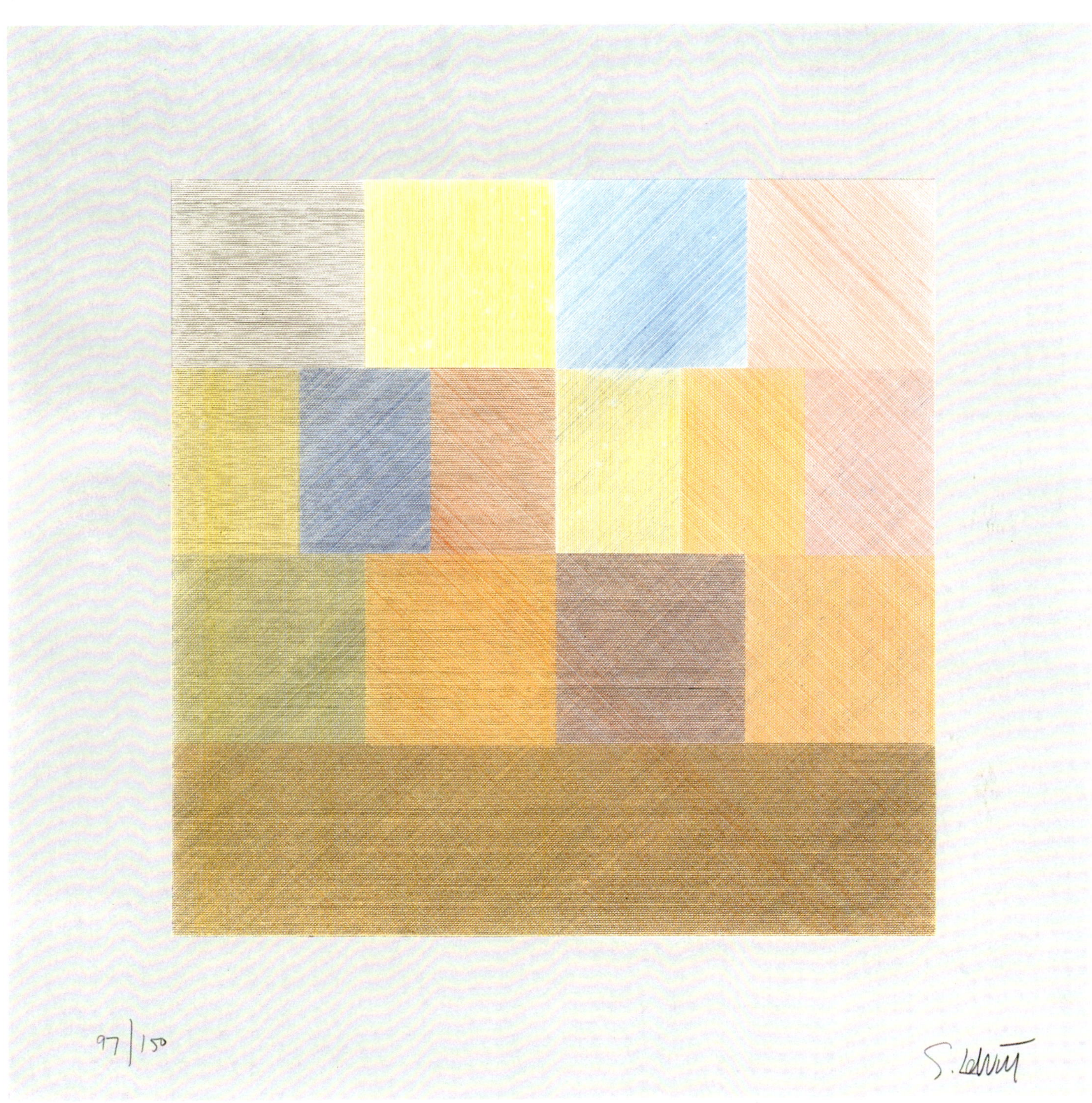

Sol LeWitt *Composite Series (Set of 5)* 1970
five screenprints (cat. no. 45)

Vito Acconci

In the 1970s Vito Acconci systematically made his own body and mental processes the medium and the subject of his work. While Body Art, a reaction to the commodity-oriented art of the 1960s, was then being practiced commonly, few other artists extended such practice into printmaking as thoroughly as did Acconci in his first three prints. In these works, published by the Lithography Workshop, Nova Scotia College of Art and Design, Halifax, in 1971 and 1972, the printmaking process became synonymous with performance.

Acconci was asked to make prints while he was participating in the college's visiting-artists program,[1] of which he recently wrote:

> The school was, consciously or not, setting itself up as the "conceptual art school" . . . they had to mark their position, publicly—printmaking was an appropriate way to do this, it provided convenient and cheap distribution for conceptual art.[2]

Although he had no practical experience with print-making, Acconci readily accepted the invitation because he believed making a print would make him "part of a group of established and soon-to-be established artists."

The first lithograph, *Kiss-Off* (1971), derives from a filmed performance piece, *Applications* (1970). In that work, Acconci directed a female performer, her lips thickly covered with red lipstick, to kiss him on the chest for twenty minutes. He then transferred her lip marks to a second male's back by rubbing his chest against it; in doing so, he says, "the three of us blend[ed] together." Taking a similar approach to make the lithograph, he began by putting lipstick on his mouth, which he then rubbed with his hand. He transferred the lipstick from his hand to the lithographic stone. Photographs showing the various steps were transferred to the lithographic plate and used as the primary images in the print.

A text, scrawled in Acconci's hand on the lower portion of the print, explicates individual images. For example, the final act involved "using this stone to wipe my hand, rubbing off my female characteristics, 'cleaning myself up.'" Aside from the writing and rubbing, no trace of his hand appears on this print. According to the artist, this was a significant aspect of the piece. "I wanted to give myself a way to be involved with the printmaking process—and I wasn't about to use my hand, let my hand

show—so I could find a way in: I could perform on the stone, act on the stone."

The use of lipstick was of utmost technical and conceptual importance in *Kiss-Off*. Lipstick is essentially grease, and as such it replaced the crayon or tusche commonly used in lithography—a process founded on the natural antipathy of grease and water. In addition to its role in creating the lithograph, the lipstick enabled Acconci to explore further an issue raised in previous performances—the possibility of understanding what it would be like to be female.

Trademarks (cat. no. 47), made simultaneously with *Kiss-Off*, related to a previous performance of the same title, in which Acconci sat naked and bit as much of his body as he could reach. As he described the event:

> When a bite was achieved, I applied printer's ink to it so I was able to have a bite print. . . . I was turning in on myself, making a closed system and then presenting the possibility of opening that system with the print. Theoretically, this is a secret activity, but the print is a possibility of revealing the secret and sharing it.[3]

Here, as in *Kiss-Off*, he used printmaking as a way of indirectly making a private act public.

A third print, *Touch Stone (for VL)*, made at the Nova Scotia college in 1972, also makes use of performance. As Acconci massaged a lithographic stone's surface, he imagined it was a woman's body and verbalized his fantasies into a tape recorder. He considered using his sweat as the drawing medium. Although this turned out to be impractical, he was apparently consoled by the fact that the ink he used was commonly called "rubbing ink."[4] He then printed his handwritten transcriptions from the tape over parts of the rubbed image.

—S.M.

---

1. For background information on the Nova Scotia College of Art and Design and the Lithography Workshop, see *NSCAD: The Nova Scotia College of Art and Design* (Halifax: Press of the Nova Scotia College of Art and Design, 1982).

2. The artist in correspondence with Elizabeth Armstrong, 4 January 1988. Unless otherwise noted, all subsequent Acconci quotations here are also taken from this source.

3. Cindy Nemser, "An Interview with Vito Acconci," *Arts Magazine* 45 (March 1971), p. 20.

4. Eric Cameron, "The Lithography Workshop," in *NSCAD*, op. cit., p. 20.

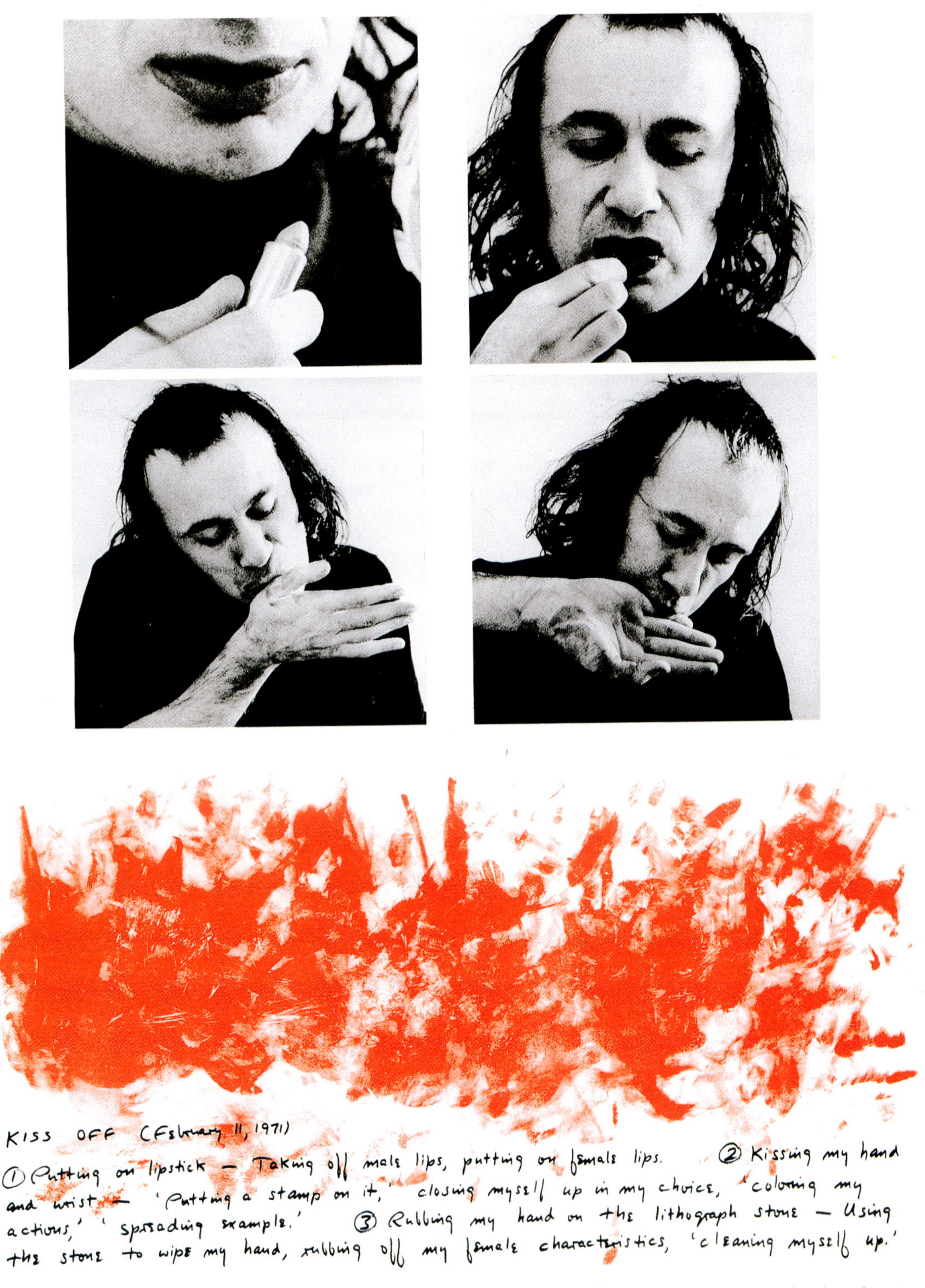

Vito Acconci *Kiss-Off* 1971
lithograph (cat. no. 46)

Ronald Davis

Ronald Davis made his first prints at Gemini G.E.L. in Los Angeles in 1971. Like his shaped paintings of the mid-to-late 1960s, these works were pioneering in that they were graphic images of three-dimensional geometric objects which, set free from the confining edges of the rectangle, seemed to exist in real space. In his paintings Davis had thrown into question the basic physical structure of the medium by experimenting with new materials—the most radical being plastic backed with fiberglass. To attain translucent interior depths he worked in reverse, beginning by pouring a clear liquid polyester resin over a waxed Formica mold. He would then paint on successive layers of colored resin to achieve the effect of geometric spaces clearly laid out in two-point perspective. He reinforced the painting by laminating on its back layers of fiberglass impregnated with resin.[1] To this he attached a wooden stretcher bar that had the same shape as the image and then peeled the completed painting from the mold. The resulting works achieved an unprecedented "congruence of literal and depicted shape."[2]

Davis' unique works and his ingenious use of unconventional materials appealed to Kenneth Tyler, whose own interest in experimentation had led him to establish Gemini G.E.L., in Los Angeles, as a workshop where artists were encouraged to take advantage of up-to-date technological resources. He invited Davis to work at Gemini, and there the artist extended his ideas into an ambitious first printmaking project.[3] Accustomed to working with a team of assistants on his paintings, Davis made the transition from studio to shop quite easily.[4]

He went to Gemini with the idea of making prints that would relate to the plastic and fiberglass paintings. If the technical virtuosity of these first prints, *Cube I, Cube II* (p. 14), and *Cube III* (cat. no. 50), belies his inexperience with printmaking, it also attests to his eagerness to break down existing distinctions between normally "flat" prints and three-dimensional objects. To attain the dimensional effect that the transparent layers of color achieve in Davis' paintings, the Gemini printers collaborated with offset printers, contracted outside the workshop.[5] They then laminated the five-color photo-offset lithographs between sheets of Mylar and plastic. The Cubes, having six edges rather than the four of a typical print, are shaped to the contours of the form they depict. This, along with their shiny surfaces and slightly raised backings, makes them at once prints and objects.

Davis and Tyler developed a compatible working relationship, which led almost immediately to a string of innovative collaborations. The artist says, "After a period of eight years of making shaped painting, I wanted to return to a rectangular format, particularly in print-making. Key in this transition were the silkscreens that I did with Tyler at Gemini in 1973–1974."[6] He has continued to investigate issues of surface and structure in a number of ambitious mixed-media printmaking projects at Gemini and, since 1979, at Tyler Graphics Ltd.

—S.M.

1. Statement by the artist in Muriel Emanuel et al., *Contemporary Artists*, 2nd ed. (New York: St. Martin's Press, 1983), p. 230.

2. Susan C. Larsen, "Los Angeles Painting in the Sixties: A Tradition in Transition," in Maurice Tuchman et al., *Art in Los Angeles: Seventeen Artists in the Sixties*, exh. cat. (Los Angeles County Museum of Art, 1981), p. 21.

3. Apart from some experimental prints he made as a student at Yale-Norfolk summer school, Davis arrived at the Gemini workshop with no printmaking experience. For a biographical sketch, see Ruth E. Fine, *Gemini G.E.L.: Art and Collaboration* (Washington, D.C.: National Gallery of Art and New York: Abbeville Press, 1984), p. 255.

4. Kenneth Tyler in a conversation with the author, 21 March 1988.

5. Fine-art printers in America were then generally hesitant to encourage artists to use commercial offset printing. Davis nonetheless insisted that his Cubes required the rigidity of "process" color separation. Tyler points out that because the Cubes could not have been printed successfully on Gemini's existing handpresses, he undertook to collaborate on the series with offset printers at Graphic Press, Los Angeles.

6. The artist in a letter to Robert M. Murdock, 20 January 1986.

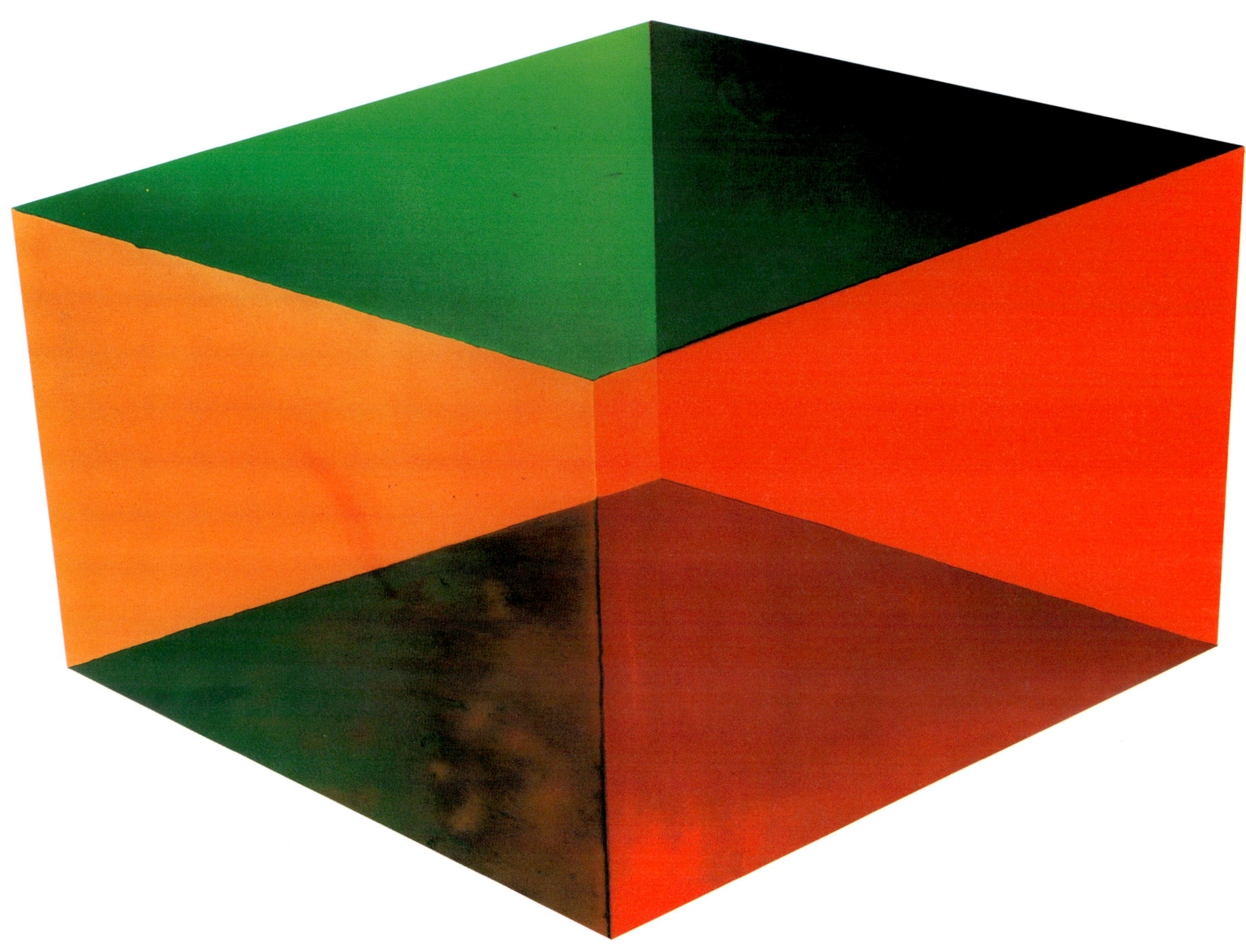

Ronald Davis *Cube I* 1971
photo-offset with laminated Mylar overlay, mounted on plastic
(cat. no. 48)

Edward Kienholz

Sawdy (1971), Edward Kienholz's first commissioned edition, reflects the trend during the late 1960s and early 1970s of artists' multiples being produced by print workshops. Under the artist's supervision, Kenneth Tyler and Jeff Sanders at Gemini G.E.L. collaborated to fabricate fifty-five pieces, each one made of a car door, a mirrored window, a screenprint, a fluorescent light, and galvanized sheet metal with applied automotive lacquer paint and polyester resin.

Other publishers had asked Kienholz to make prints before Tyler invited him to make a multiple sculpture at Gemini.[1] He turned down these offers because of his conviction that making two-dimensional prints was incompatible with his artistic approach. Then, as now, he made subversive life-size tableaux from a variety of materials, many of which were gathered from salvage shops. Tyler's offer to edition a three-dimensional object gave Kienholz the opportunity to extend the powerful message of his *Five Car Stud*, then under way. The tableau graphically depicts a group of whites castrating a black man they have caught sharing a drink with a white woman. For the artist, *Five Car Stud*, though an invented scene, was symbolic of "minority strivings in the world today."[2]

The central element of *Sawdy* is a black-and-white screenprint made from a photograph of *Five Car Stud* and placed behind the car-door window. As Tyler points out, viewers who do not like the subject matter can shut it out: "You roll the window down and see the terrible castration scene, and then you roll it up."[3] Although some of the details are lost in the reproduction, the horrible rubber masks of the white captors are disturbingly visible. Kienholz and his friends had to set up the tableau—which had never before been fully assembled—in Gemini's parking lot in order to take the nighttime photograph for this screenprint.

Kienholz submitted a prototype for *Sawdy*, constructed from a salvaged car door, which the Gemini printers used to determine what materials would be necessary to realize the edition. Primary among these were the car doors themselves, which they ordered in a variety of colors from a Datsun factory in Japan. The doors were shipped in nearly one hundred pieces each, requiring Jeff Sanders to learn the fine art of car-door assembly from a local Datsun dealer. But this was just the first step in the complicated process of manufacturing

Sawdy. A sheet-metal fabricator devised a pattern that enabled the printers to solder a shadow box holding the printed image to the door's exterior. The design also had to allow for the placement of a fluorescent light fixture that would illuminate the print mounted on the back of the shadow box.

When assembly was complete, Kienholz came in and dripped resin on each of the doors, not only to identify them with his other work but also to impart to each an individual element. Tyler considers this to have been a forward-looking action and is convinced that other artists then working at Gemini took notice and saw the value of individualizing their pieces.[4]

The layers of meaning embedded in Kienholz's car door are meticulously recorded with photographs and the artist's personal remarks in another Gemini edition, *Documentation Book: Five Car Stud and Sawdy* (cat. no. 52), published in 1972. In true scrapbook fashion, the volume includes everything from the bills of sale for the salvage vehicles used in *Five Car Stud* to photographs of the installation of the tableau in the Gemini parking lot. Kienholz has compiled unique documentation books for many of his projects; this one, issued in an edition of fifty-five, makes his ideas somewhat more accessible.

In 1972 he also produced an edition entitled *Souvenir License Plate for Sawdy* (cat. no. 53) at Gemini, a die-stamped, painted license plate with a chrome frame and plastic reflectors; and *Marriage Icon*, a three-dimensional work contained within a wooden frame, which combines photographs, photo-offsets, nylon lace, and hand-coloring. Since 1977 Kienholz has been making series of television-related multiples at Gemini that incorporate a variety of unconventional objects, including radios, light bulbs, and old shoes.

—S.M.

---

1. The artist in correspondence with Elizabeth Armstrong, 11 January 1988.

2. Edward Kienholz, *Documentation Book: Five Car Stud and Sawdy* (Los Angeles: Gemini G.E.L., 1972), pp. 4–5.

3. Tyler in a conversation with the author, 21 March 1988.

4. Ibid.

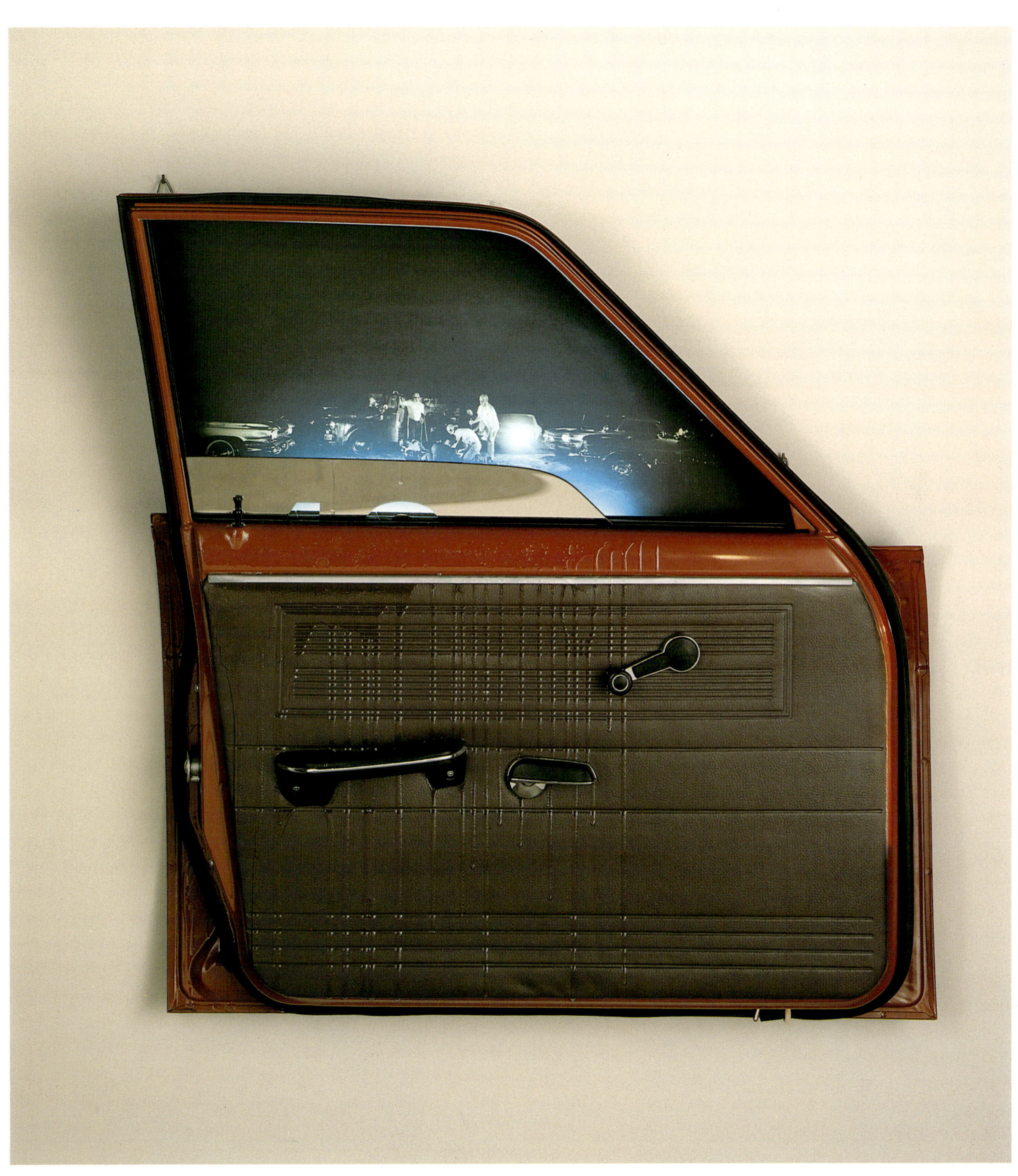

Edward Kienholz *Sawdy* 1971
car door, mirrored window, screenprint, fluorescent light, galvanized sheet metal, automotive lacquer, polyester resin (cat. no. 51)

Ed Paschke

Media-generated imagery of freaks, deviants, and other subculture types has informed Ed Paschke's art since the late 1960s. His technically polished, exaggerated characterizations of such subjects linked him with a group of artists, which included Jim Nutt and Karl Wirsum, now widely known as the Chicago Imagists. His frequent reliance on photographic imagery and investigations into how media images function, however, separated him from these artists. Garish, often discordant colors liken his figures to those in carnival sideshow posters and other such sensational forms of advertising.

The artist's early fascination with popular imagery led him to employ graphic media to express his ideas. As a student at the School of the Art Institute of Chicago in the 1960s, he studied etching, aquatint, silkscreen, and lithography.[1] From 1968 to 1970 he independently produced eight color silkscreens and two etchings that rely heavily on newspaper imagery. Paschke's first invitation to print professionally, however, came in 1971, when Jack Lemon of Landfall Press in Chicago invited him and four other local artists to participate in a portfolio project.[2]

The resulting lithograph, *Hairy Shoes* (1971), is integrally related to a concurrent group of paintings and drawings of elaborately decorated shoes that occupied Paschke for nearly two years. In these works he demonstrated his interest in the similarities between flesh and leather by depicting hair, scars, warts, tattoos, and scales covering stylish shoes, baseball gloves, and purses. "I was caught up with the idea that human beings frequently treat themselves in an object-like way,"[3] he says, in reference to the way people often stamp and puncture their skin for decorative reasons. A triad of tattooed bearded shoes in the painting *Hairy Shoes* (1971) explicitly points up this connection. Related works, such as the painting *Painted Lady* (1971), present fully tattooed people as curiosities, objects on display.

Paschke says he based the lithograph *Hairy Shoes* on an existing drawing because he "felt a little insecure taking risks with a medium [he] was out of touch with."[4] Further, he felt that the strong value contrasts in the drawing would translate well into multiple colors. In the work three shiny customized loafers with frizzled beards are set against a disconcertingly empty background. Each of the shoes is of a different style, but it is the artist's meticulous modeling that endows them with individual personalities. Thus the print is linked to those well-known surrealistic images in which nonsensical subjects are rendered with masterful realism.

The process of printing the lithograph in stages—beginning with the basic black-and-white image and successively adding colors—relates closely to the painting style Paschke had evolved over the years. By building up thin layers of transparent oil paints over a colorless underpainting, he achieves brilliant surface colors. To finish a work, he emphasizes the textural details and those areas that show the play of light on different surfaces. Paschke sees a parallel between this progression and the one from black and white to color in "the historical development of printing, film and T.V. images."[5] The artist's interest in this subject has led to his current work, which deals with depersonalized video and television images.

—S.M.

---

1. See Dennis Adrian and Richard A. Born, *The Chicago Imagist Print: Ten Artists' Works, 1958–1987, A Catalogue Raisonné*, exh. cat. (David and Alfred Smart Gallery of the University of Chicago, 1987), pp. 108–125, for a complete illustrated listing of Paschke's graphic work. As this book indicates, students at the School of the Art Institute of Chicago were encouraged to study printmaking, and many went on to pursue it actively.

2. Lemon in correspondence with the author, 16 June 1988. He also invited Roger Brown, Jordan Davies, Ed Flood, and Karl Wirsum.

3. Quoted in "Ed Paschke," *Profile* 3 (September 1983), p. 17.

4. The artist in correspondence with Elizabeth Armstrong, 7 March 1988.

5. Ed Paschke, "A Personal Statement," in the Renaissance Society at the University of Chicago, *Ed Paschke: Selected Works, 1967–1981*, exh. cat. (Renaissance Society at the University of Chicago, 1982), p. 3.

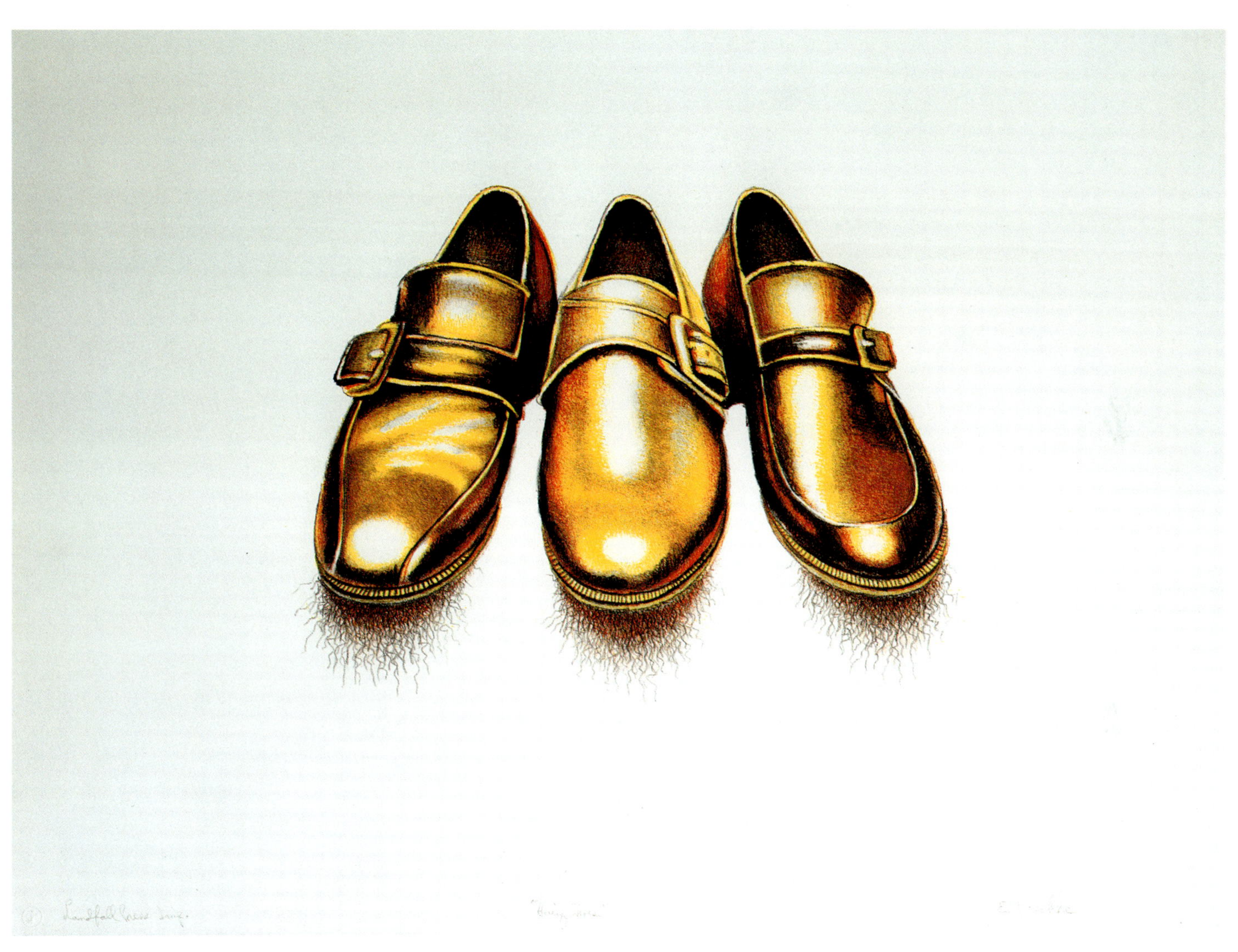

Ed Paschke *Hairy Shoes* 1971
lithograph (cat. no. 54)

Nancy Graves

By the early 1970s Nancy Graves had employed sculpture, painting, drawing, and film to express her artistic ideas. In 1972, when she accepted an invitation from the publisher Carl Solway to make lithographs at Landfall Press in Chicago, she added printmaking to this repertoire. Her first prints, the *Lunar Maps*, at once scientific and lyrical, encourage the viewer to contemplate their surfaces as though from a satellite. At the same time, the complex arrangements of color, line, pattern, and, in some cases, texture in these images demand close-up examination.

In the late 1960s Graves concentrated on ethnographically oriented subjects expressed in camel sculptures, bone constructions, shaman pieces, films, and intricate drawings. Though most of her work then was three-dimensional, she constantly concerned herself with surface effects, both planar and painterly. Late in 1971 she began a number of paintings and gouache drawings that took camouflaged sea animals and, slightly later, bathymetric and topographical maps, as their points of departure. Created from hundreds of dabs of paint, their colorful surfaces fluctuate between appearing unrestrained and tightly controlled.

Maps increasingly attracted Graves' attention because they lent themselves to her interest both in the natural environment and in exploring new ways of seeing. After making paintings based on maps of the ocean floor, she took on the moon, which, she says, "was not only poetically but scientifically, considered to be a fossil of the earth."[1] Satellite photographs with superimposed color diagrams of recent geologic discoveries formed the basis of eight lunar paintings and ten related drawings. She transposed and overlayed images from various maps to achieve satisfying compositions. Because these maps were inherently colorless, the artist developed her own color schemes.

In 1972 Graves decided to adapt variations of these lunar maps for her first editioned prints. Lithography was a natural choice, since she had worked in the medium as a student at Yale and later, in 1964–1965, at Atelier Mourlot in Paris.[2] Collaborating with printer David Keister at Landfall, she produced the *Lunar Maps*, comprising ten lithographs, each one designed to interact with the others. The maps she took as her sources were photo-offset lithographs of dot patterns used to convey varying levels of depth; she wanted to expand upon them to produce different spatial configurations, using any lithographic means available. Owing to some of the uncommon materials she and Keister chose—and to the complexity of her imagery—their collaboration time, prior to proofing, lasted over three weeks.

The second lithograph in the series, *Fra Mauro Region of the Moon*, illustrates the contrast between naturalism and formalism prevalent in much of Graves' art. The colored dots assert themselves not only as representing the lunar surface but also as unabashed bursts of pure color. A circus of eight colors spreads across the print; by contrasting dense areas of color with open ones, Graves generates a terrific energy. For the third lithograph, *Maestlin G Region of the Moon* (cat. no. 56), she printed six colors on six sides of three sheets of Shin-Ten-Gu rice paper. She then laminated these to a sheet of heavier paper to achieve an eloquent, if not quite tangible, pastel surface color. The transparency of the layered rice paper allows all six printed sides to appear simultaneously but prevents any one from dominating. To achieve an even greater illusion of depth in *Sabine D Region of the Moon* (cat. no. 59), the ninth in the series, a black pattern was printed on Mylar and then laminated to the paper, on which a dazzling composition of layered dots had already been printed.[3]

Graves recently wrote that making prints "expanded my perception of drawing, color, and process."[4] In 1977 she spent some time at Tyler Graphics Ltd., where she made a number of hand-colored, mixed-media prints that address the lack of personal touch inherent in standard printmaking processes. She continued to personalize her prints in numerous projects, including a group of thirty-one monoprints she made with Kenneth Tyler in 1981.

—S.M.

---

1. The artist in a conversation with Joan Seeman, 6 June 1979, in Linda Cathcart, *Nancy Graves: A Survey, 1969/1980*, exh. cat. (Buffalo, N.Y.: Albright-Knox Art Gallery, 1980), p. 22.

2. The artist in a conversation with the author, 9 May 1988. Dissatisfied with the results of her collaboration at Mourlot, Graves did not edition the prints.

3. According to Jack Lemon, the use of Mylar in this print and the layering of Japanese paper in *Maestlin G Region of the Moon* were both new procedures for Landfall. Correspondence with the author, 16 June 1988.

4. In correspondence with Elizabeth Armstrong, 3 February 1988.

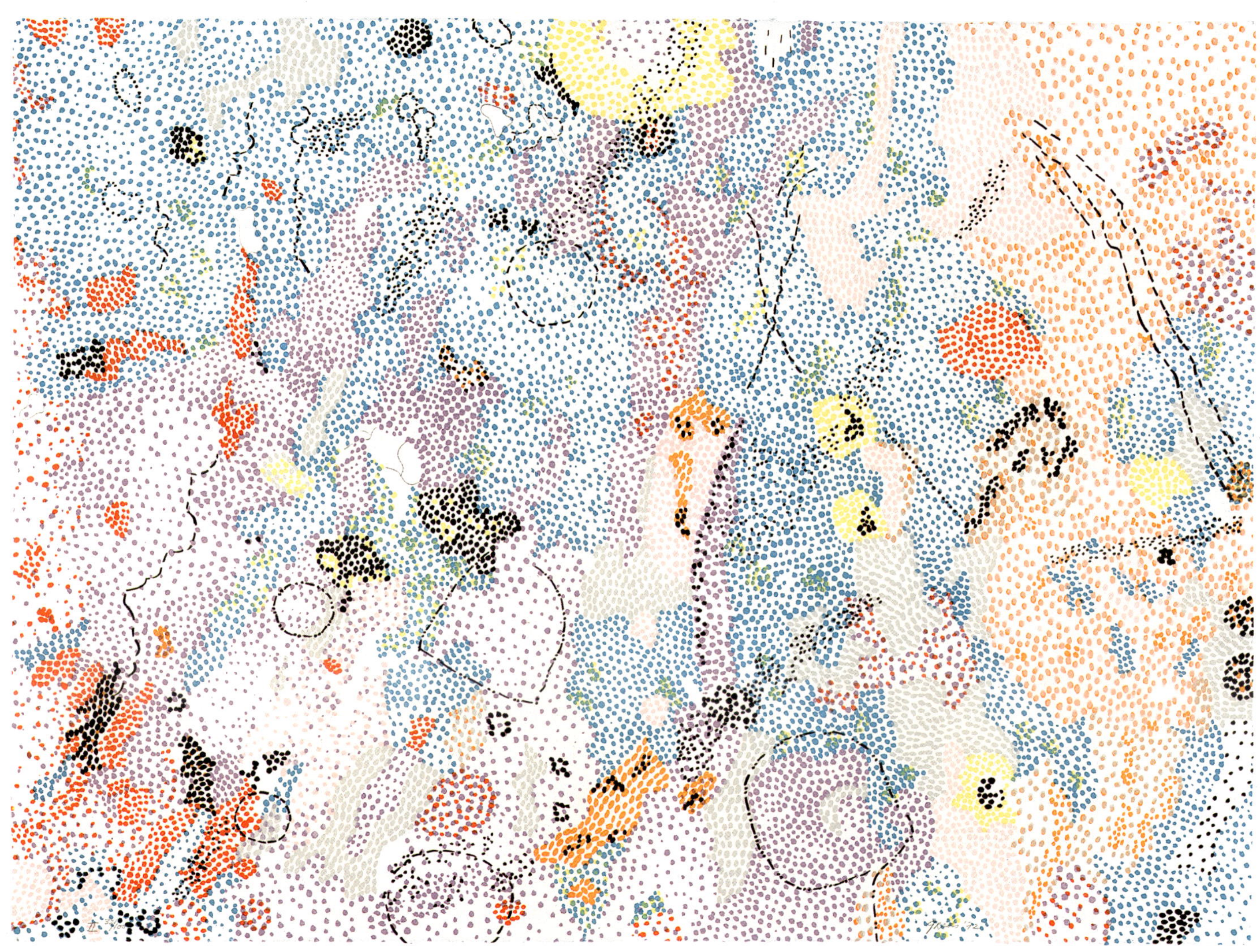

Nancy Graves *Fra Mauro Region of the Moon* 1972
lithograph (cat. no. 55)

Chuck Close

When Robert Feldman of Parasol Press in New York City first approached Chuck Close about making a print, the painter was understandably wary. Having spent time during graduate work at Yale as assistant to the prominent printmaker Gabor Peterdi, he had firsthand knowledge of how printers' technical expertise can strongly affect an artist's working process. In order to avoid this kind of dependency, Close told Feldman he wanted to work with mezzotint, one of the most difficult of graphic techniques, and proposed to make the largest mezzotint ever printed. "Since no one had made a mezzotint in years and years," he remembers, "it would be on-the-job training for me and the printer as we both tried to figure out how to do it. And it didn't give [the printer] a leg up. That kind of interested me."[1] In fact, this mutual lack of expertise was one of the things that convinced Close to publish his first print, *Keith*, in 1972. In addition, the mezzotint's ability—with its extraordinary tonal range—to simulate a photographic image made it a desirable one for the Photorealist painter.

Feldman could not have found a more compatible printer for this challenging project than Crown Point Press, a small etching workshop in Oakland, California, directed by Kathan Brown. Close described it as a shop that "becomes whatever you need it to be,"[2] and this was certainly the case with *Keith*. Crown Point had never made a print larger than twenty-two by thirty inches; Close wanted the work to measure at least three by four feet. This would require a new press and specially made copper plates. It was only after Brown had accepted the idea of working in this large format that Close delivered the even more daunting request to work in mezzotint. As Brown explained to Feldman in an effort to convince him and the artist to choose another medium, "Only a few people have done [mezzotint] in the past hundred years, and even . . . when they were popular their size range was about 9 × 12 [inches]."[3]

In a mezzotint the artist begins with a completely black plate and works from dark to light. Traditionally, the medium's dark ground is achieved through the laborious process of hand-rocking, which covers the plate with tiny pits and burrs needed to hold the ink. Lighter areas are then created by smoothing out this surface, an arduous process that yields subtle variations of shadow and light. Because of its size, the plate for *Keith* would have taken too long to hand-rock, presenting yet another problem for the Crown Point crew. This, too, they solved—with the help of photography. They revamped their studio to accommodate a commercial photo-engraving machine (the apparatus that, ironically, was responsible for the mezzotint's fall into disfavor in the late nineteenth century), brought in especially for the project. This machine enabled them to transfer a photographic halftone screen to the large plate with a finer resolution than that achieved with the traditional mezzotint rocker.[4]

When Close works on a painting, he begins with a photograph that has been overlaid with a grid and then transfers the image, unit by unit, onto the canvas. After the mezzotint plate for *Keith* was prepared, Close adopted the same strategy, dividing the surface into dozens of one-inch squares. Although he worked from the same photograph he had used to make a painting of his friend Keith in 1970, the process was the opposite of the way he painted. Instead of putting black paint on a white canvas, he worked in reverse, scraping and burnishing the plate to carve the image out of its dark surface. Accustomed to seeing the results of his hand, Close found this experience extremely disconcerting, and so he asked for a large number of proofs from the plate during the early stages of his work. While this enabled him to see how the image was progressing, it also had the effect of eroding the delicate copper plate.

This erosion, which is evident in the lighter mouth and eye areas of the final print, did not displease Close. As Brown later explained, it serves as a "record of the struggle put into the print." Close was also intrigued by the appearance of the grid, which surfaced in certain areas of the mezzotint. This grid made manifest his highly systematic approach to realism; he incorporated the grid into a series of drawings he made of Keith in 1973, and it has become a dominant element in his work since.

—E.A.

---

1. The artist in a conversation with the author, 13 June 1988.

2. Supra, note 1.

3. Quoted in a portfolio entitled *The Chuck Close Mezzotint "Keith" 1972* (cat. no. 63). Subsequent Brown quotations here are also taken from this source.

4. Nancy Towley, "In Conversation with Kathan Brown," *The Print Collector's Newsletter* 8 (November–December 1977), p. 133.

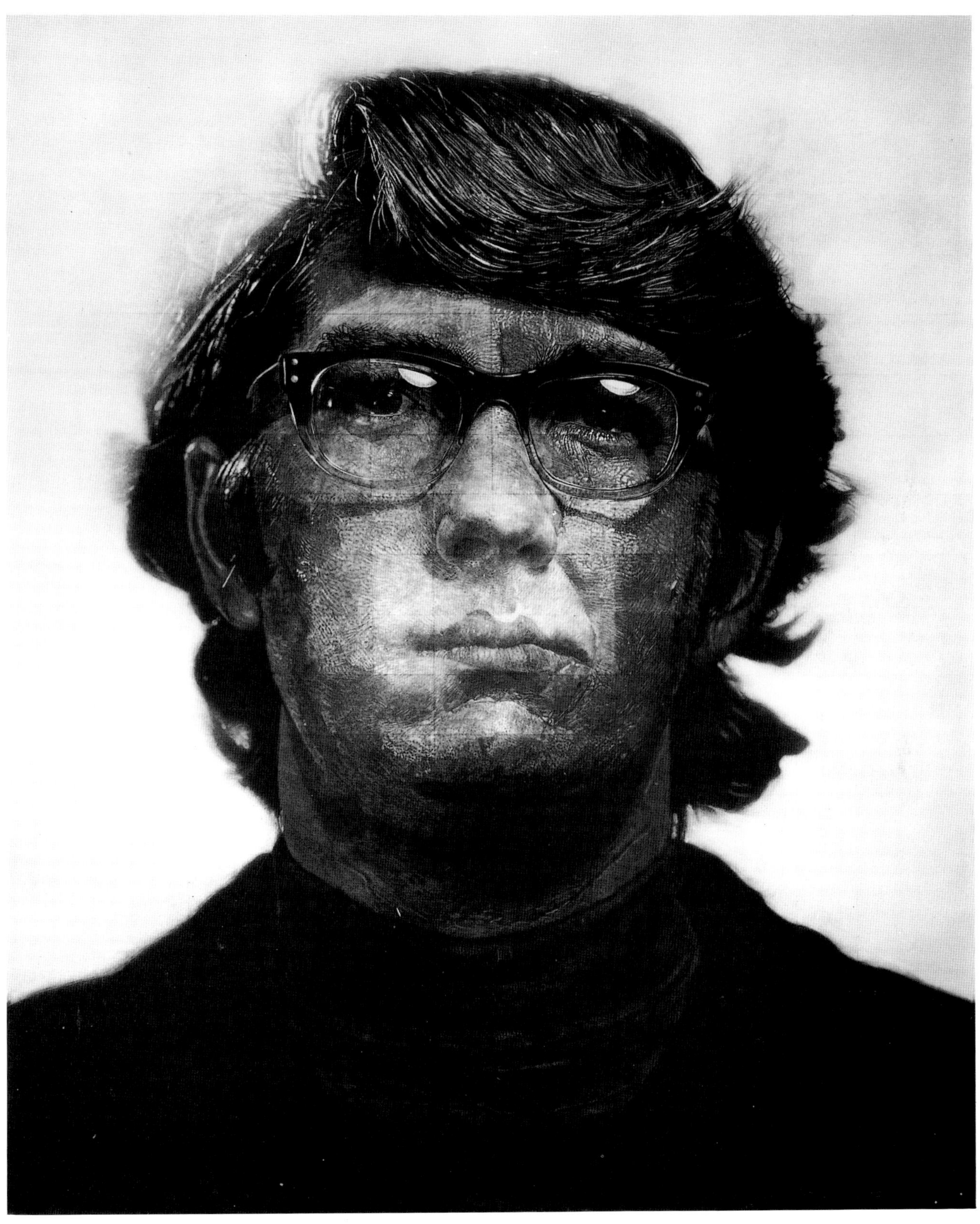

Chuck Close *Keith* 1972
mezzotint (cat. no. 60)

Richard Estes

Richard Estes' pseudo-photographic paintings of urban scenes epitomize Photorealism during its formative years, the late 1960s. His overt use of his own photographs to crystallize the streets and storefronts in these canvases overshadowed his painterly technique and innovative manipulations of objective reality. A profound interest in picture-making led him to remove people and trash from his scenes and to adjust the perspectives, reflections, and tonalities of the original photographs in the final paintings. Sometimes he would even reposition a building.

In 1971 Robert Feldman, director of the then burgeoning Parasol Press in New York City, asked Estes to make prints. Although he had no prior experience with printmaking, the painter was interested in working in a new medium;[1] this, the two of them decided, would be lithography. They then set out to find the right printer for the job. But, perhaps because of the complexity of Estes' images, they were unable to find a lithographer who could print them satisfactorily. So they decided to pursue silkscreen instead. Estes went to Stuttgart to collaborate with Michael Domberger, a printer who had an excellent reputation in the medium.[2]

No print medium could have been better suited to Estes' Photorealist imagery than silkscreen. For years silkscreen had been associated only with commercial advertising and photomechanical reproduction. The medium experienced a rush of popularity with the Pop artists in the 1960s, and Estes played a key role in elevating its status again during the 1970s—at a time when his realist colleagues preferred to edition color-offset reproductions of their paintings.[3] His first printmaking effort, *Urban Landscapes I* (1972), a portfolio of eight multicolored screenprints, stretched the limits of the medium by using an average of between 50 and 115 colors on each impression.[4]

The prints in *Urban Landscapes I* are essentially devoid of narrative. As in the paintings, the play of light off various surfaces is the key subject. Although Estes' realist style is somewhat restrained and softened by the silkscreen medium, he creates quite complex compositions that fully demonstrate his command of illusionistic reflections. The myriad details of city life reflected in the glass facade and revolving door in *560* (cat. no. 67) bring to mind the art critic John Canaday's observation that in Estes' paintings "reality and reflections of reality become all but indistinguishable from one another, until reality

becomes a kind of fantasy in spite of rigidly explicit factual details."[5] The same could be said of the highly reflective storefront in *Grant's* or of the multipaneled windows in *Danbury Rubber Tile* (cat. no. 65).

The art historian Richard Field recently described Estes' *Urban Landscapes I* as "an object lesson in the fabrication of illusion." "Each element of each reflection," he elaborates, "is reduced to discrete areas of opaque, planar color, befitting the flat, stenciled screenprinting medium."[6] The individuality of each mark forces the viewer to reconsider the apparently photographic quality of the subjects. The artist's expert manipulation of perspective and vigorous use of pattern also contribute to the composed nature of these printed images. The bounty of richly patterned surfaces in *Ten Doors* (cat. no. 66) and the bold cropping in *St. Louis Arch*, for example, illustrate Estes' tendency toward abstraction.

Estes still makes prints with Domberger. "Over the years," he says, "I have learned to work easily with him. He has learned to deal with my eccentricities and I with his." Many projects, including the technically complex, large-scale screenprint *Untitled* (1974) and two subsequent *Urban Landscapes* portfolios, attest to the success of this collaboration.

—S.M.

1. The artist in correspondence with Elizabeth Armstrong, 11 March 1988. All subsequent Estes quotations here are also taken from this source.

2. Ibid.

3. See Richard S. Field, "Printmaking since 1960: The Conflicts between Process and Expression," in Richard S. Field and Ruth E. Fine, *A Graphic Muse: Prints by Contemporary American Women*, exh. cat. (New York: Hudson Hills Press in association with Mount Holyoke College Art Museum, 1987), p. 17.

4. Domberger and Estes prepared the screens for *Urban Landscapes I* from a series of gouaches made especially for the project. For illustrations of these gouaches, see Louis K. Meisel, *Richard Estes: The Complete Paintings, 1966–1985* (New York: Harry N. Abrams Publishers, 1986), pp. 72–73.

5. John Canaday, *Richard Estes: The Urban Landscape*, exh. cat. (Boston: Museum of Fine Arts and New York Graphic Society, 1978), p. 14.

6. Field, op. cit., p. 17.

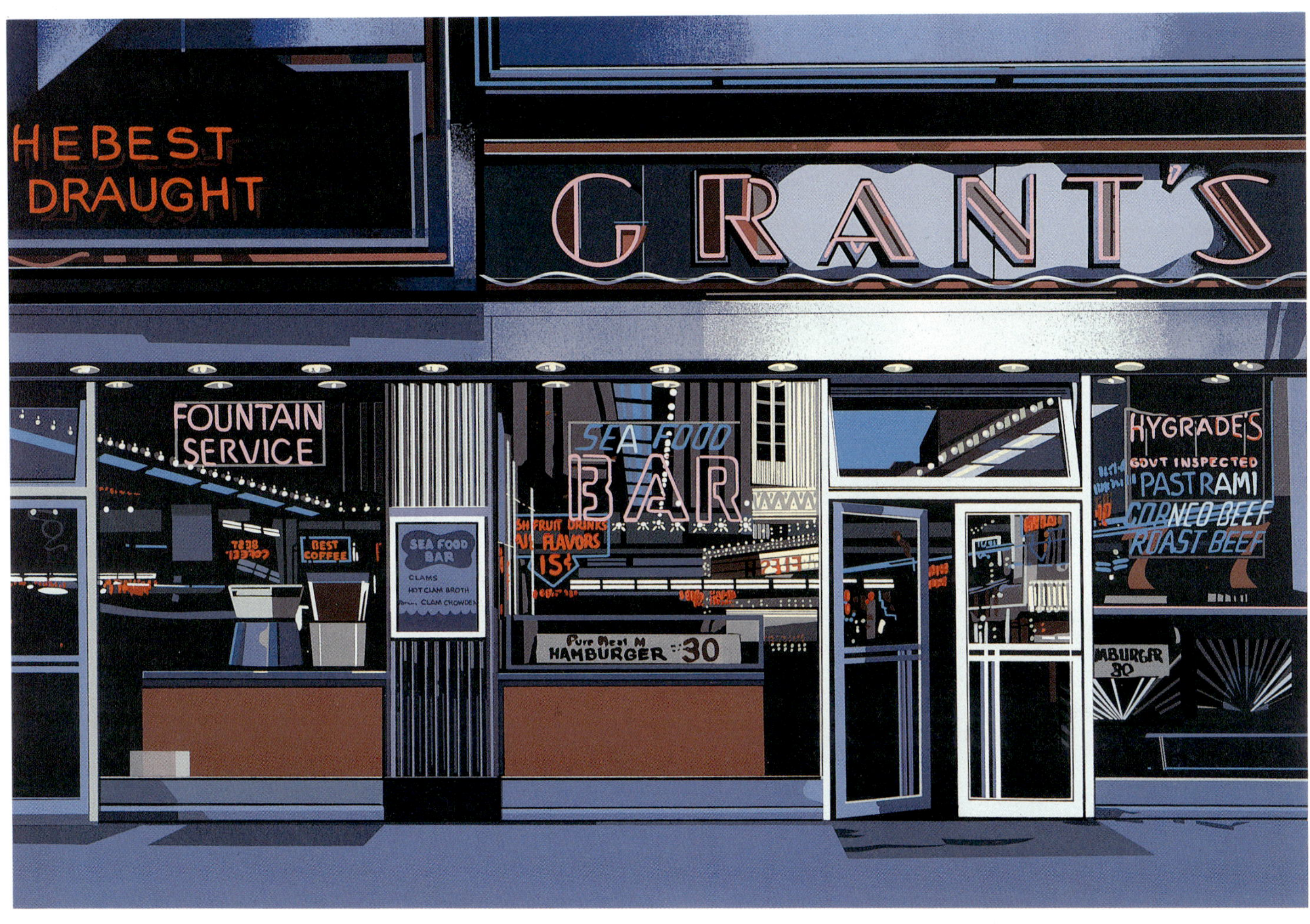

Richard Estes *Grant's* 1972
screenprint (cat. no. 64)

William Wiley's first exposure to printmaking was at the San Francisco Art Institute, where he earned his B.F.A. in 1960 and M.F.A. in 1962, studying under Nathan Oliveira. Upon graduation, Wiley began teaching at the University of California, Davis, where, he acknowledges, he was influenced by students such as Bruce Nauman—whose emphasis on ordinary, nontraditional materials and antiformal approach to art-making Wiley shared.[1] Wiley's private, idiosyncratic sensibility, in turn, exerted significant influence on Nauman and many of his contemporaries.

By the late 1960s Wiley had developed a highly personal style, which, in contrast to the dominant aesthetic of that period, was a complex combination of figuration, abstraction, and commentary. Narrative text played—and continues to play—an active role in his drawing, painting, and sculpture; it generally takes the form of random thoughts that occur while he is creating. Such text is especially evident in his printmaking, which has been described as "the medium through which he makes conversational contact with his audience."[2]

Wiley made a few prints on his own between 1967 and 1971. His first published works were commissioned by Studio Marconi in Milan in 1971, while he was preparing for an exhibition at that gallery.[3] But because he spoke no Italian and so was restricted in his communication with the printers, he felt that the four lithographs produced there were inadequate. His first significant collaboration took place a year later at Jack Lemon's Landfall Press in Chicago. Visiting the city for his first retrospective exhibition,[4] which was then at the Art Institute, Wiley accepted the latest of the master printer's many invitations to make prints with him. Although the shop's low-key atmosphere agreed with Wiley, he nonetheless "embarked on the project with all the misgivings (and enthusiasms) of a novice."[5]

Moon Mullings (1972), one of the first prints he made at Landfall, displays Wiley's typically informal, punning use of the language. For a start, the title is a play on the name of the venerable, derby-hatted comic strip character Moon Mullins, whose lowbrow humor undoubtedly appealed to Wiley. The text takes the form of a hand-written letter to Wiley's wife, in which he poetically recounts, with intentional misspellings not unlike those in the comic strip, the ups and downs of working on the Landfall prints. "Eyes gwine plumb crazy here in the winter workin with the printers," reads the first part of the extended caption. Was he going crazy, or was it just eyestrain? He ends with the casual salutation, "Well nice chattin with you."

Above the text rests an image within the image, a dense maze of quirky lines and ambiguous, cartoonlike forms. The yellow crescent moon embedded in these markings anchors them so that they almost coalesce into an abstracted landscape. A patchwork of abstract markings covers the background of *Moon Mullings*, making it look something like an old piece of paper that has been crumpled and then flattened out. In each corner are spheres—forms that often appear in Wiley's work—which seem to orbit around the central image like portentous symbols on an astrologer's chart.

While at Landfall, Wiley decided to try printing on chamois; during the preceding two years, he had made many paintings and drawings on animal hides. Lemon was willing to experiment with this material: the varying nap and stretch of each hide presented a technical challenge. Delighted with the success of the first edition, *Little Hide*, Wiley and Lemon made a second chamois object, *Coast Reverse*, a diptych in which the same image (roughly shaped like a map of the United States) was printed twice, first on paper and then on chamois. Wiley then hand-colored the hides with acrylic paints and ballpoint pens, further differentiating each print in the edition.

Wiley's two-week stay at Landfall produced ten lithographs and led to numerous return visits. During one of these, a few years later, he began work on a book of etchings entitled *Suite of Daze*, a project he and Lemon had discussed in 1972. Wiley refers to this book, which combines fourteen etchings with original text, as a kind of culmination of his initiation into printmaking at Landfall, a "book about the making of the book," in which he immersed himself in the exploration of various etching processes.[6] In recent years he has come to favor etching, collaborating extensively with Timothy Berry, who printed *Suite of Daze* at Landfall Press in 1976, and with Crown Point Press in Oakland, California, among others.

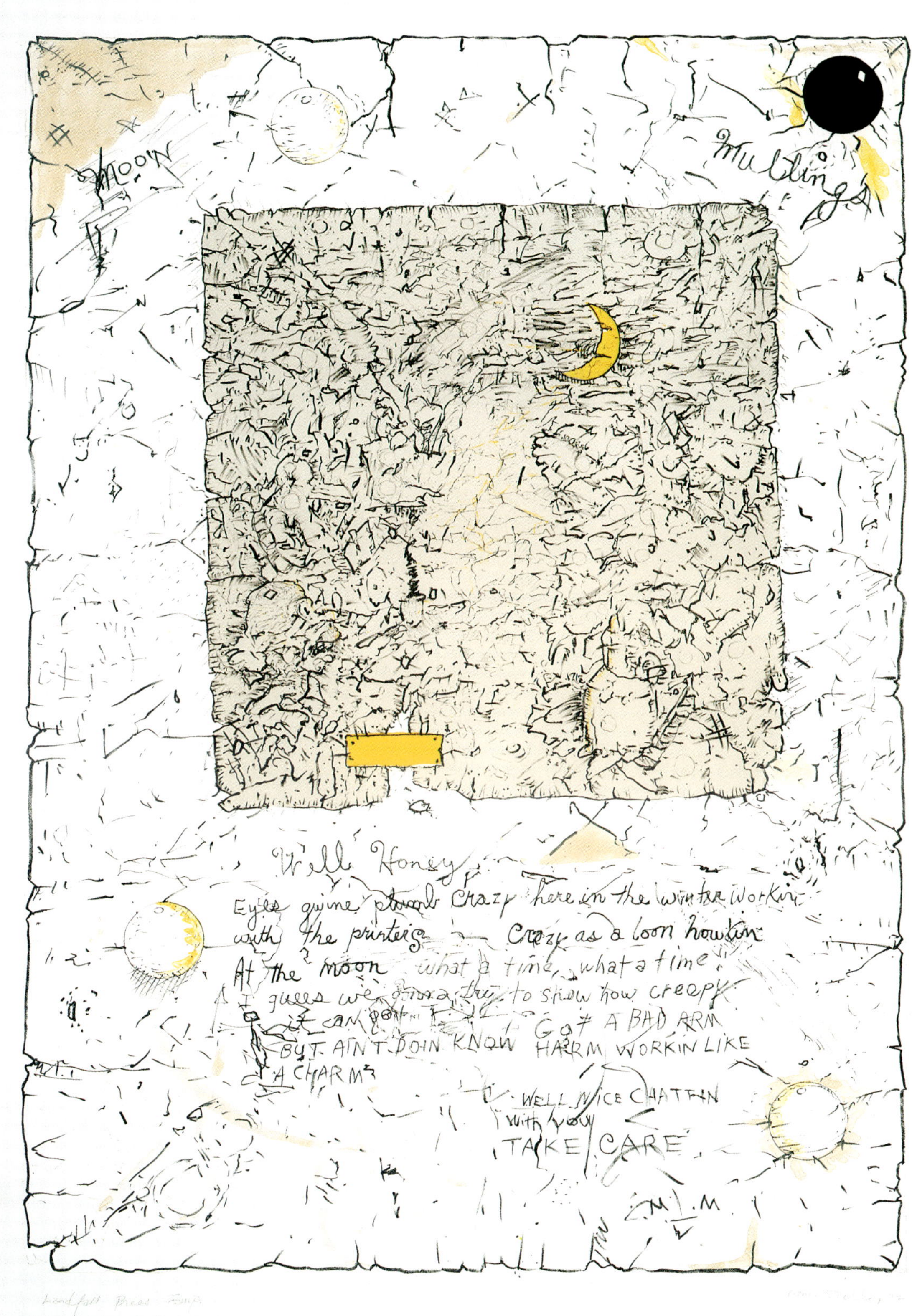

William T. Wiley *Moon Mullings* 1972
lithograph (cat. no. 68)

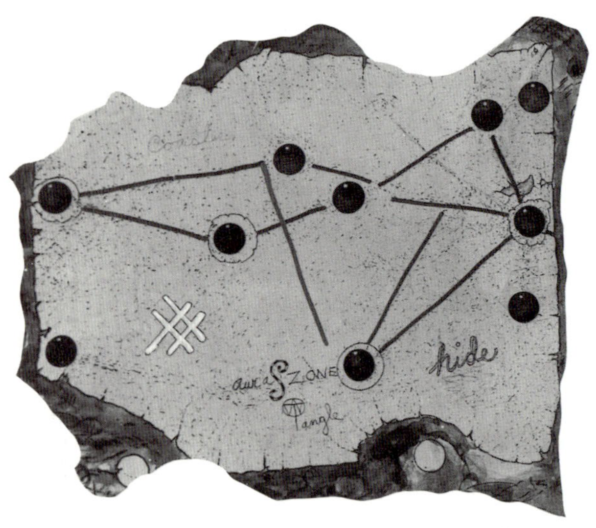

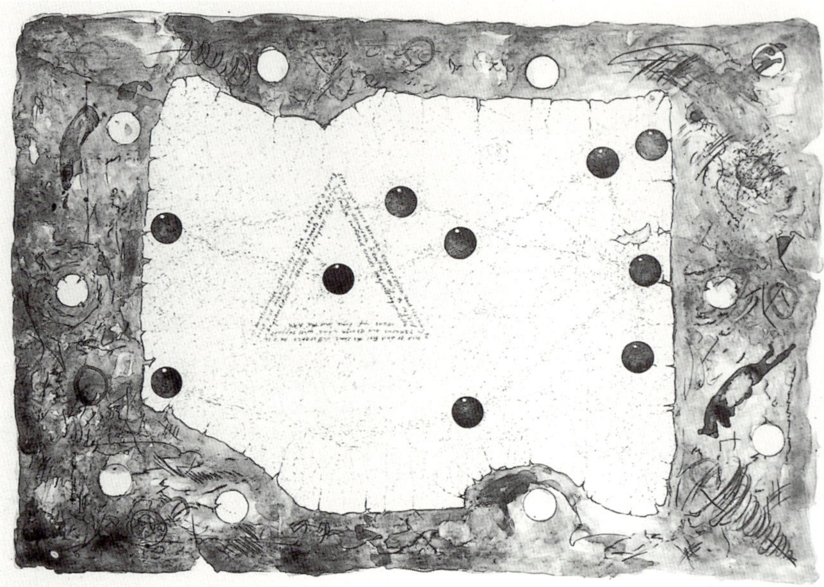

William T. Wiley *Coast Reverse* 1972
two lithographs (cat. no. 70)

Wiley explains his attraction to printmaking in characteristic stream-of-consciousness style: "I have always ? liked prints. . . . The history of images and marks and gestures etc. that can be caught ? on a plate . . . worked and reworked. Images layering—ghost images—unintentional marks and so on—the tools—the materials—the alchemy."[7]

—E.A.

1. See John Perreault in *Wiley Territory*, exh. cat. (Minneapolis: Walker Art Center, 1979), p. 9.

2. Brenda Richardson, *William T. Wiley Graphics, 1967–1979* (Chicago: Landfall Press, 1980), p. 6.

3. These four early prints are illustrated and documented in ibid., pp. 16–19.

4. Organized by Brenda Richardson at the University Art Museum, Berkeley, the 1971–1972 exhibition *William T. Wiley* traveled to the Institute of Contemporary Art, University of Pennsylvania, Philadelphia, and to the Art Institute of Chicago.

5. Richardson, op. cit., p. 5.

6. The artist in correspondence with the author, 1 February 1988.

7. Ibid.

Yvonne Jacquette

In 1973 the print publisher Brooke Alexander invited twenty-four artists to make hand-colored lithographs for a group portfolio.[1] Some of the artists he approached, such as James Rosenquist and Edward Ruscha, were already experienced printmakers. Others, including Yvonne Jacquette, had had virtually no previous involvement with graphic media. Until this time Jacquette had considered printmaking too "stamped out" for her sensibility.[2] She agreed to participate in Alexander's project, however, because hand-coloring left open the option for varying her images. "This seemed to be a chance to 'dive-in' half-way," she recalls. "Since I intended to get the touch of my hand and the use of many materials in the hand-coloring, the print part of it was to be a way to get the drawing structure down, to vary by colors of ink the kind of feeling that would help trigger the hand-coloring response."

Alexander's dedication to this project and the support he extended were, Jacquette says, key factors in the success of her first prints. He suggested different papers to her, showed her a variety of other prints, and delivered the lithography stone to the artist's studio. According to Jacquette, Alexander's first piece of advice was, "Don't go looking up anything about printmaking." For the artist, he was the catalyst: "He was sticking pins into what I had in my mind, but it was never about technique, it was always about enlarging the vision."[3]

For the hand-colored lithograph (1973), she chose an image that she was painting in oils at the time, *East 12th Street* (1972–1973), a view of a hanging traffic light set against an expanse of sky. She recognized its potential for many variations: the traffic signal itself could be red, yellow, or green, and the light and quality of the sky could change dramatically depending on the weather or time of day depicted. The prospect of exploring changes within a single image excited her: "I wanted to play with a wide variety of emotional responses—to start, red traffic lights for 'restriction,' green for 'freedom,' yellow for 'caution.'"

Not content to confine variation to the colors in the image, Jacquette, in collaboration with printer Paul Narkiewicz, expanded her first printmaking endeavor to include experiments with a variety of smooth, bumpy, and tinted papers, as well as with different inks and ink consistencies.[4] She made yet other modifications by using different techniques of hand-coloring, including watercolor, gouache, and pastel. This was her first extensive use of pastel, a medium that would become essential to her way of seeing and working. "At first the pastels seemed completely fat and unwieldy," she remembers, "but after I got the touch and made separate marks rather than blending it, I got very excited by what the colors did."[5] She discovered that pastels enabled her to work more intuitively and came to see them as a sketch medium that was "more flexible and portable than watercolor."

The collaboration on *Traffic Signal* proved fruitful for Jacquette, who felt "the print was more alive than my paintings." Her future work was greatly affected by the experience. Besides leading her to use pastel, the prints encouraged her to find new ways of depicting light. The moonlit versions of *Traffic Signal* led to the series of nighttime paintings she would undertake four years later.

—S.M.

---

1. Each of the prints is illustrated in the catalogue that accompanied a touring exhibition of the portfolio organized by Brooke Alexander, Inc. Carter Ratcliff discusses their range of techniques and styles in his introduction to this catalogue, *Hand Colored Prints* (New York: Brooke Alexander, Inc., 1975), unpaginated.

2. The artist in correspondence with Elizabeth Armstrong, 31 December 1987. Unless otherwise noted, all subsequent Jacquette quotations here are taken from this source.

3. Quoted in Judith Goldman's introduction to *Brooke Alexander: A Decade of Print Publishing*, exh. cat. (Boston University Art Gallery, 1978), unpaginated.

4. Upon completing the twenty-seven different hand-colored prints, Jacquette and Narkiewicz made three other editions from the stone: one in black, one in grays, and one in red and black.

5. Interview with Kate Horsfield, in "Yvonne Jacquette," *Profile 2* (November 1982), p. 17.

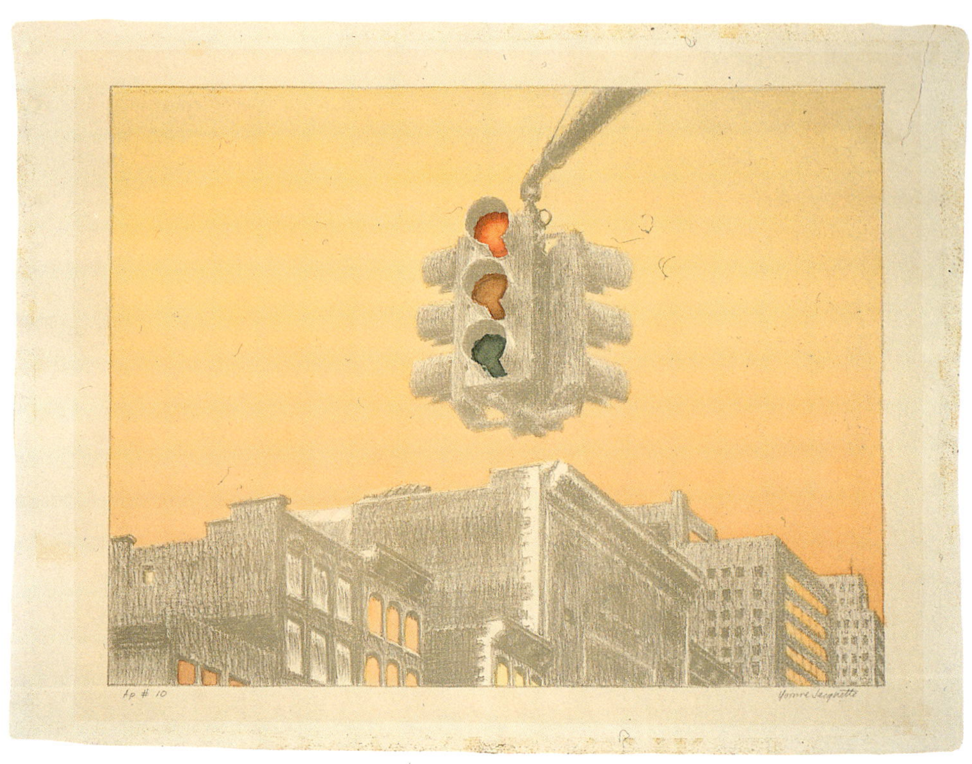

Yvonne Jacquette *Traffic Signal* 1973
lithograph, hand-colored with watercolor (cat. no. 71)

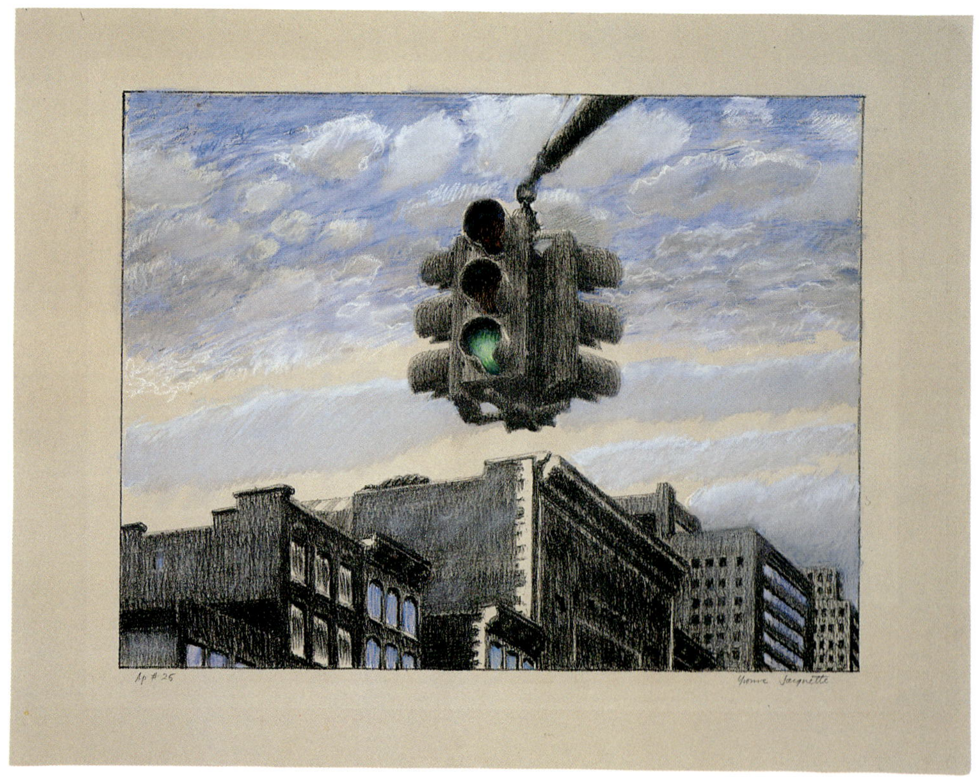

Yvonne Jacquette *Traffic Signal* 1973
lithograph, hand-colored with pastel (cat. no. 72)

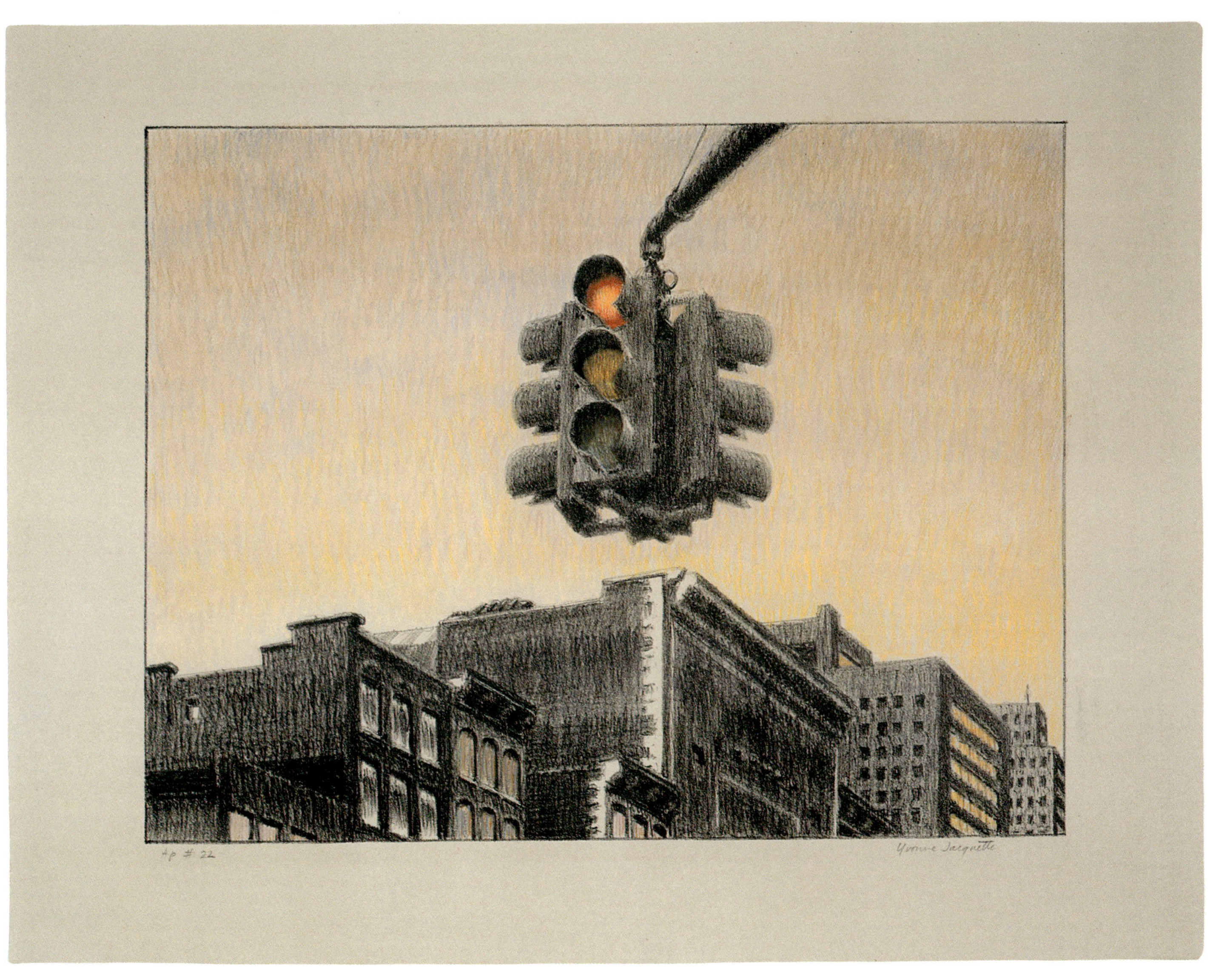

Yvonne Jacquette *Traffic Signal* 1973
lithograph, hand-colored with pastel (cat. no. 73)

Pat Steir

Pat Steir has always valued printmaking as a medium through which to explore her interest in the relationship between language and art. Graphic-media studies at Pratt Institute in Brooklyn led her to work as a book designer and an art director at Harper and Row during the 1960s. Although she painted in her spare time, she lacked the equipment to pursue printmaking independently. In 1970 she left the publishing firm to concentrate exclusively on paintings that investigated form, illusion, and myth as individual components of art. Impressed by a group of these paintings, Jack Lemon invited Steir to make lithographs at Landfall Press in Chicago in 1973.

At Landfall in 1974, Steir produced five lithographs— *Roll Me a Rainbow*, *Between the Lines* (cat. no. 75), and *Wish Series #1*, *#2*, and *#3*—which both show an ambitious approach to the medium and make the very elements of lithography one of their primary subjects. Because she loved working on stones, she "used them [as] freely as paper" to improvise on images from her drawings and paintings of the same period. "That work," she explains, "was intensely involved in process, so printmaking was a logical extension."[1]

Roll Me a Rainbow, the first lithograph Steir made at Landfall, exemplifies her interest in the syntax of lithography and the meaning of printed marks. Lining the left side of the image is an inventory of lithographic marks: a splatter of tusche, an opaque stroke of tusche, and lines scribbled in wax crayon. Immediately below these, a drawn flower represents the concept of illusions with images constructed of line, color, and shape.

Steir contrasts her spontaneous application of tusche, dripping from the center of the print, with the technical virtuosity of a rainbow roll above. In response to her request that the color scale be printed across the top, Lemon instructed his printer to "roll me a rainbow." To him this was merely a technical phrase indicating "print a rainbow roll," but to the artist it rang romantically—as she says, "Roll me a rainbow. It sounds like a movie from 1940."[2] She decided to use it as the title of the print.

Between the Lines, her next print, also takes the syntax of lithography as one of its subjects. Recognizable images drawn between the ruled lines in the bottom section offer a wry critique of the then prevalent Minimalist aesthetic, in which formal elements such as line and color are dominant.[3] Steir's comments about this image reveal another level of deep-seated humor:

They were jokes to the printers about the printing process. . . . Between the lines each of those little images was printed in a different way, a different method of lithography, a different technique. So each of those little images was a different way of combining colors—with line, with wash, with scraping, with drawing. . . . and the printers really enjoyed that print more than anybody else did.[4]

Printmaking helped Steir clarify her "thinking about art both philosophically and in terms of process." In the three *Wish* lithographs she uses the idea of transformation from state to state and the technical act of overprinting, both unique to graphic media, to illustrate the ways in which images or "illusions" become associated with myth, memory, and history. Representational elements in her work function as universal signs. The iris, for example, has many layers of meaning for Steir—including an element of self-portrayal, since her given name is Iris.

By 1976, when Steir returned to Landfall, Lemon had acquired an etching press and an experienced intaglio printer, Timothy Berry. He trained her in drypoint, a technique she used to produce two complex groups of prints, *The Burial Mound Series* (1976) and the *Line Poems* (1976). With these and subsequent projects, including the complicated triptych etching *Abstraction, Belief, Desire*, made at Crown Point Press in 1981, Steir has reached the point where she can participate in, and control, all phases of print production. After fifteen years the medium still excites her, a condition she attributes to having worked with some of the "best printmakers available."

—S.M.

---

1. The artist in correspondence with Elizabeth Armstrong, 26 May 1988. Unless otherwise noted, all subsequent Steir quotations here are also taken from this source.

2. Quoted in Elizabeth Broun, *Form, Illusion, Myth: Prints and Drawings of Pat Steir*, exh. cat. (Lawrence, Kans.: Spencer Museum of Art, 1983), p. 29. This book includes a complete illustrated catalogue by Jan Howard of the prints Steir produced from 1973 to 1982.

A rainbow roll, also known as blend inking, is a technique by which the printer's roller can pick up a blended succession of different colors from a slab and transfer that sequence to a printing element.

3. Ibid., p. 28.

4. Ibid.

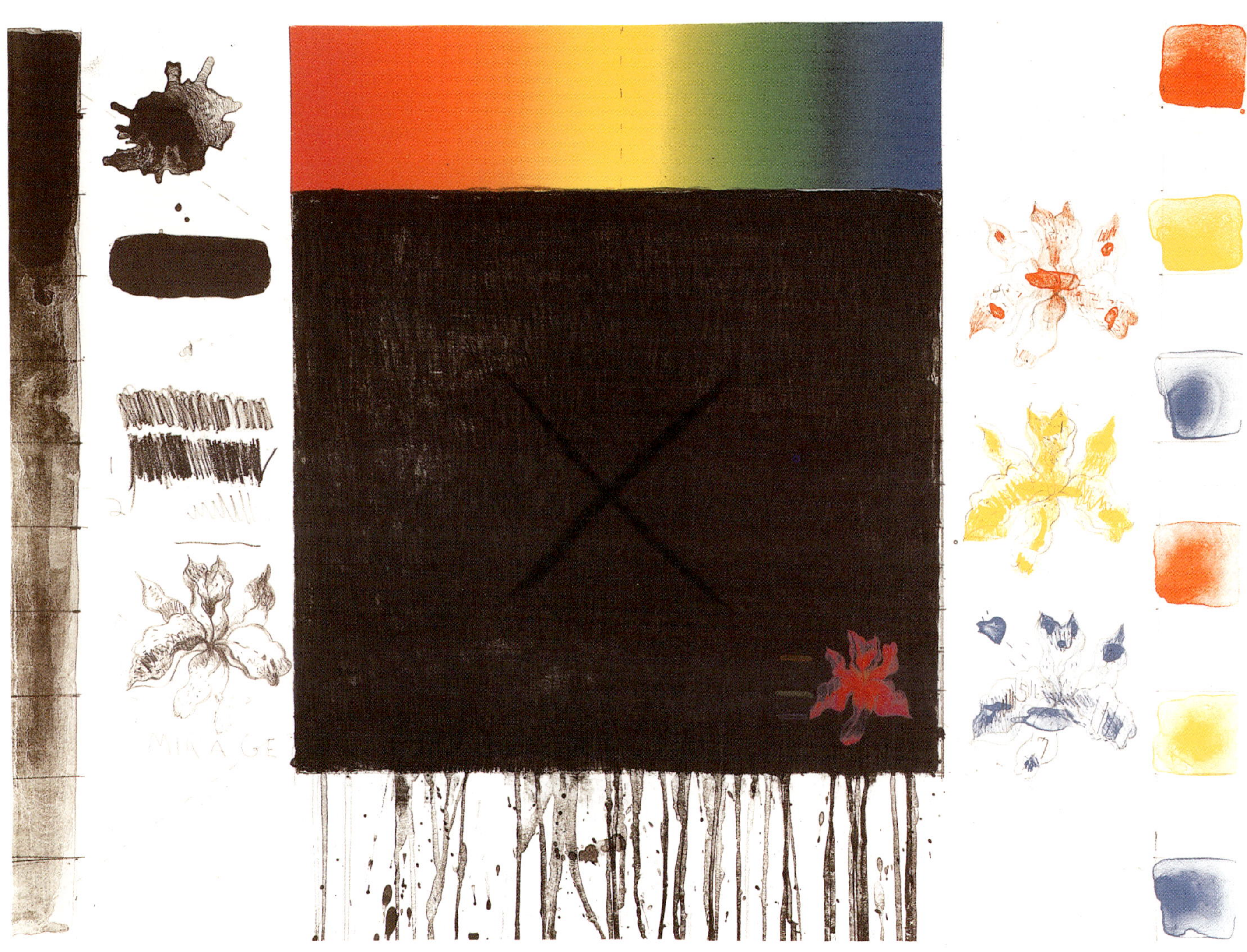

Pat Steir *Roll Me a Rainbow* 1974
lithograph (cat. no. 74)

Michelle Stuart

In 1974 a favorable review of Michelle Stuart's art by Lawrence Alloway appeared in *Artforum* magazine.[1] Alloway described the unique process Stuart used in her wall works: she began with a form of frottage, placing muslin-mounted rag paper on top of rocks or sand and rubbing it with sticks of graphite to make an impression from the earth's surface. In the process she produced scroll-like works (some as large as twelve by five feet) with shimmering, textured surfaces. The resulting pieces resembled the terrain that spawned them and yet, when hung on the wall, had an extraordinarily ethereal quality.

Later that year, perhaps in response to the Alloway piece, Clinton Adams invited Stuart to make prints at Tamarind Institute in Albuquerque. Adams, who had served as associate director of the Tamarind Lithography Workshop in Los Angeles in 1960 and 1961 under June Wayne, became director when the press relocated to the University of New Mexico in 1970. Like Wayne, Adams focused the workshop's activities on lithography; he undoubtedly saw Stuart's "rubbings" as a logical extension into this medium. For her part, Stuart accepted Adams' invitation to Tamarind largely because of its location. She was deeply interested in the Southwest—in the colors of the earth, in the light, and in native American myths, beliefs, and ceremonies. She chose to work there from November to January, a time when a number of important celebratory events would be taking place in the pueblos.[2] She spent her first weekend in New Mexico at a Zuñi dance ceremony called Shalako, which included Comanche and Mudhead dancers. Though outsiders are discouraged from attending such ceremonies, Stuart's knowledge of native American traditions, as well as several key contacts she had made among anthropologists in the community, facilitated this and subsequent visits to the pueblos.

She filled a journal with notes about the land around Albuquerque, in particular the Jemez Mountains. "Ancient trails criss cross the area," she wrote, "and shrines on mesas and summits have been used by the Indians within recent times. . . . Tunyo is sacred to the San Ildefonso Indians but permission to climb the mesa may be obtained from the Governor of the Pueblo." Her notes make references to native American history and folklore as well as to the topography of the region. "Zuni Mts . . . composed of Precambrian core and flanked by sediments ranging from Pennsylvanian to recent. The uplift is the plateau type." These geographical jottings reflect Stuart's readings, as well as her experience as a mapmaker for the U.S. Army Corps of Engineers.

Stuart went to Tamarind with an idea for making prints that related directly to the process she used to create her wall works. She planned to use rocks, instead of printing elements, to emboss the paper as it went through the press. According to Stuart, Adams was less than enthusiastic about this approach. He was undoubtedly concerned about the effect this procedure might have on the press, and he also felt that the final products would have little to do with lithography. While drawn to Stuart's work in frottage, which seemed directly applicable to lithography, he was not aware until she arrived at Tamarind that her method of working had undergone a significant change. Instead of making rubbings of the earth, Stuart, in July 1974, had begun smashing rocks directly onto her paper surfaces. Now, as she began making prints, she was looking for a technique consonant with this process that would give them the embossed quality she was after.

For her first prints Stuart drew directly on the lithographic stones and plates as Adams had encouraged her to do. She thought about using handmade paper to help achieve the desired rough surface effects but discovered there was not enough time to have paper made to her specifications. In each of her first three prints[3]— *Taaiyalone, Maxwaluna,* and *Tunyo* (all 1974)—she conveyed her concern for natural forms by floating a single shaped image within the linear borders of the paper. She also tried multiple printings to get some surface buildup. Stuart worked diligently on these first prints but was not satisfied with the results. On her fourth piece, *Redondo* (1974), she convinced the workshop to make a plate of raised sculpmetal (a malleable synthetic metal) that would simulate a rocky terrain. When the paper was run through the press, the plate left the indentations she wanted. For this print Stuart also had each sheet of paper torn on a template to resemble the deckle edges of the handmade paper she originally desired.

Having established a working harmony with the Tamarind printers in the course of her visit, Stuart felt a new confidence in her printmaking instincts and ca-

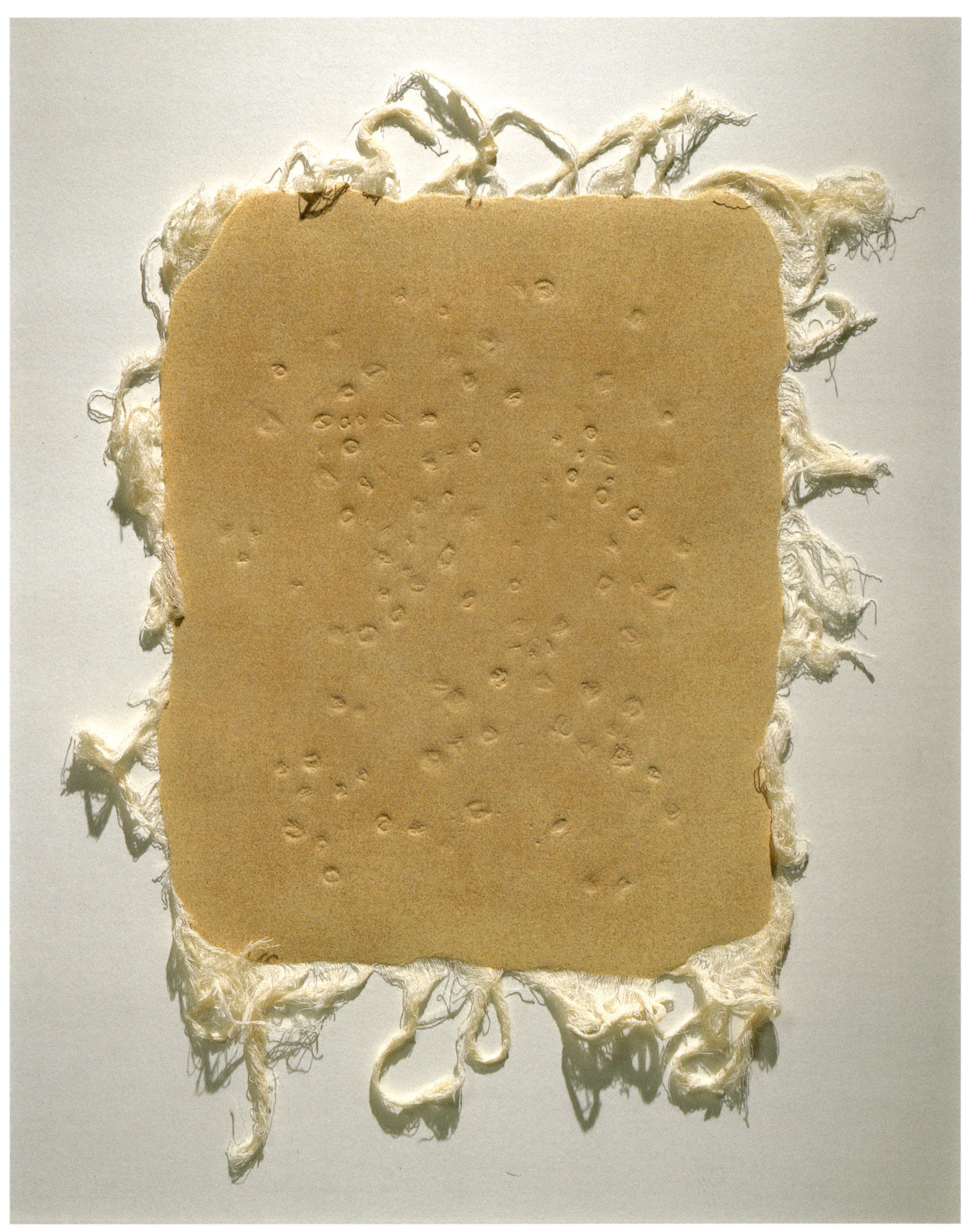

Michelle Stuart *Tsikupuming* 1975
lithograph (cat. no. 77)

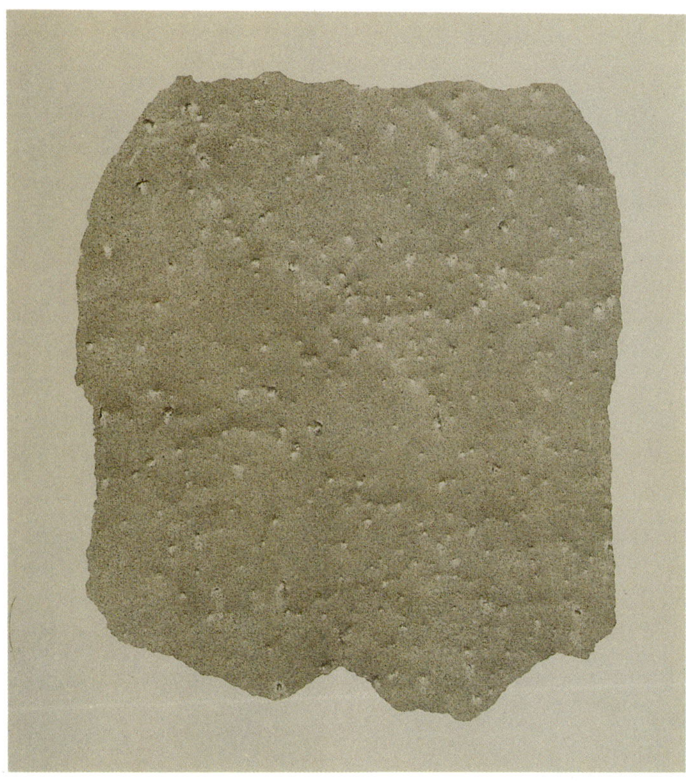

Michelle Stuart *Tunyo* 1974
lithograph (cat. no. 76)

pabilities. Thus her final project there, a suite of five lithographs entitled *Tsikomo* (1975), was her most successful. As noted in her journal, Tsikomo is the highest peak in the Jemez range, the spiritual "Center of it All." Each of the works from the *Tsikomo* suite has a tangible quality; they have been aptly described as more works *of* paper than works *on* paper.[4] *Tsikupuming*, in particular, has a fetishlike appearance. Each piece of paper in the edition, torn to a template, was mounted on cheesecloth and the edges raveled. As with the other prints in the suite, a sculptmetal plate was used to give the piece texture. Stuart's choice of color, a pink beige, lends the work an earthy quality that is further emphasized by the embossed ruts. *Tsikomo* (cat. no. 78), another print from the suite, was mounted on natural handmade Nacre paper treated by the artist to look frayed around the edges. In contrast to the tabletlike rectangle of Stuart's previous prints, *Tsikomo* is circular. In the three remaining prints, Stuart folded her shaped papers over to hang in layers. The four outside layers of *Okuping* are a muted olive green, while the underside of each of the three top layers is printed in bright red, orange, and yellow. When suspended, the underside colors reflect onto the sheets beneath—an effect that approximates the sun setting in the desert. As Stuart had hoped, these tactile pieces evoke the unique light, colors, and textures of the New Mexican landscape.

—E.A.

1. Lawrence Alloway, "Michelle Stuart: A Fabric of Significations," *Artforum* 12 (January 1974), pp. 64–65.

2. The artist in correspondence with the author, 3 January 1988.

3. The titles of these and subsequent prints made by Stuart at Tamarind are taken from the Tewa language, one of several used by the Pueblo Indians, and are names for mesas, buttes, and other geographical landmarks in the region.

4. See *The Tamarind Papers* 2 (Autumn 1978), p. 4.

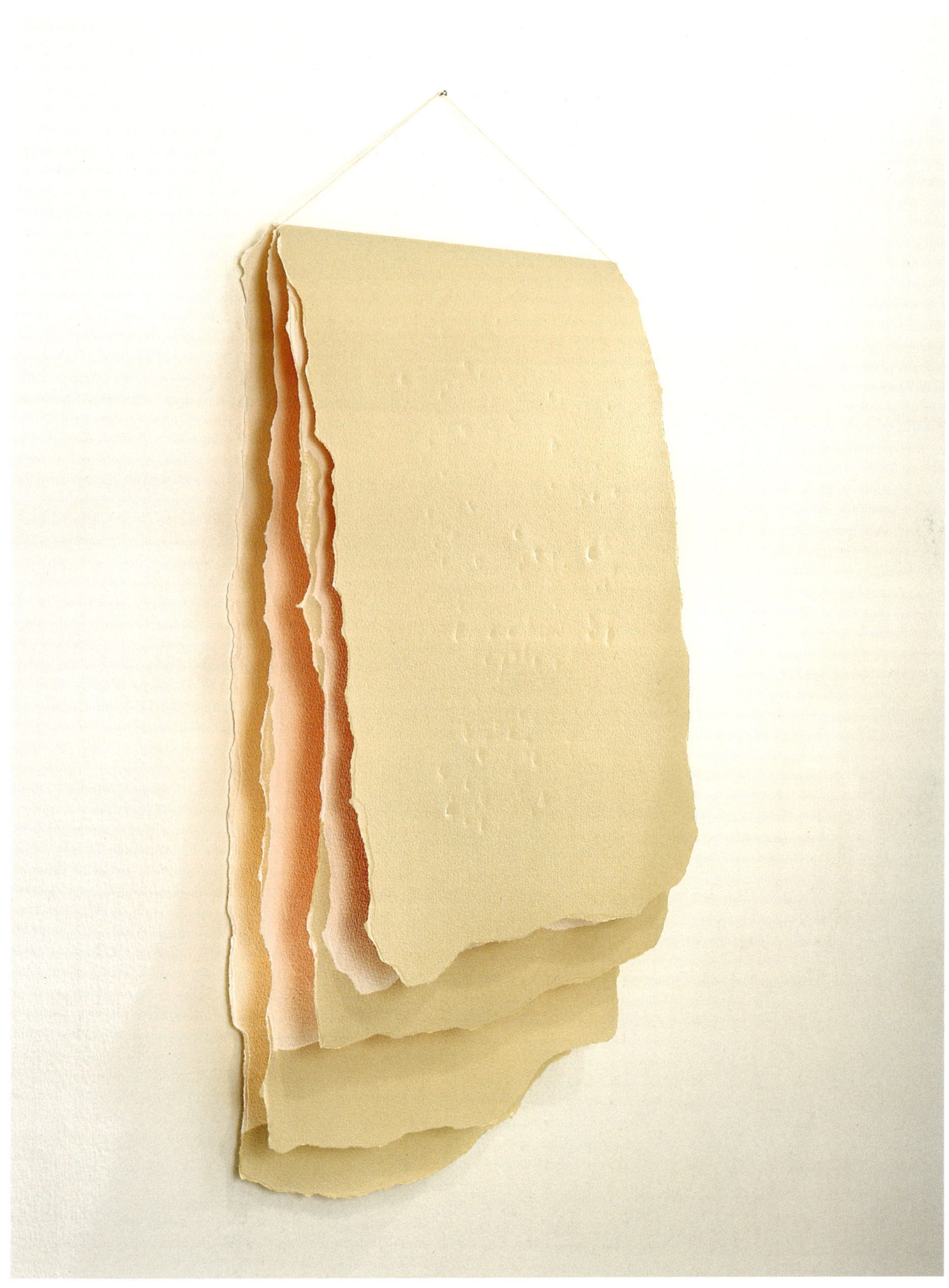

Michelle Stuart *Okuping* 1975
lithograph (cat. no. 79)

Susan Rothenberg

In 1973 Susan Rothenberg began making horses the subject of her paintings. She did so in order to explore the formal aspects of the medium through figure painting, at a time when the human figure as subject was out of favor with much of the art world. Further, as she only later realized, the equine canvases comprised a sort of continuing self-portrait.[1] In these largely expressionistic works she frequently bisected the horses with a line or bar in order to flatten and clarify the images. The lines, she explained at the time, "allow the viewer to read, reassemble, or in some way get involved with two different kinds of occurrences. The center line keeps one from illusionism, from reading depth into the painting."[2] This approach forces one to consider the formal relationships between figure and ground, form and edge, part and whole.

In 1977 Sidney Singer, director of Prestige Art Limited in Mamaroneck, New York, invited Rothenberg to make prints. An art collector who owned several of her paintings, Singer recognized the potential of translating the rich horse images into intimately scaled lithographs. He arranged for her to collaborate with Maurice Sanchez, the director of Derrière L'Etoile Studios, which had opened in New York City the previous year. Rothenberg recalls a preliminary meeting with Sanchez and James Rosenquist, with whom the printer had previously worked, during which they discussed the benefits of printmaking.[3] This meeting helped assuage her initial ambivalence about working in the medium. Lured by their enthusiasm and by the potential financial rewards they hinted at, she agreed to give the project her best effort.

Rothenberg admits, however, that she was her own worst enemy when it came to learning lithography procedures. Having never actually produced a print—save for one linoleum block in college—she was hesitant to make marks on the stones. Fearful of having to draw in reverse, she worked relentlessly on transfer paper. She felt that "working on the stone was too scary—too direct— so I kept working on paper as long as possible." She finally made a sensuous drawing of two galloping horses in profile, one in front of the other, their bodies bisected by a horizontal line. Since she was already comfortable with the horse, it was a natural choice as the subject of her first print, *Untitled* (1977). Helped by Derrière L'Etoile printer Chris Erickson, Rothenberg executed this lithograph in soft silver and black inks. She doubted the quality of the edition and almost immediately undertook the ambitious task of hand-coloring every impression with pencil, gouache, crayon, and pastel until each of eighteen lithographs became truly unique.

Having established the lithograph's basic image, she had the freedom to make compositional experiments. The rear horse visible in some of the impressions fades away almost completely in others and, in yet others, convincingly commands the forward position. Rothenberg also manipulated the critical dividing line to achieve distinctively different fields of perception. A crossbar in one early version slightly distances the viewer from the horses, making it seem that they are being seen through a window, while a star configuration resolutely holds a gray horse in place in a later variation.

Perhaps of primary consideration in these images is Rothenberg's diverse use of her limited palette of black, silver, white, and red. In one print (p. 16) a blazing red horse and its shadowy black counterpart run against an equally vivid field of red. Sketchlike marks enhance the immediacy of this image. In contrast, a more consistent evocative gray surface suffuses the final print in the series.

Rothenberg's next lithograph was also produced with Chris Erickson. This striking image of two galloping horses—one black, one white—stands without the aid of hand-coloring or other manipulation. Since 1977, as her editions in etching, spitbite, aquatint, woodcut, and lithography testify, Rothenberg has steadily gained printmaking confidence.[4] Shedding her early ambivalence, she has become one of the consummate print practitioners of the 1980s, able to produce startling images in every technique she tackles.

—S.M.

---

1. See Peter Schjeldahl, "Putting Painting Back on Its Feet," *Vanity Fair* 43 (August 1983), p. 85.

2. Artist's statement, in Richard Marshall, *New Image Painting*, exh. cat. (New York: Whitney Museum of American Art, 1978), p. 56.

3. The artist in a conversation with Elizabeth Armstrong and the author, 17 March 1988. All subsequent Rothenberg quotations here are also taken from this conversation.

4. For a listing of Rothenberg prints through 1987, see Rachel Robertson Maxwell, *Susan Rothenberg: The Prints* (Philadelphia: Peter Maxwell, 1987).

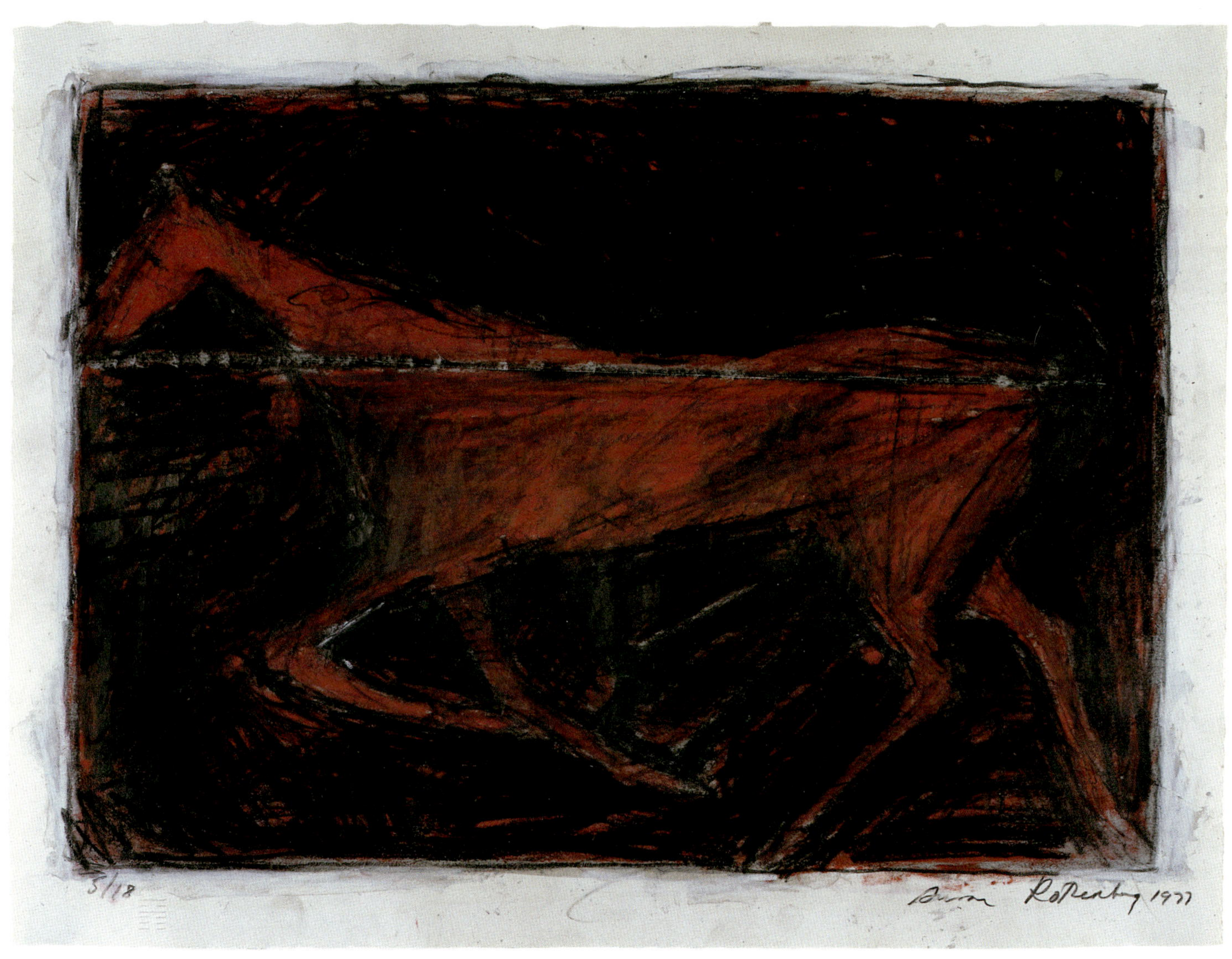

Susan Rothenberg *Untitled* 1977
hand-colored lithograph (cat. no. 82)

Jenny Holzer

The anonymity of Jenny Holzer's *Truisms* (1977–1979), which consist simply of a list of declarative statements set in a black, neutral typeface and printed on white paper, is striking: they contain no name, signature, or chopmark by which to identify the artist. Holzer had them printed at a commercial press that ran them off in unlimited editions; she then randomly pasted them on building walls and fences around Manhattan—alongside the usual array of advertising posters and political broadsides.

The *Truisms* were Holzer's first mature works, made shortly after she arrived in New York City from graduate school at the Rhode Island School of Design. Seeking to make art that communicates with a large public, she employed the print medium—in this case, the offset poster—as it was originally used, to disseminate ideas and information. In the *Truisms* she juxtaposes seemingly commonplace remarks (such as HUMOR IS A RELEASE) with provocative pronouncements (such as PRIVATE PROPERTY CREATED CRIME). It was her intention that each statement, or "truism," be presented in the same visual tone. She achieved this by having each occupy a separate line on the poster. Removing value judgments would, she believed, allow viewers to read and interpret the statements on their own terms. In Holzer's words, these texts have "something to offend almost anyone or something to agree with."[1]

The *Truisms* series was partially motivated by the weighty reading list Holzer was provided when she attended the Whitney Museum of American Art's Independent Study Program in 1976 and 1977. In response to the overwhelming range of ideas represented by the books on this list, her thought was to do "Jenny Holzer's *Reader's Digest* version of Western and Eastern thought. . . . I thought maybe I could translate these things into language that was accessible."[2] Each *Truisms* poster was derived from a page-long typed list of short declarative statements. The statements were a mixture of texts and pronouncements Holzer had altered, along with remarks of her own, often phrased to sound like clichés. She typeset the text, made photostats, had them printed, and then posted them around the city. She ultimately composed some three hundred individual statements for the series. Because of their easily adaptable form, the *Truisms* were subsequently enlarged to fill storefront windows, used for electronic billboards, printed on T-shirts, and, most recently, engraved in benches Holzer designed.

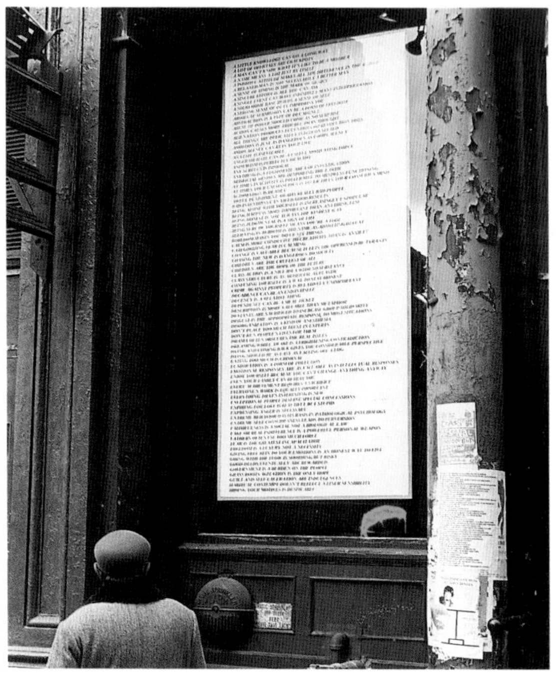

Jenny Holzer *Truisms* (installed in New York City, 1979)

All of Holzer's work exists either in multiple form or in a medium that has the potential for mass communication.[3] With their impersonal style, which was carried into two later series—the *Inflammatory Essays* (1979–1982) and *Living* (begun in 1980 and still in progress)—they are created primarily to provoke viewer reaction. Public response to the *Truisms* was indeed lively; people sometimes checked off the statements they liked or disliked and even, on occasion, explained why. Holzer continues to scrutinize the authoritativeness of the printed word in her work today, using language as her primary vehicle of expression.

—E.A.

1. Quoted in "New York Studio Events, Jenny Holzer," *ICI Newsletter* 2 (Spring/Summer 1987), unpaginated.

2. From an interview with Bruce Ferguson, in *Jenny Holzer: Signs*, exh. cat. (Des Moines Art Center, 1986), p. 67.

3. For example, from 15 to 30 March 1982, nine of Holzer's *Truisms* were beamed in forty-second sequences on the Spectacolor sign above Times Square. The project was conducted under the auspices of the Public Art Fund.

ABUSE OF POWER COMES AS NO SURPRISE
ALIENATION PRODUCES ECCENTRICS OR REVOLUTIONARIES
AN ELITE IS INEVITABLE
ANGER OR HATE CAN BE A USEFUL MOTIVATING FORCE
ANY SURPLUS IS IMMORAL
DISGUST IS THE APPROPRIATE RESPONSE TO MOST SITUATIONS
EVERYONE'S WORK IS EQUALLY IMPORTANT
EXCEPTIONAL PEOPLE DESERVE SPECIAL CONCESSIONS
FAITHFULNESS IS A SOCIAL NOT A BIOLOGICAL LAW
FREEDOM IS A LUXURY NOT A NECESSITY
GOVERNMENT IS A BURDEN ON THE PEOPLE
HUMANISM IS OBSOLETE
HUMOR IS A RELEASE
INHERITANCE MUST BE ABOLISHED
KILLING IS UNAVOIDABLE BUT IS NOTHING TO BE PROUD OF
LABOR IS A LIFE-DESTROYING ACTIVITY
MONEY CREATES TASTE
MORALS ARE FOR LITTLE PEOPLE
MOST PEOPLE ARE NOT FIT TO RULE THEMSELVES
MOSTLY YOU SHOULD MIND YOUR OWN BUSINESS
MUCH WAS DECIDED BEFORE YOU WERE BORN
MURDER HAS ITS SEXUAL SIDE
PAIN CAN BE A VERY POSITIVE THING
PEOPLE ARE NUTS IF THEY THINK THEY CONTROL THEIR LIVES
PEOPLE WHO DON'T WORK WITH THEIR HANDS ARE PARASITES
PEOPLE WON'T BEHAVE IF THEY HAVE NOTHING TO LOSE
PRIVATE PROPERTY CREATED CRIME
ROMANTIC LOVE WAS INVENTED TO MANIPULATE WOMEN
SELFISHNESS IS THE MOST BASIC MOTIVATION
SEX DIFFERENCES ARE HERE TO STAY
STARVATION IS NATURE'S WAY
STUPID PEOPLE SHOULDN'T BREED
TECHNOLOGY WILL MAKE OR BREAK US
THE FAMILY IS LIVING ON BORROWED TIME
THE LAND BELONGS TO NO ONE
TIMIDITY IS LAUGHABLE
TORTURE IS BARBARIC
YOU ARE GUILELESS IN YOUR DREAMS
YOU MUST REMEMBER YOU HAVE FREEDOM OF CHOICE

Jenny Holzer *Truisms* 1977
photo-offset (cat. no. 83)

Steven Sorman

Steven Sorman taught himself printmaking during the mid-1970s. As an assistant at Dayton's Gallery 12 in Minneapolis, he constantly handled graphic works and developed an interest in printing processes. Having no access to a shop or press, he began making prints by scratching on Plexiglas plates.[1] He hand-pulled the images, printed with Speedball ink. Between 1973 and 1976 he pulled sixteen small editions by hand in media that included drypoint, linocut, woodcut, and collography.[2] Ten of these were used in a book, *Coyote Stories* (1976), which he produced in an edition of sixteen with his friend the writer Lee Blessing.

The experimental nature of these early prints was in keeping with Sorman's inventive approach to art-making. In the mid-1970s he began literally to construct his paintings on the floor of his studio, often working on up to five at a time. Because he relied on collage as a central element in the paintings, creating several simultaneously enabled him to interchange materials freely and, in doing so, to develop close links between the works. Although largely abstract, Sorman's paintings often reveal a basis in observed fact—especially landscape and architecture. Their sketched marks and generally organic quality belie the fact that they frequently rely on underlying geometric structures and forms. He made his collage paintings on nylon drapery sheer, coated with polymer medium to achieve a somewhat stiff surface. On top of this, he would collage different types of paper, more sheer, charcoal, crayon, various kinds of paint, and gold and silver leaf.

In 1977 Sally Mitchell of Bird Island Publishing in Minneapolis, a consortium of private collectors, invited Sorman to make prints at the recently opened Vermillion Editions, also located in Minneapolis.[3] "I loved making prints and a professional shop opened within walking distance," he writes. "It was irresistible." He worked with Vermillion's director and master printer, Steven Andersen, on his first print, *The First Building Project According to What Plan* (1978).[4] The three-panel work combines etching, aquatint, and lithography with collage elements.

The simple outline of a house, etched in yellow on the left panel, was for Sorman "a literal reference to this first professional shop experience." In the right panel the house reappears with extensive aquatint additions. At once a common and personal image for the artist, it had appeared in his work for about a year. The central panel, a lithograph, presents a loosely painted box shape, printed in gold ink on blue paper. The title was rubber-stamped in lowercase letters across this and the right panel. According to Sorman, the two small red rectangles collaged to the lower corners of the piece function "very much like quotation marks." A work he made to "pry open the door," he considers it his most methodical and literal print to date.

Sorman compares making prints to nailing boards together to build a house: "If you're going to make something you can use—that serves you—you think about it and then cut the wood so you waste as little as you can."[5] Indeed, *The First Building Project* exhibits a remarkable economy of means in spite of its ambitious use of mixed media and collage. It also displays his ability successfully to adapt the mechanical aspects of the medium to his additive approach to art-making.

During the past decade printmaking has become a significant medium for Sorman, who views the producing of prints and paintings as parallel activities that continually borrow from one another. His prints have ranged from extremely delicate, self-published drypoints with monotype and chine collé, printed on his own etching press, to the monumental mixed-media prints with collage made at Tyler Graphics Ltd. in 1984 and 1985.

—S.M.

---

1. Philip Larson, "Steven Sorman: An Interview," *The Print Collector's Newsletter* 11 (May–June 1980), p. 42.

2. The artist in correspondence with Elizabeth Armstrong, 27 May 1988. Unless otherwise noted, all Sorman quotations here are taken from this source.

3. This was Bird Island Publishing's first project as well.

4. Sorman says he had made some prints at a shop in Wisconsin in 1975 but was dissatisfied with the results and did not edition them.

5. Quoted in Larson, op. cit., p. 42.

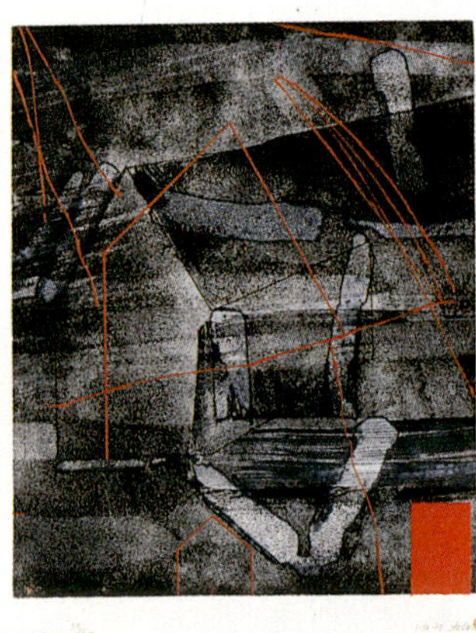

Steven Sorman *The First Building Project According to What Plan* 1978
lithograph, etching, aquatint, collage (cat. no. 84)

Lynda Benglis

Over the years Lynda Benglis has explored a wide range of unusual materials in her art. She first made her mark on the post-Minimal art scene in 1969 with latex-and-foam sculptures. Taking Jackson Pollock's floor paintings (which ultimately ended up hanging on walls) a step further, she poured intensely colored liquid rubber into piles on the studio floor, piles that eventually hardened into free-form sculptures. During the same period she produced sensual sculptures of layered wax. In the late 1970s she began forming sculptures of gessoed cotton batting shaped over wire and elaborately decorated with glitter, gold leaf, and polypropylene flounces.

She extended her interest in such materials to her first publication, *Lagniappe I* (1978), an edition of twenty-six cast-paper reliefs made with A. Lynn Forgach. The two met in 1978 at Kent State University, where Benglis was then a visiting artist and Forgach a graduate student. Later that year, having just begun to operate a print-making shop in her studio in Cleveland, Forgach invited Benglis to make prints with her. Considering two-dimensional graphics incompatible with her other work, the artist declined this offer but suggested that they join forces instead on a paper project. Forgach, an experienced papermaker, accepted Benglis' counterproposal, and the project got under way.[1] Because the artist was working in New York City at the time, Forgach was constantly traveling there from Ohio to discuss the early proofs with her. Finally, Benglis convinced her to set up shop in a temporary studio she had in New York. They produced the edition there under the name Exeter Press; it was published by Benglis' dealer, Paula Cooper.

Trial pieces for *Lagniappe* were made with a richly pigmented paper pulp cast in two molds that Benglis had fashioned for a bronze sculpture. Each working proof was assembled from two pieces of cast paper. Prior to casting each *Lagniappe* relief, Benglis decided on a color scheme and drew a configuration in the molds to indicate how the paper pulp should be arranged. After a relief was dried and cured, she would take it to her studio and paint and decorate it as befit the particular colors and shapes. While she left a few of the reliefs untouched, she liberally decorated the majority with combinations of acrylic, glitter, gold leaf, and polypropylene. Derived from Mardi Gras figures,[2] they more than do justice to their title, which, as the artist comments, means "a little something extra."[3]

The critical and financial success of *Lagniappe I* prompted Benglis and Forgach to begin work almost immediately on a second edition, *Lagniappe II* (1979). These reliefs are wider and more bulbous than those in the first edition, and some of their designs are even more spectacular, but the underlying concept remains the same. The Lagniappe series led the artist and printer to work on another pair of related multiples, *Gujurat* and *Mold* (both 1980), and subsequently to team on many other projects.

During 1978, while Benglis was making the first Lagniappes, she accepted an invitation from Jack Lemon to make a lithograph at Landfall Press in Chicago. There she made her first and only nonunique print, *Untitled* (1979), for a portfolio to benefit the NAME Gallery in Chicago. This project led her to produce monoprints at Landfall with Lemon and printer Timothy Berry. In monoprints Benglis discovered the graphic medium most suitable to her experimental style. Since then, having made several trips to India, she has become involved in a number of projects incorporating collage, handmade papers, hand-coloring, and, not surprisingly, the vacuum-forming of paper.

—S.M.

---

1. A. Lynn Forgach in a conversation with the author, 13 June 1988.

2. Benglis' Lagniappe forms grew out of a collaboration with the painter Ida Kohlmeyer, a former teacher of hers, for the exhibition *Five from Louisiana* at the New Orleans Museum of Art in 1977. They put together an environmental sculpture, *Louisiana Prop Piece* (1977), comprising large papier-mâché heads and figures, once used in Mardi Gras parades, which they decorated with colorful tissue-paper collars, ties, and flounces. The work was illustrated in *Art in America* 65 (July–August 1977), p. 22.

3. The artist in a conversation with the author, 6 May 1988. Specifically, a lagniappe is a small gift given by a merchant as a bonus to a paying customer. In broader terms, it can be considered something that is given gratuitously.

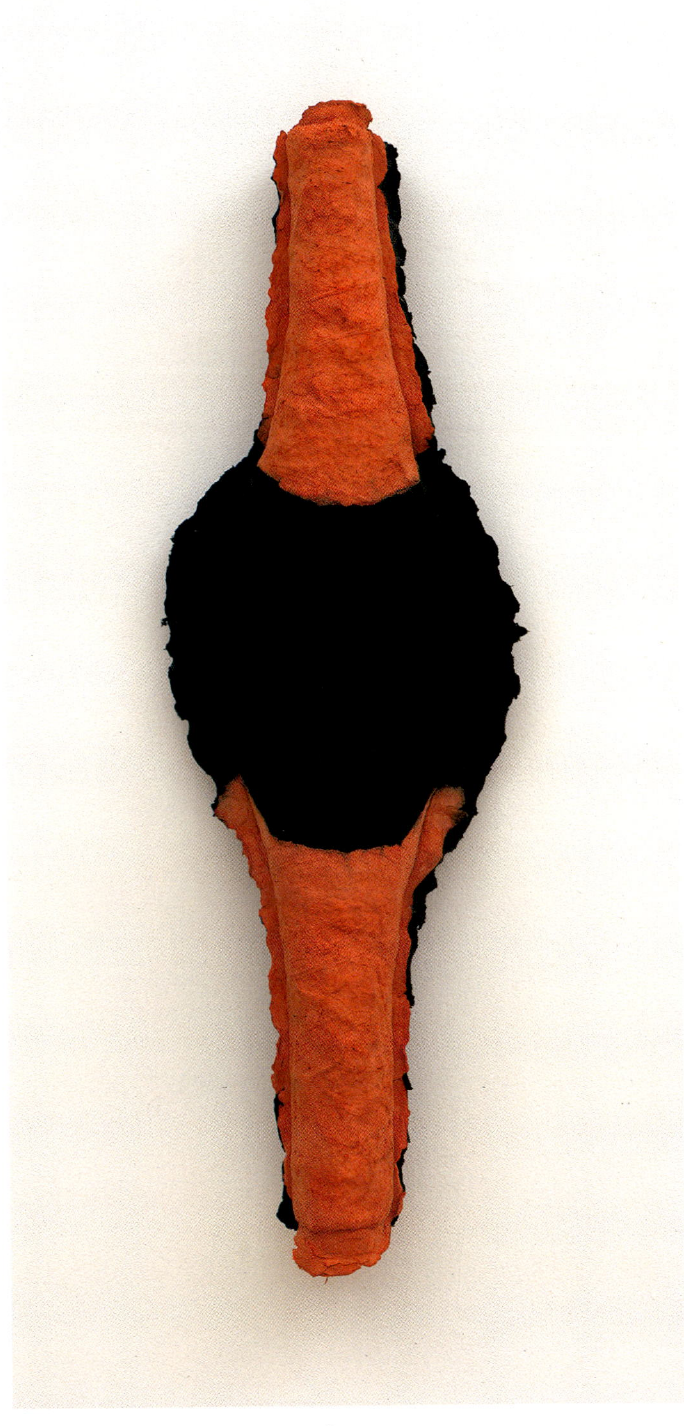

Lynda Benglis *Lagniappe I* 1978
cast paper with acrylic (cat. no. 85)

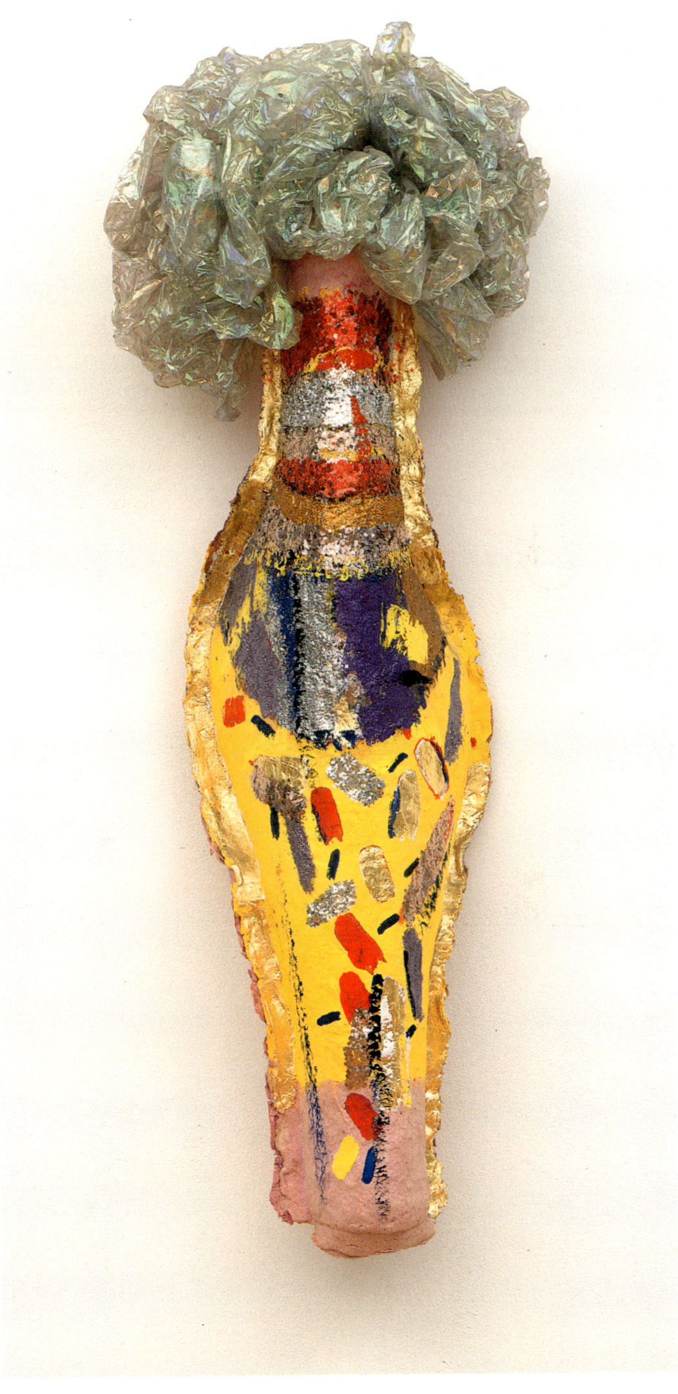

Lynda Benglis *Lagniappe II* 1979
cast paper with acrylic, glitter, gold leaf, polypropylene (cat. no. 86)

Jennifer Bartlett

A small, childlike image of a house emerged out of Jennifer Bartlett's abstract plate paintings of the late 1960s and, without affecting her systematic approach to picture-making, became a continuing and potent symbol in her art. An artist who works in series, she completed thirteen large and numerous smaller paintings incorporating the generalized house image between 1969 and 1977.[1] As the series of paintings focused on this subject developed, she became increasingly interested in the passage of time and in the related effects of changing light on the dwelling. Her explorations of color, style, and technique culminated in images such as *27 Howard Street/Day and Night* (1977), in which two houses are placed side by side beneath two tumultuous skies: a day sky, ablaze with impressionistic dabs of color; and a night sky, filled by darker, more angular crosshatchings.

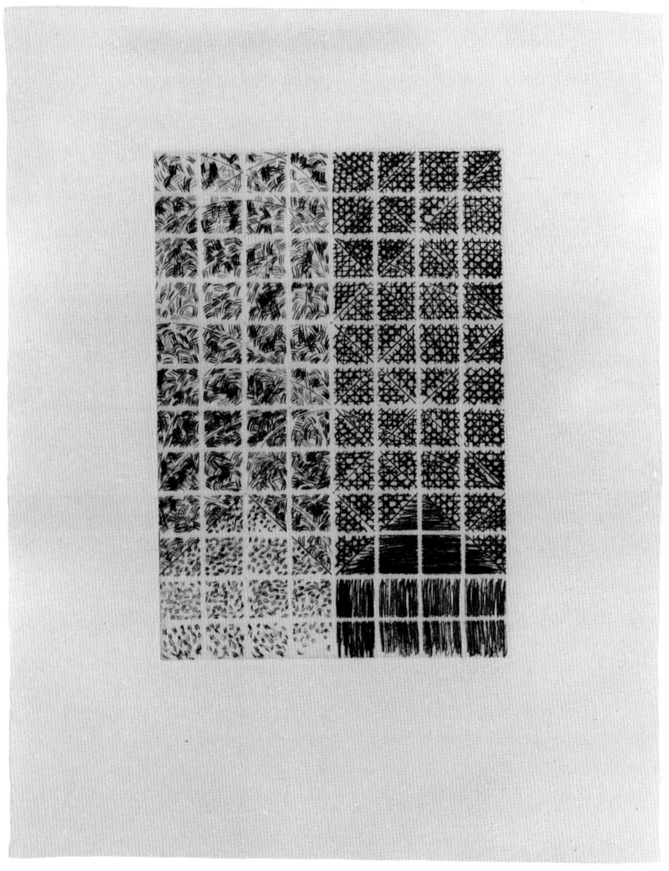

Jennifer Bartlett *Day and Night* 1978
drypoint (cat. no. 87)

Bartlett chose *27 Howard Street/Day and Night* as her starting point when she tried her hand at printmaking a year later. Invited by Marian Goodman of Multiples, Inc., New York, to make prints, she thought the Howard Street painting would translate well into etching. Although she had made a couple of obligatory prints in college, this was her first real immersion in any one printmaking technique. It was greatly facilitated by printer Pat Branstead of Aeropress, who was a painter herself and had some experience making prints with artists just being introduced to the medium.

With its battery of markings—vertical and horizontal lines, curved strokes, dots, and crosshatchings—the painting *27 Howard Street/Day and Night* lent itself to experimentation in etching, a technique that relies on mark-making. Bartlett immersed herself in the process with characteristic energy and drive. Branstead suggested that they make several small test plates using both drypoint and etching, and these were so successful that they became the first three prints in the Day and Night series. The first drypoint (1978) has a soft, velvety quality inherent in the medium. Working directly on the plate, Bartlett made an image with a spontaneous, sketchy feel that is relatively rare in her paintings from this period. Using the structure of the original painting, which is composed of ninety-six enamel squares, she etched a twelve-by-eight-inch grid into the copper plate. The intaglio also incorporates the painting's short, slightly curved lines on the daytime (left) side and sharper, longer strokes on the nighttime (right) side. In the next etching Bartlett separated each of the ninety-six squares, further mimicking the composition of her enamel-plate paintings. In the third print she made her markings more emphatic and, perhaps due to the increasing density, reversed the positions of the lighter and darker houses.[2]

Pleased with the test plates and particularly with the effects of drypoint, Bartlett continued the series on a slightly larger scale—thirty-one by twenty inches. In the first of these images, the long vertical and horizontal lines of the nighttime house merge to become a solid dark form that stands out from the airy strokes in the surround. In the last two prints Bartlett utilized the same printing plates in order to focus exclusively on the use of color. Markings that had begun to blend together become discrete, illuminating the contrast between her depiction of day and night and adding a new dynamic to the series.

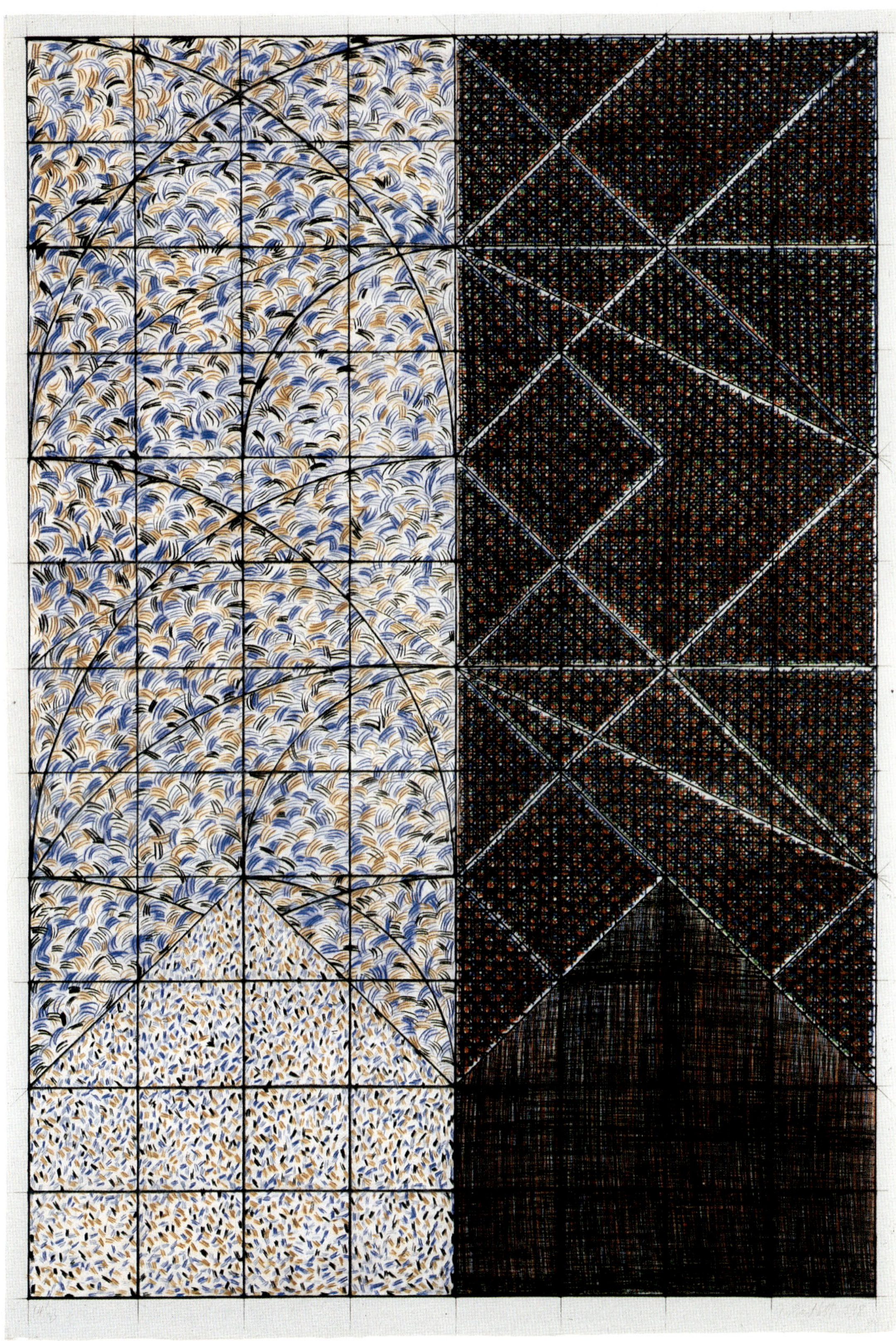

Jennifer Bartlett *Day and Night* 1978
drypoint (cat. no. 88)

While Bartlett's preoccupations with process, technique, and the nature of depiction often neutralize the emotional impact of her work, the Day and Night images carry subjective associations for her. In addition to the familiar connotations of home and family spawned by the generic house form, the domicile in the Day and Night print series is associated with 27 Howard Street in New York City, where, just a few years earlier, Bartlett's friend Hiroshi Kawanishi had set up his own print shop, Simca Print Artists. Hiroshi honed his printmaking skills with Jasper Johns—with whose sensuous brushwork Bartlett's has often been compared—becoming in the process a peerless master of the screenprint. In 1980 Hiroshi would collaborate with her on one of her most ambitious projects, *At Sea, Japan*, a complex work involving ninety-five screens and eighty-six woodblocks that is a tour de force of contemporary printmaking.

—E.A.

---

1. Marge Goldwater, *Jennifer Bartlett*, exh. cat. (Minneapolis: Walker Art Center and New York: Abbeville Press, 1985), p. 50.

2. In an excellent article on Bartlett's printmaking, Richard S. Field discusses these prints in some detail: "Jennifer Bartlett: Prints, 1978–1983," *The Print Collector's Newsletter* 15 (March–April 1984), pp. 2–6.

Donald Sultan

In 1978 Donald Sultan's work was featured in group exhibitions at the New Museum of Contemporary Art and at the Mary Boone Gallery, both in New York City. His paintings from this period are dominated by dark, weighted images of such recognizable forms as industrial-looking buildings and boats and were made from such unconventional materials as linoleum floor tiles and Butyl roofing tar. Shortly after the two exhibitions closed, he was approached by Robert Feldman, director of Parasol Press in New York, who felt Sultan's work would translate well into etching. At the time, Feldman, who had started publishing in 1970, was having most of his projects executed by Crown Point Press in Oakland, California. Under the direction of Kathan Brown, Crown Point specialized in etching, a medium with which Sultan also had some experience.[1] Feldman was characteristically relaxed in his involvement with this project; he chose the printer and medium but remained behind the scenes during production.

For his part, Sultan approached the experience as an opportunity to explore etching, and he experimented with different methods in each of the plates. Aquatint, hard ground, soft ground, drypoint, scraping, and burnishing were all employed in slightly different ways and to various effects. Working with the constant assistance of printers David Kelso and Hidekatsu Takada, Sultan spent two weeks at Crown Point making numerous preliminary drawings in black ink and more than forty plates before arriving at the eight prints that were to comprise the series. He called it *Water under the Bridge* (1979) "because of the boat imagery, and also the fact that I now understood etching in a way, and that was that. It was kind of a pun."[2]

The series serves as a primer not only for Sultan's etching technique but for his imagery as well. An examination of *Water under the Bridge* as a whole reveals Sultan's playful use of metamorphosis—about which much has been written—his way of allowing one image to evolve into the next. The thin line between representation and abstraction in his work, not to mention his enjoyment of visual double entendre, lend themselves to this sort of progression. When turned upside down, the first image of a boat in the series becomes a table, as its title, *Boat/Table, March 20, 1979*, indicates. The boat/table is a motif he had previously explored in drawing and painting. The next image, *Sailor Hats, March 21, 1979*,

was a new one. This is followed by *Half Hats, March 22, 1979* and by *Half Hats and Whole, March 24, 1979*; when turned on its side, the latter resembles the factory image then prevalent in Sultan's work. As the metamorphosis continues—almost daily, as the dates in his titles show—the motifs become increasingly obscure; without their descriptive titles as clues, several of the prints would seem to be totally abstract.

The last print in the series is a case in point. Reading left to right, a cascading white mass funnels into a long, white, horizontal rectangle. Entitled *Cigarette/Stack, March 28, 1979*, it provided Sultan with a particularly fecund image. A year later its smoking cigarette became the subject of *Smokers*, a series of large-scale aquatints also made at Crown Point Press. Turned on its side, the cigarette became the factory smokestack found in his industrial landscapes of the early 1980s.

This initial visit to Crown Point proved so productive that Sultan returned the following year to make six more aquatints. While the relatively small size of the *Water under the Bridge* prints related directly to the twelve-by-twelve-inch paintings he was making during this period (dimensions dictated by the size of the standard household linoleum squares he used in these works), the new aquatints reflected the much larger format that he also used.

In addition to working in woodcut and linocut, Sultan has immersed himself in etching, making more than twenty etchings and aquatints, many on a very large scale, since the 1979 series. The appeal of printmaking, he has said, lies in its industrial nature. In keeping with his use of tar, plaster, tile, and other manufactured materials in his paintings—especially those employed for buildings—he now often utilizes roofing copper, which is softer and more pitted than fine printing copper, for his etchings. This is also the only copper available in sheets large enough to make the accomplished, five-foot-high prints Sultan now produces.

—E.A.

1. Sultan first studied etching at the University of North Carolina, Chapel Hill, and later at the School of the Art Institute of Chicago.

2. Quoted in Ceil Friedman, *Donald Sultan Prints, 1979–1985*, exh. cat. (Boston: Barbara Krakow Gallery, 1985), unpaginated.

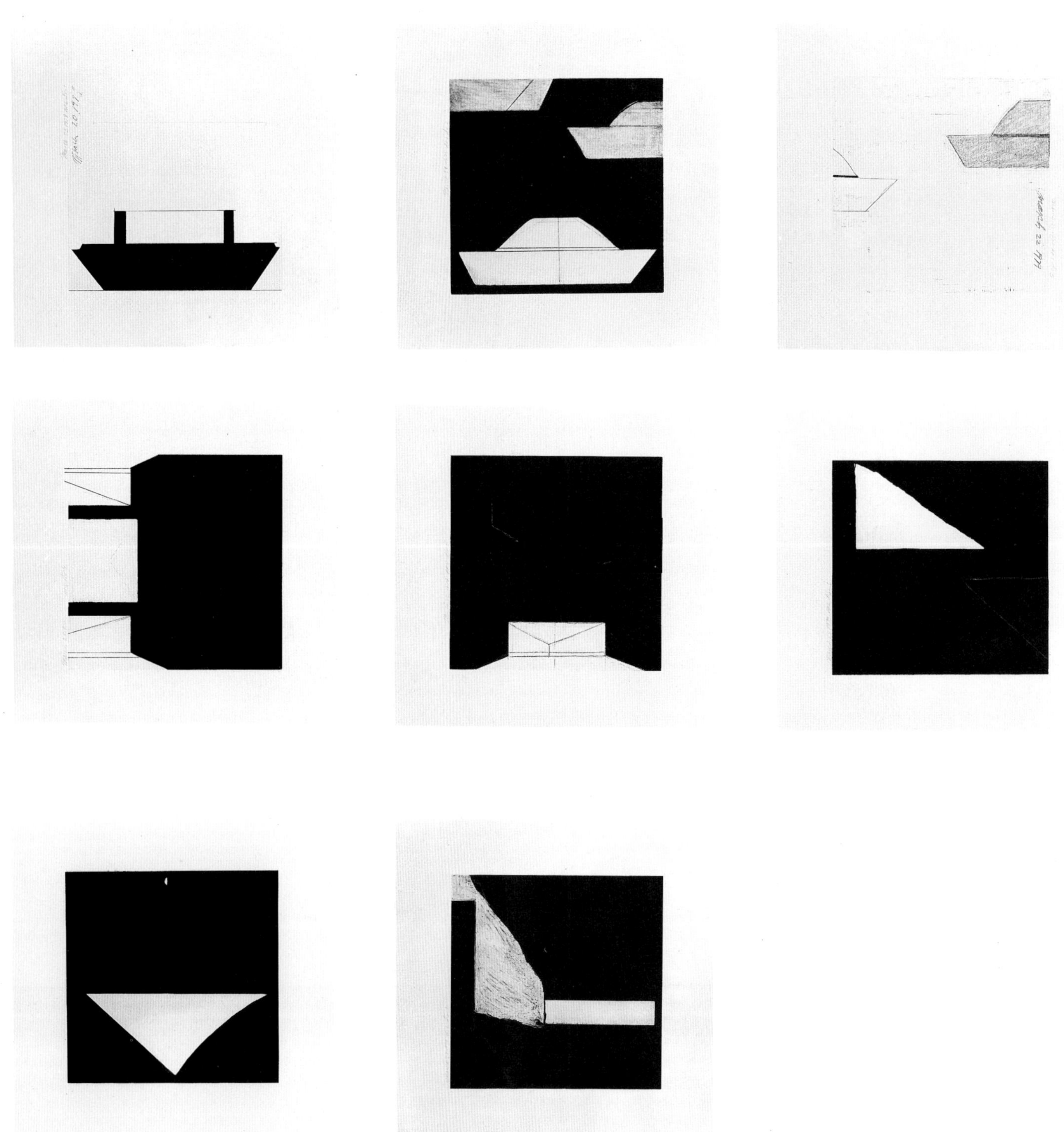

Donald Sultan *Water under the Bridge* 1979
eight aquatints (cat. no. 89)

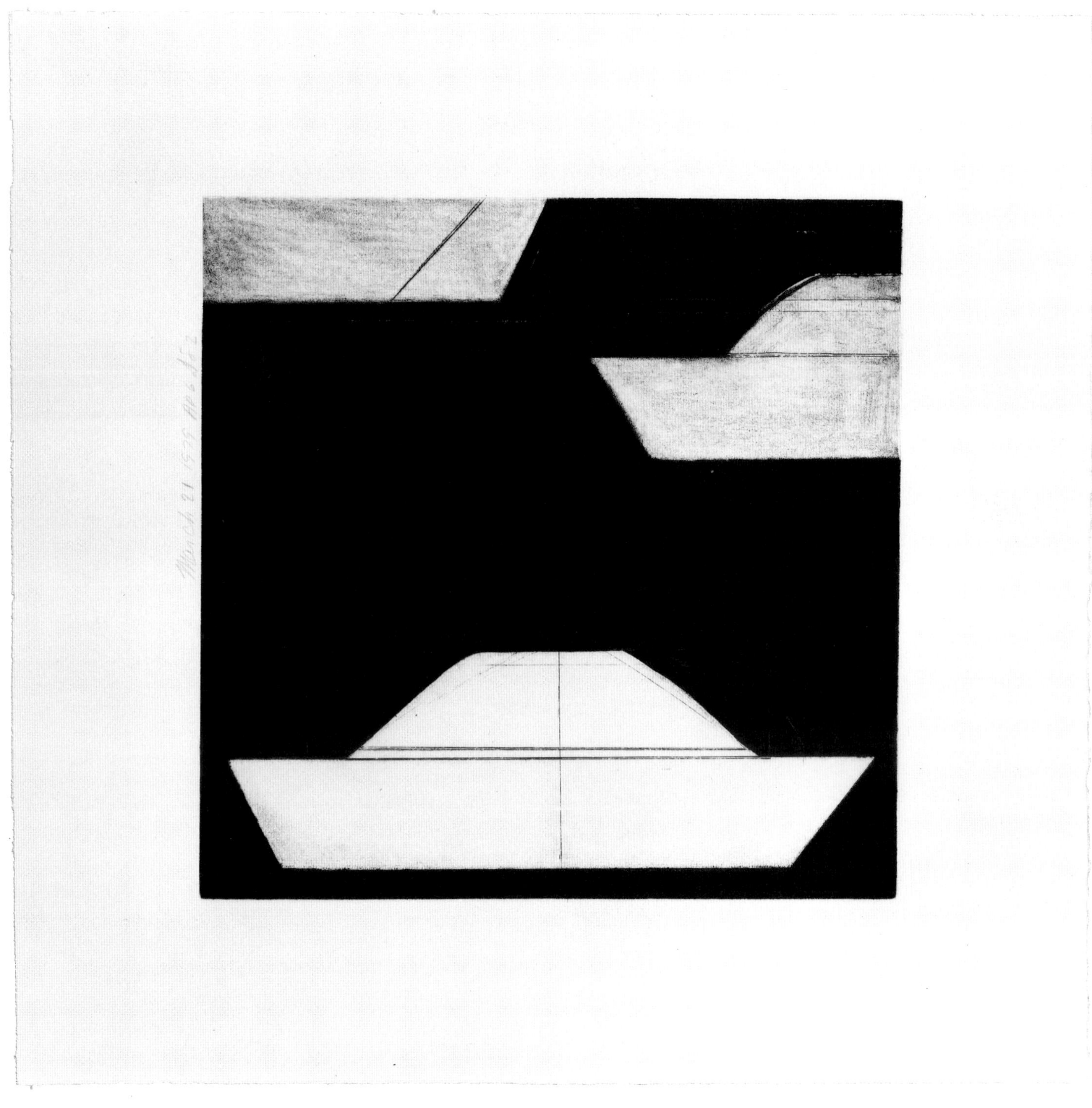

Donald Sultan *Sailor Hats, March 21, 1979*
aquatint with drypoint (cat. no. 89)

Nicholas Africano

born Kankakee, Illinois   1948

The Whitney Museum of American Art's *New Image Painting* exhibition in 1978 drew attention to a new generation of figurative artists.[1] Nicholas Africano, one of the ten painters in that exhibition, focused on the figure with particular intensity, emphasizing humanistic concerns over formal ones. At the time of the Whitney exhibition, he was painting three-dimensional miniature human figures that he either isolated against large fields of monochromatic canvas or, sometimes, hung directly on the wall. The figures themselves were built up from the surface, thick with pigment that was often mixed with wax. Their plasticity, especially in contrast to the surrounding void, channeled attention to the mise en scène—usually a domestic drama focusing on the relationship between two or among three figures.

The overt narrative content of these paintings deviated somewhat from the work of the other *New Image* painters. In fact, Africano started out as a writer whose first images were small drawings made to punctuate his texts. These evolved into large-scale paintings that carried with them a few words. He found that he could express himself more directly through painting: "I had been a writer of short, non-discursive prose. I was trying to make a direct and immediate image and began to substitute small drawings for words within the writing. Eventually the emphasis fell on the visual imagery, for it seemed more effective and was more fulfilling to me."[2]

The images in Africano's work usually derive from personal experience and make an unabashed appeal to the emotions of the viewer. "I try to reproduce the nature of experience," he has said, "rather than the figure itself."[3] His first prints, a series of four etchings entitled *The Shadow* (1979), present a typical Africano figure—small, thick, slightly awkward—boxing with his shadow. The last three prints capture figure and shadow in sync, in a sequence of boxing positions, but it is the first image that provides the punch(line). In it the shadow stands alone beneath the legend "I beat this fucker up," written in Africano's childlike scrawl. The four images arose from his efforts to amuse a fatally ill relative. He painted several small images of the boxer on cardboard, making the backgrounds particularly bright in consideration of the invalid's failing eyesight. Although the shadow can be seen as an image of death—and the title page expresses his anger over the impending death of this man—the artist meant the imagery to be humorous. A self-portrait of sorts, it can also be seen as a comment on the futility of doing battle with oneself.

Technically, *The Shadow* represents the sophistication of the resources available to artists who took up printmaking in the 1970s. Under the direction of Pat Branstead, at Aeropress, one of the best etching printers in New York City, a combination of processes was incorporated in these prints, including hard ground, soft ground, spitbite, and embossing on handmade paper. The intensely saturated taxicab-yellow paper, made to order at Twinrocker, a paper mill in Indiana, provides a brilliant backdrop for Africano's boxer, whose heavily embossed body mimics the bulging figures in his paintings. The prints are intimate in scale, small enough to be hand held. Every detail—down to individual chest hairs—is vividly conveyed. Aquatint, generally used by printmakers to produce areas of allover tone, is skillfully applied to form the boxer's brown shadow.

While a series of paintings developed out of *The Shadow*, Africano did not make prints again for some time. Not particularly interested in the crafting of these first publications, he had remained distant from their production. When he returned to the medium, in 1985, working with Steven Andersen at Vermillion Editions in Minneapolis, he again felt too much emphasis was being placed on trying to approximate his paintings and that the processes used were overly complicated. His most recent series of prints, begun at Vermillion in 1987, eschews the multimedia fervor that characterized the field in the 1970s. Rejecting the use of multiple plates, he has started to draw his primary image on a single stone in an effort to make the simplest, most direct impression possible. This minimal kind of drawing has, he says, been very useful to his painting, and he has come to see the print shop as a second studio.

—E.A.

---

1. See Richard Marshall, *New Image Painting*, exh. cat. (New York: Whitney Museum of American Art, 1978).

2. Quoted in ibid., p. 14.

3. The artist in a conversation with the author, 3 June 1988.

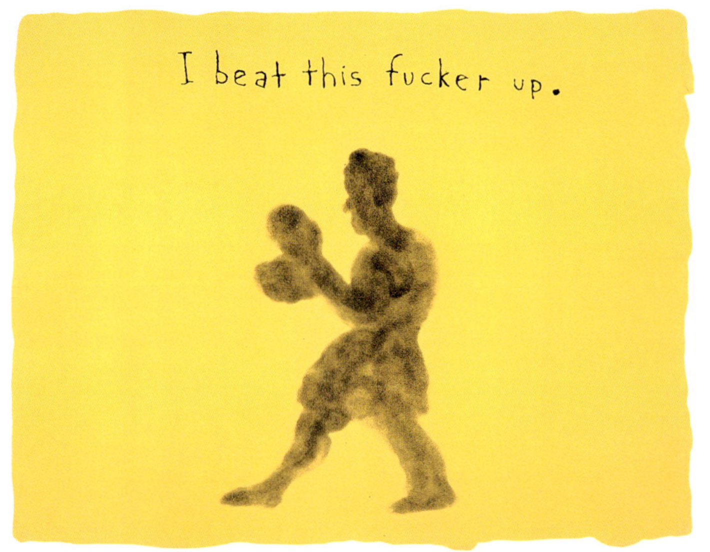

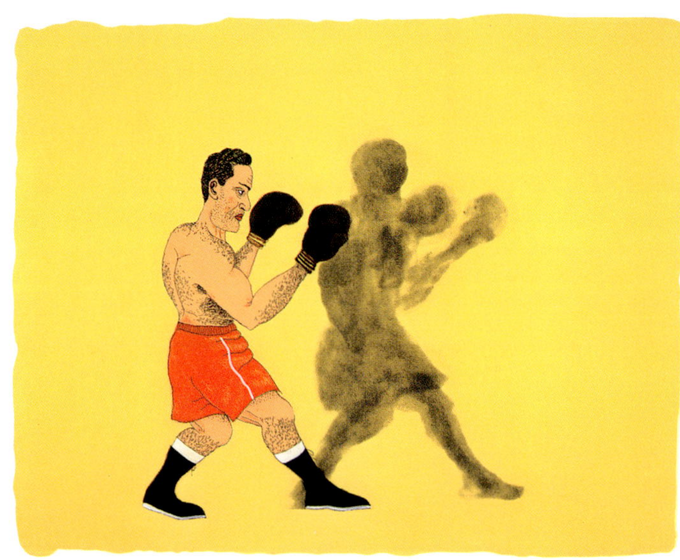
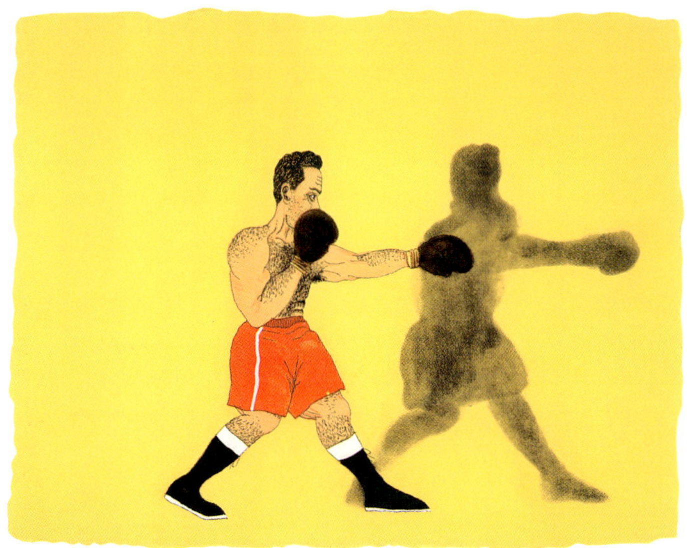
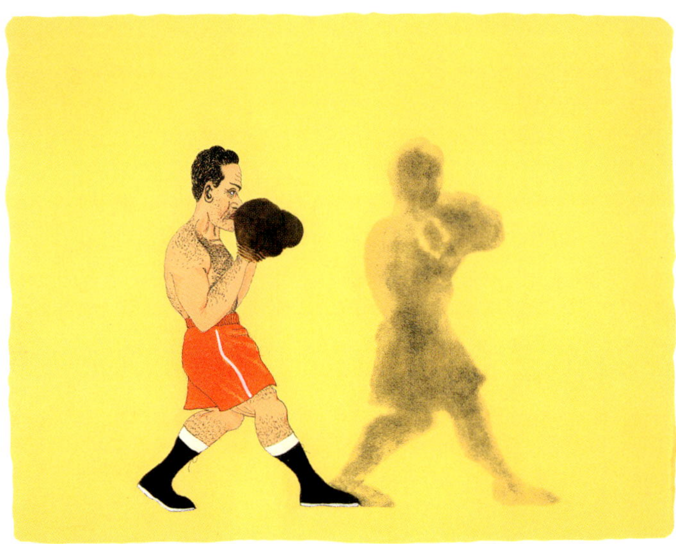

Nicholas Africano *The Shadow* 1979
four etchings with aquatint, spitbite, embossing (cat. no. 90)

Elizabeth Murray

When the print publisher Brooke Alexander first approached Elizabeth Murray about making prints, she had little desire to work in the medium. Although she had taught the subject while at Rosary Hill College in Buffalo, New York—her first teaching job—and had even started a printmaking department there in 1965, she found the delicate processes involved ill suited to her creative approach. Also, very few prints by contemporary artists excited her. For these reasons she turned down invitations from several publishers, Alexander included, until 1980.

Up to that time Murray had concentrated almost exclusively on making monumental and, later, eccentrically shaped paintings and dense, multilayered pastel drawings. Her imagery, typically biomorphic and semi-abstract, is rooted in her personal life. References to her role as an artist take the form of a brush or palette and coexist with domestic objects such as kitchen tables and coffee cups. These sometimes sensual, even sexual, forms are often given rich, brilliantly colored surfaces.

What spurred Murray on to make prints was a series of eleven Minotaur prints by Pablo Picasso, which she saw in the massive retrospective of his work at the Museum of Modern Art, New York, in 1980. The Picasso prints sequentially displayed alterations the artist had made from one state to the next as he worked through the increasingly abstract series of images. His interest in a gradual transformation as expressed in these prints appealed to her own sensibilities and inspired her to pursue printmaking seriously, with Alexander, whose persistence was finally rewarded. As she later said, "I finally felt it was time for me to expand into prints. To sort of stick my nose up in the air about them felt ridiculous."[1]

Once committed to her first printmaking project, Murray used it as an opportunity to get deeply involved in the process of drawing on the stone. Her first set of lithographs, *Untitled, States I–V* (1980), copublished by Brooke Alexander and Paula Cooper, derives from a single stone, which she continually worked and reworked. The entire development—the erasures and additions—can be traced when viewing the prints together. In fact, the artist feels so strongly about the composite impact of the images that she thinks of the five prints as one work.

Murray's emphasis on drawing is underscored by her determination that her first print be in black and white.[2] Although color is vital to her paintings, she did not like the appearance of color lithographs in general and felt, moreover, that color-related considerations would diminish the directness and spontaneity of making marks on the stone. By the time she arrived at the fourth state, however, she felt compelled to add a specific shade of medium-dark red. She was influenced in this by Ingmar Bergman's potent use of red in his 1972 film *Cries and Whispers*. As she later explained, the print "began to feel like a film in a sense. The structure is filmlike—the narration or the frames or the forms changing."[3]

Maurice Sanchez, master printer at Derrière L'Etoile Studios in New York City, collaborated with Murray on *Untitled, States I–V*. Together they sought ways to keep the stone open, slightly grinding it down only when Murray could no longer see what she was doing through the compounded layers of crayon, tusche, and ink. They were midway through the project before Sanchez explained to her that Picasso had started from scratch for each print in his Minotaur sequence. But this did not deflect her from her purpose; like Jasper Johns in his first 0–9 portfolio (pp. 28–29), she wanted each image to retain the residue of preceding images.

Murray used the first state of the print primarily as a means for planning and distributing light and dark. The second state reveals the traces of a large Z shape that the artist, after proofing, decided to erase. She carefully scratched out some parts of the Z and drew lively circular shapes over other parts of it. She found the third state even more challenging since, by then, the stone was so layered with previous marks that she could barely see to work on it. Scratching the surface to create areas of light, and introducing more lines, she achieved more depth in this state than in the preceding two. A large upside-down comma, already part of Murray's repertoire, dominates this image. For the last two images, she worked closely with Sanchez to delete portions of the previous states, in order to ensure that the red would pull through the black. Despite Sanchez's suggestion that she stop with the fourth

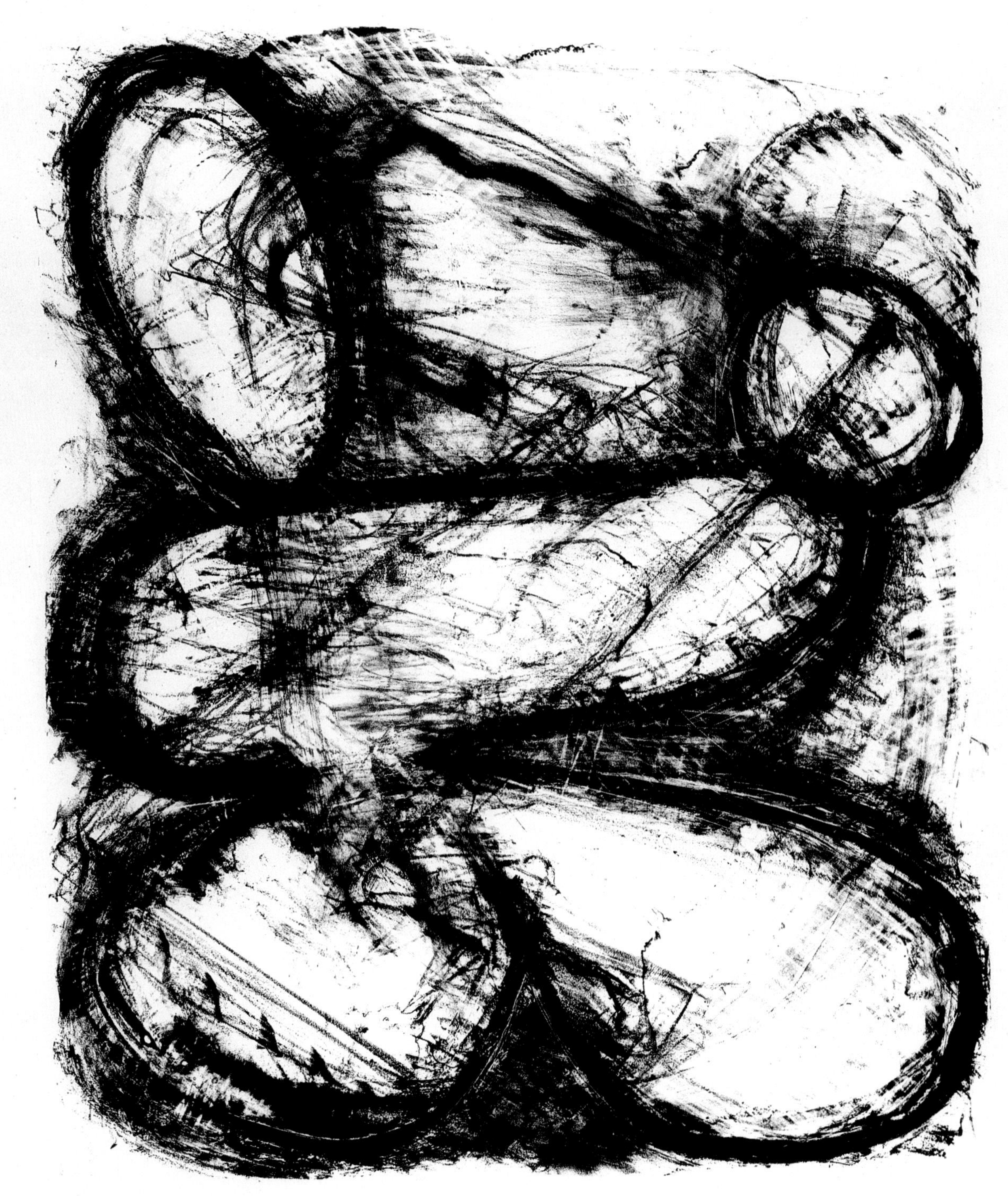

Elizabeth Murray *Untitled, State II* 1980
lithograph (cat. no. 91)

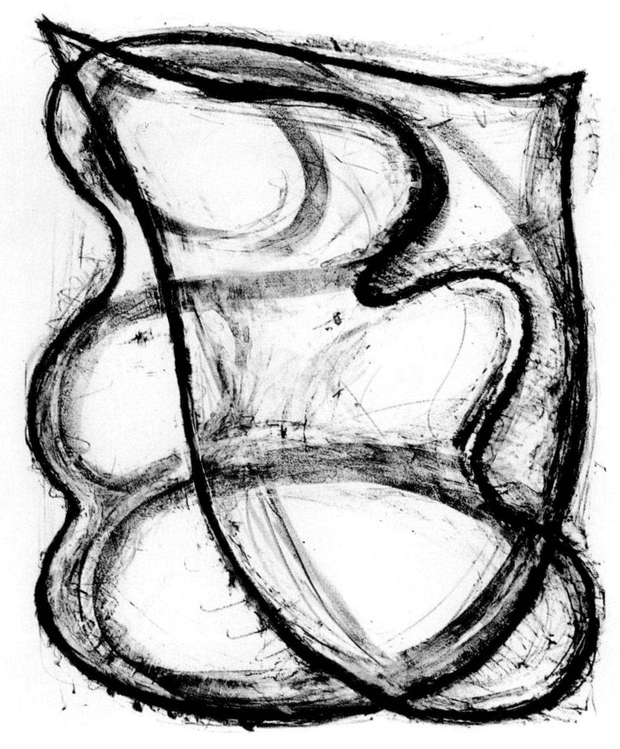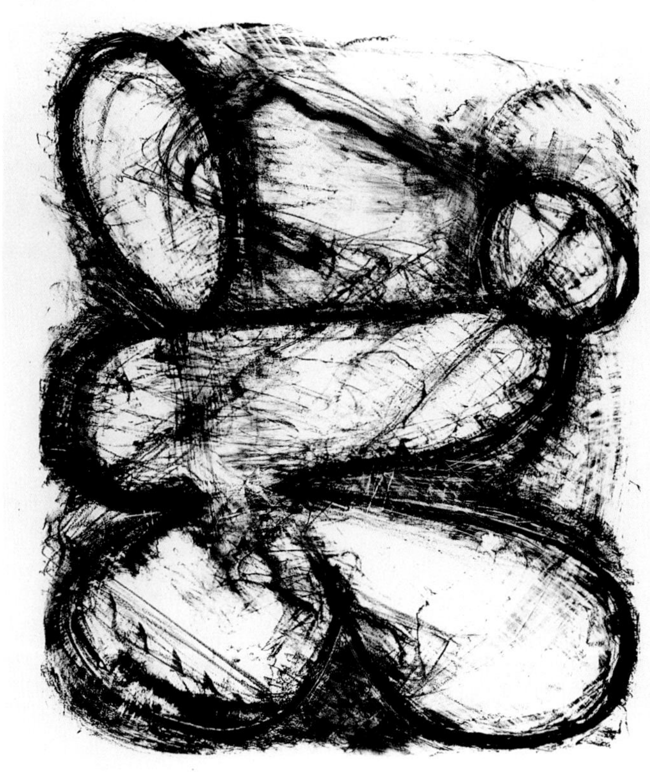

Elizabeth Murray *Untitled, States I–V* 1980
five lithographs (cat. no. 91)

print, she insisted on making one more because she wanted an image that would suggest intertwining figures. This effect was achieved in the fifth state by reprinting the fourth image on top of itself, upside down.

Untitled, States I–V is, in Murray's words, "about showing these layers that in a painting get covered up."[4] But indeed her paintings retain a history of shapes since she does not sand down the pigment, even after deciding to cover one form with another. Their marks and ridges become active parts of the work and reveal its evolution. Similarly, each state in *Untitled, States I–V* bears the record of its own making.

—S.M.

1. Quoted in Jacqueline Brody, "Elizabeth Murray, Thinking in Print: An Interview," *The Print Collector's Newsletter* 13 (July–August 1982), p. 74.

2. Ibid.

3. Ibid., p. 75.

4. Ibid., p. 76.

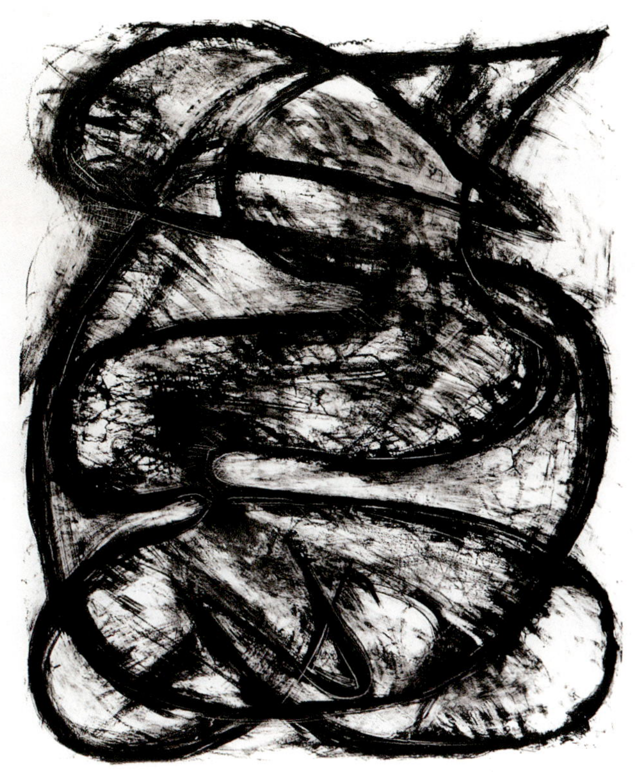

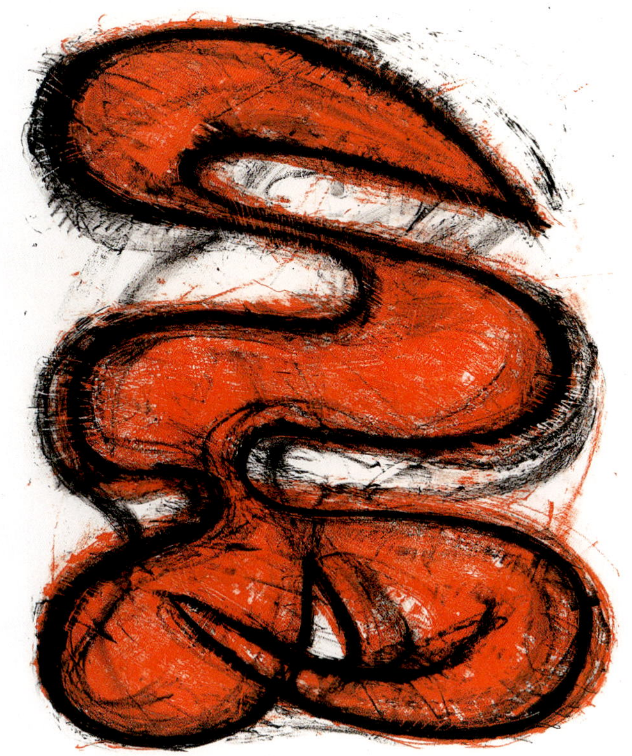

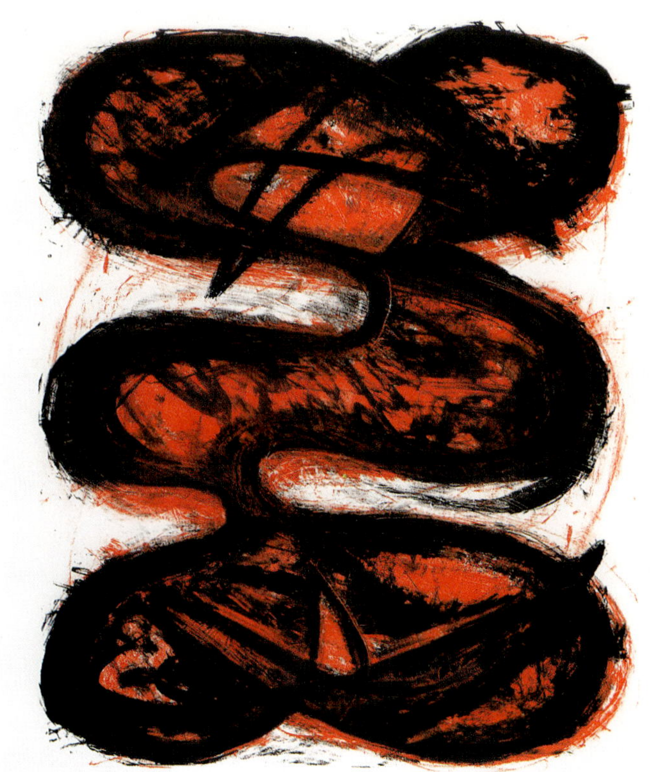

Richard Bosman

Richard Bosman excels at capturing the human figure in moments of crisis. Loading his brush thickly with paint or gouging deeply into his woodblocks, he imparts expressionistic angst to his anonymous characters, while at the same time making it seem that they are disconnected from their perilous situations, as if in a dream.

The son of a Dutch sea captain, Bosman grew up in such exotic port cities as Madras, Suez, Singapore, and Perth. In the late 1960s he attended art school in London, and in 1969 he moved to New York City; he studied art at the Studio School there from 1969 to 1971. He worked in sculpture, then painting, and, in the late 1970s, started making prints. His first ones were fashioned from linoleum blocks he bought when he could not afford paint and canvas. The lines he cut into the linoleum were, for him, related to drawing; he sometimes used these prints as studies for his paintings. In fact, Bosman attributes the predominance of night imagery in his early work to the linocuts, the backgrounds of which he left uncut so that they printed black.[1]

In 1981 the print publisher Brooke Alexander invited him to make a woodcut. At this time Bosman was deriving most of his imagery from an international array of popular sources, especially Asian comic books, B movies, and television, as well as from his own experiences. *Man Overboard* (1981), the night-world image of a figure plunging off a ship, was inspired by an episode from an ocean voyage Bosman made from Australia to Europe as a child. During the trip a priest threw himself overboard; the artist clearly remembers that the man left his shoes on deck. In the print the priest has been replaced by a paper doll-like everyman, fully dressed in a striped suit and red tie but wearing no shoes. More striking, however, is the graceful abandon with which he plummets into oblivion, injecting an incongruous element of humor into an otherwise dark scenario.

If the print originated in personal incident, its composition is based, the artist says, on the cover of a detective novel his wife had bought him entitled *Inspector West's Holiday*. The caricature of the plunging figure also reflects the influence of Alex Katz—an artist known for his highly stylized portraits—with whom Bosman studied at the Studio School. The affinity of *Man Overboard* with Japanese ukiyo-e woodblock prints is also noteworthy; there is a strong correspondence in such compositional elements as the print's verticality, the dominance of its flattened central figure, the rhythmic pattern of the waves, and the hint of wood grain showing through the ink. Bosman's primitive, vehement execution, however, has more in common with that of the German Expressionists, who also loved the graphic media, the woodcut in particular.

Man Overboard was the first of many projects the artist was to undertake with printer Chip Elwell, who specialized in woodcut. In 1981 alone they collaborated on five more woodcuts, and Bosman has continued to embrace the technique.

—E.A.

---

1. An interview with the artist conducted by the author on 12 January 1984 provided the basis for this entry. Portions of the interview text also appear in Elizabeth Armstrong et al., *Images and Impressions: Painters Who Print*, exh. cat. (Minneapolis: Walker Art Center, 1984), p. 10.

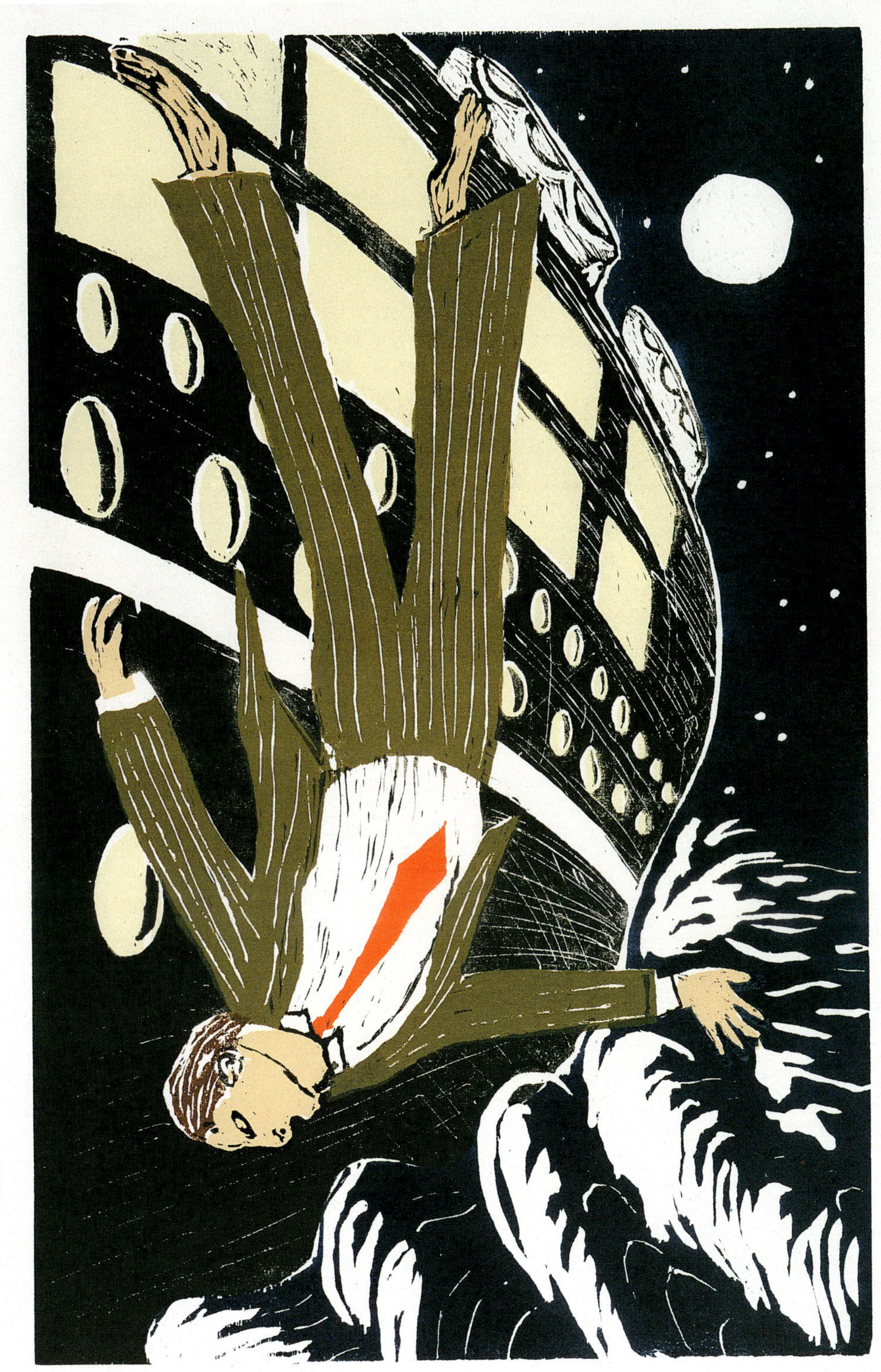

Richard Bosman *Man Overboard* 1981
woodcut (cat. no. 92)

John Buck

John Buck's sculptural environments of the late 1970s bear the stamp of his days as a graduate student at the University of California, Davis, where his humorous tendencies prospered under such teachers as Robert Arneson, Jim Nutt, and William T. Wiley. His installations of larger-than-life painted wooden figures in wildly colorful settings are packed with personal symbols and humor alluding to typically American influences, be they naïve art or the sensational, oversized figures seen on roadside billboards and carnival midways.

A trip Buck made to Jerusalem in 1980 brought about major changes in the mood and meaning of his constructions; flat freestanding sculptures, each one a frontal male figure modeled in low relief, made up a group of works from 1981 exhibited under the title *A Month of Sundays*. The somber tone of these works evolved from the artist's reflections on his experiences in that ancient city.

It is from these contemplative pieces that Buck's first published print, *Les Grande Eclipse* (1982), evolved. He had made a small woodcut during a workshop at the Visual Arts Center of Alaska, Anchorage, in 1980, which he sent to Jack Lemon at Landfall Press in Chicago. Buck had known Lemon when he was teaching printmaking at the Kansas City Art Institute in the late 1960s. He now wanted him to see that he had made a print. Lemon received his print enthusiastically and suggested that they collaborate on a large handmade woodcut.

The collaboration was a rather unusual one. Buck made his woodblock—attacking parts of it with a bandsaw—in his studio in Montana and then sent it to Landfall. He describes the woodblock as a "great big puzzle" that consisted of various interlocking pieces: the figure, the crescent moon, the background, and the border.[1] He assumed that each part would be inked separately, in different colors, and joined together for printing. This approach related closely to the way he was making sculptures at the time; he fabricated them from various pieces of wood cut to fit together. Unaware of Buck's practice, Lemon, upon receiving the pieces, glued them all together before printing. Nonetheless, they were able to move forward with the project.

Printing the edition was a physically demanding task. In order to have his image achieve the particular hardness he wanted, Buck required that the prints be pulled by the spooning method. In this method, a sheet of paper is laid directly onto the inked block and rubbed with a spoon until the ink is completely transferred to the sheet. Owing to the monumental scale of the prints, each one could take up to a day to print. Buck and printer David Holzman proofed the six-foot-tall *Les Grande Eclipse* in several different color combinations before the artist concluded that color was incidental to its content. He decided to execute it in black with a red border.

When Buck had visited the Western Wall in Jerusalem, he had been profoundly impressed by the masses of people clothed in black who came there to pray. In addition, the sight of the Moslem crescent moon on the Dome of the Rock mosque on the Temple Mount above the Wall invoked memories of an eclipse he had witnessed in Montana just a few months earlier. He used black to evoke these two experiences in the painting-construction *Eclipse* (1981), in which a figure whose head consists in a crescent moon stands in front of a canvas depicting the Western Wall. White lines scratched into or painted over dark impasto areas repeat the patterns of the backdrop to make the figure appear transparent.

Les Grande Eclipse relates directly to *Eclipse* without replicating it. A rigid male figure dominates the monumental woodcut, and a moon literally eclipses his skeletal face. To capture the feeling of looking through the figure in the print, Buck drew a skeleton within the body. An abundance of other, smaller figures, crudely drawn symbolic images, and random marks surround the dual figure to imbue the surface with great energy. Buck impressed many of these images into the surface of the pine panels using a pencil and a ballpoint pen, and he created other marks by pounding washers, nuts, and bolts into the surface.

Buck's contribution to the American woodcut revival of the 1980s extends beyond his unique imagery and the monumental scale of the prints to his method of constructing the blocks and his innovative treatment of the wood's surface. The act of cutting the woodblock came naturally to him. As he explains, "Since I knew I could take rubbings from my relatively flat sculpture, doing a print was a short step to make."

—S.M.

---

1. The artist in a conversation with the author, 27 June 1988. The following account of Buck's experiences at Landfall and in Jerusalem was also drawn from this conversation.

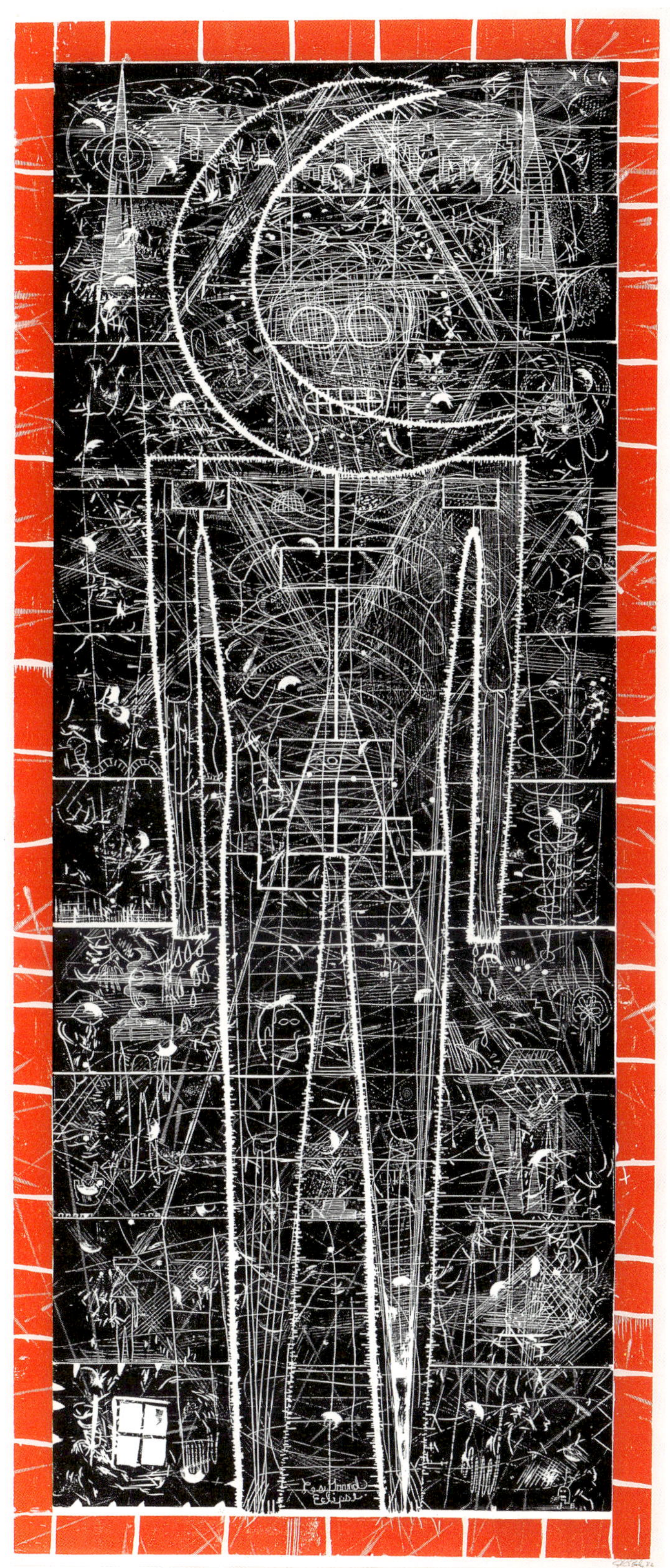

John Buck *Les Grande Eclipse* 1982
woodcut (cat. no. 94)

Eric Fischl

Eric Fischl is one of the few contemporary American artists whose work explicitly focuses on life in the suburbs. His quasi-narrative images dig beneath the surface of everyday middle-class life to reveal, for better or worse, its underside. Depicting private dramas that occur at home, on the beach, or around the backyard pool, Fischl probes the terrain of the contemporary American psyche and, in the process, has become a compelling painter.

To Pat Branstead, director of Aeropress in New York, Fischl's figurative style seemed well suited to prints.[1] Originally a painter herself, she had been diverted by printmaking during the 1970s and had become interested in introducing other young artists to the medium. In the early 1980s she made the transition from printer to printer-publisher, and Fischl was one of the first artists she approached in this new capacity. Prior to his project with her, in 1982, he had had limited experience with printmaking.[2] By way of initiation, Fischl worked at Aeropress part of every day for a two-week period, making test plates and trying different techniques. As publisher, Branstead was careful not to pressure him but, at the end of two weeks, realized that they needed to try a different approach to the medium. Visiting Fischl at his studio, she came up with the idea of making prints based on the format he used in his large-scale drawings on glassine.

An unusual drawing surface, glassine provided Fischl with translucent layers and a straightforward way of making composite imagery. Branstead noted that the separate etching plates, printed in succession, would produce the same kind of overlay that Fischl created in his drawings. In both prints made at Aeropress, *Digging Kids* and *Beach Balls* (cat. no. 96), the indentation left by the pressure of each printed plate emphasizes their separate drawing substrates. Each of the three figures in *Digging Kids*, for instance, is contained by a lightly embossed rectangular background that serves, ever so

subtly, to isolate one from the other. A delicate green tone added over all the plate areas approximates glassine. As in the composite drawings, Fischl's overlapping of the figures is blatantly made so that, for example, the bottom half of the boy on the right can be seen through the woman's head. The transparency of these images finds a parallel in the figures' nakedness.

The imagery in both *Digging Kids* and *Beach Balls* involves an ambiguous form of voyeurism. In *Beach Balls* a young boy who has just emerged from the water (he still has his flippers on) stands wrapped in a towel over a smaller, naked figure sleeping under a beach umbrella. Although quite possibly innocuous, the boy's dark, dripping presence has a menacing quality, especially in contrast to the repose of the other figure. In *Digging Kids* a woman sits on a beach chair, facing two young boys digging sand on the beach. The intensity of their activity is countered by her seeming disengagement. She appears to be lost in her thoughts, focusing neither on the boys nor on her magazine. From a vantage point just behind the sunbathing woman, the viewer can only guess at the direction of her gaze—and at her state of mind. But the image conveys a certain malaise, just as *Beach Balls* suggests potential unpleasantness, a feeling underlying many of Fischl's pictures of contemporary American life.

—E.A.

1. Branstead in a conversation with the author, 8 July 1988.

2. Fischl had worked on two lithographs in 1975 while teaching at the Nova Scotia College of Art and Design, Halifax, but he does not consider them to have been successful and had little interest in seeing them distributed. Largely abstract, they predate Fischl's mature figurative style.

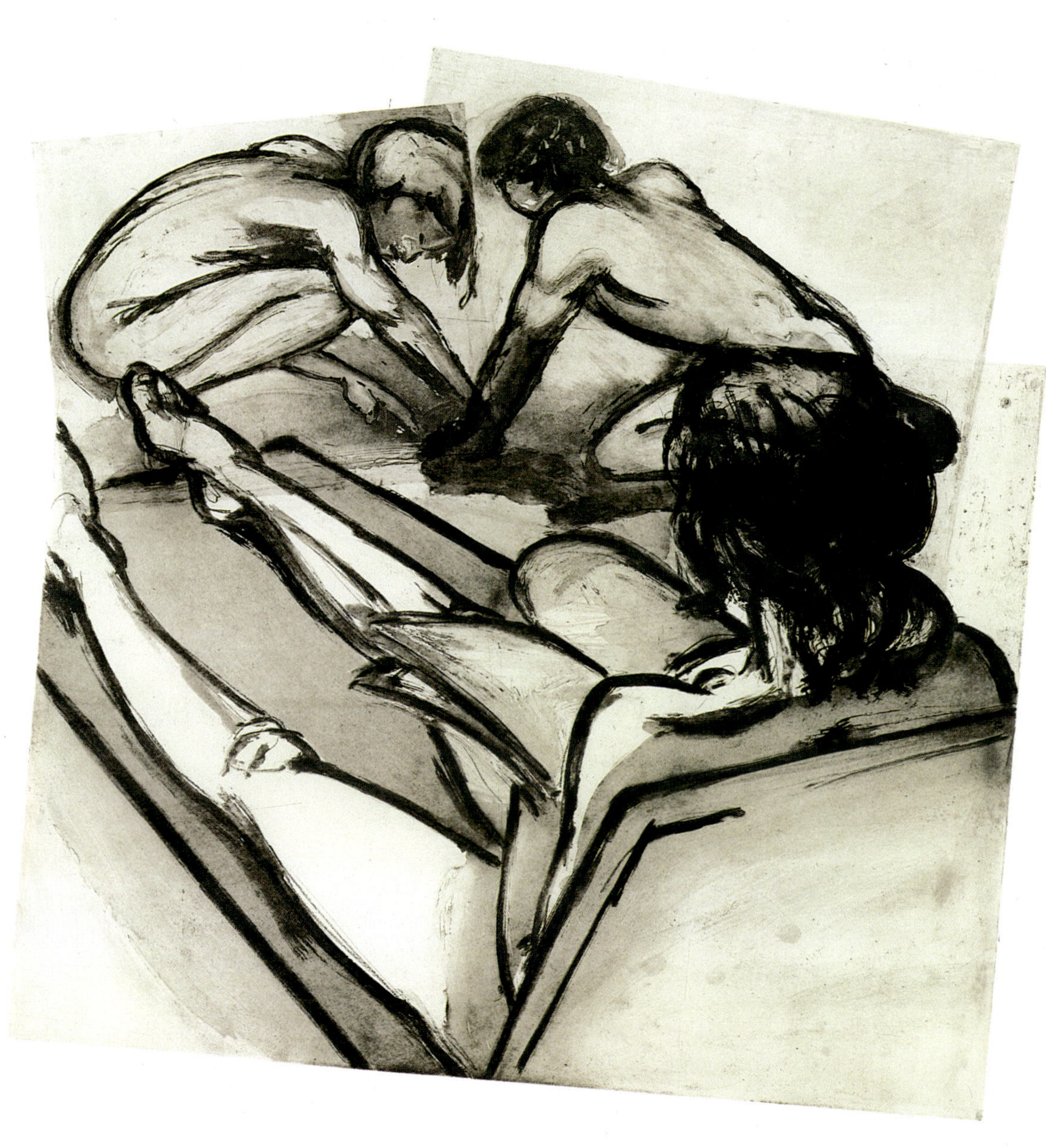

Eric Fischl *Digging Kids* 1982
etching, aquatint (cat. no. 95)

T. L. Solien

Although T. L. Solien was influenced by Abstract Expressionism and Conceptual Art while at the University of Nebraska, where he graduated with an M.F.A. in 1977, his interest in making his works narrative and personal became predominant soon afterward. In his paintings and drawings of the late 1970s, he developed a kind of visual shorthand to relay events from his own life, especially those involving his family. Essential in this shorthand was a repertoire of invented characters—many of which were alter egos—including a tin man, a jester, and a bull.

In 1982 Solien was invited by Steven Andersen, director of Vermillion Editions in Minneapolis, to make prints there. He was initially inclined to turn down the offer, "thinking that prints lacked the 'painterly' quality and physicality that I was employing at that time."[1] Indeed, his paintings of this period were thickly impastoed with oil paints mixed with wax. Andersen, however, had been experimenting with heavy inks that could be applied to prints with the viscosity of paint. Solien was impressed by what Andersen showed him at Vermillion and agreed to try making one or two prints. He was also naturally interested in increasing his ability to make a living from his art, which the production of graphic works seemed likely to help him do.

Solien arrived at Vermillion with several cartoonlike drawings that were similar to his paintings of that period. Once there he made a full-scale drawing on which the first print was closely based. This image, *The Three Sailors* (1982), reflects Solien's interest in "trying to find symbolic images to represent a three person nuclear family."[2] He does this in *The Three Sailors* by picturing his family at the time, representing his daughter as the yellow-faced troll at the left, his wife as the crying head at the right, and himself, in the center, as a vessel-shaped cyclops. A fourth figure in the print injects a further note of autobiography: a tiny blue conelike form between the two parents alludes to the infant child Solien and his wife had lost a few years earlier; its presence explains the soulful expressions of the adult figures.

The Three Sailors and a second multimedia print made at Vermillion in 1982, *Nightwatchman*, have richly varied and distinctively textured surfaces. Andersen created these surfaces by combining lithography with intaglio and screenprinting, thus giving the prints the painterly quality Solien was after. As the printers prepared plates and mixed inks for these prints, Solien found himself with

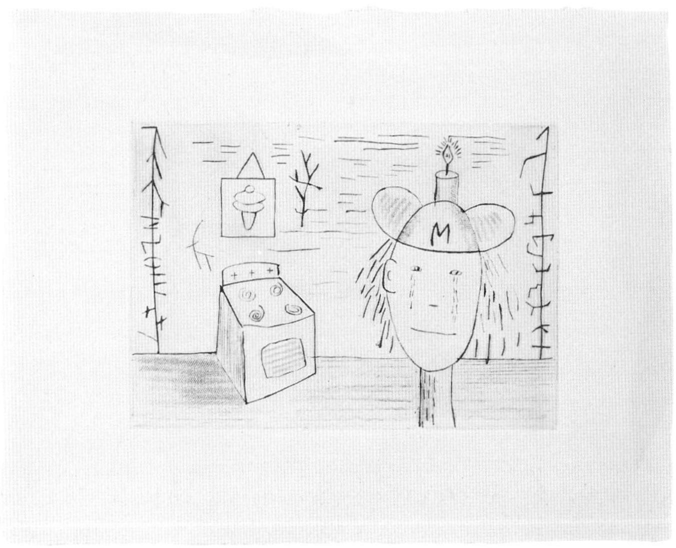

T. L. Solien *Fragments of Hope* 1982
drypoint (cat. no. 98)

time on his hands. It was suggested that, while waiting, he try working in drypoint or making monotypes. He quickly generated a suite of six drypoints entitled *Fragments of Hope*[3] and a series of monotypes. In *Fragments of Hope*, executed, like *The Three Sailors*, in a deliberately childlike pictographic manner, Solien fully vents his feelings about the loss of his child. The delicate handworking of these drypoints corresponds to the tender character of their imagery. The monotypes Solien made at Vermillion led to his immersion in this medium, which requires a spontaneity that particularly appeals to the artist. Some of his fiercest imagery to date has been created using the monotype process.

—E.A.

1. The artist in correspondence with the author, 11 June 1988.

2. Ibid.

3. The complete suite is reproduced in Elizabeth Armstrong et al., *Images and Impressions: Painters Who Print*, exh. cat. (Minneapolis: Walker Art Center, 1984), p. 55.

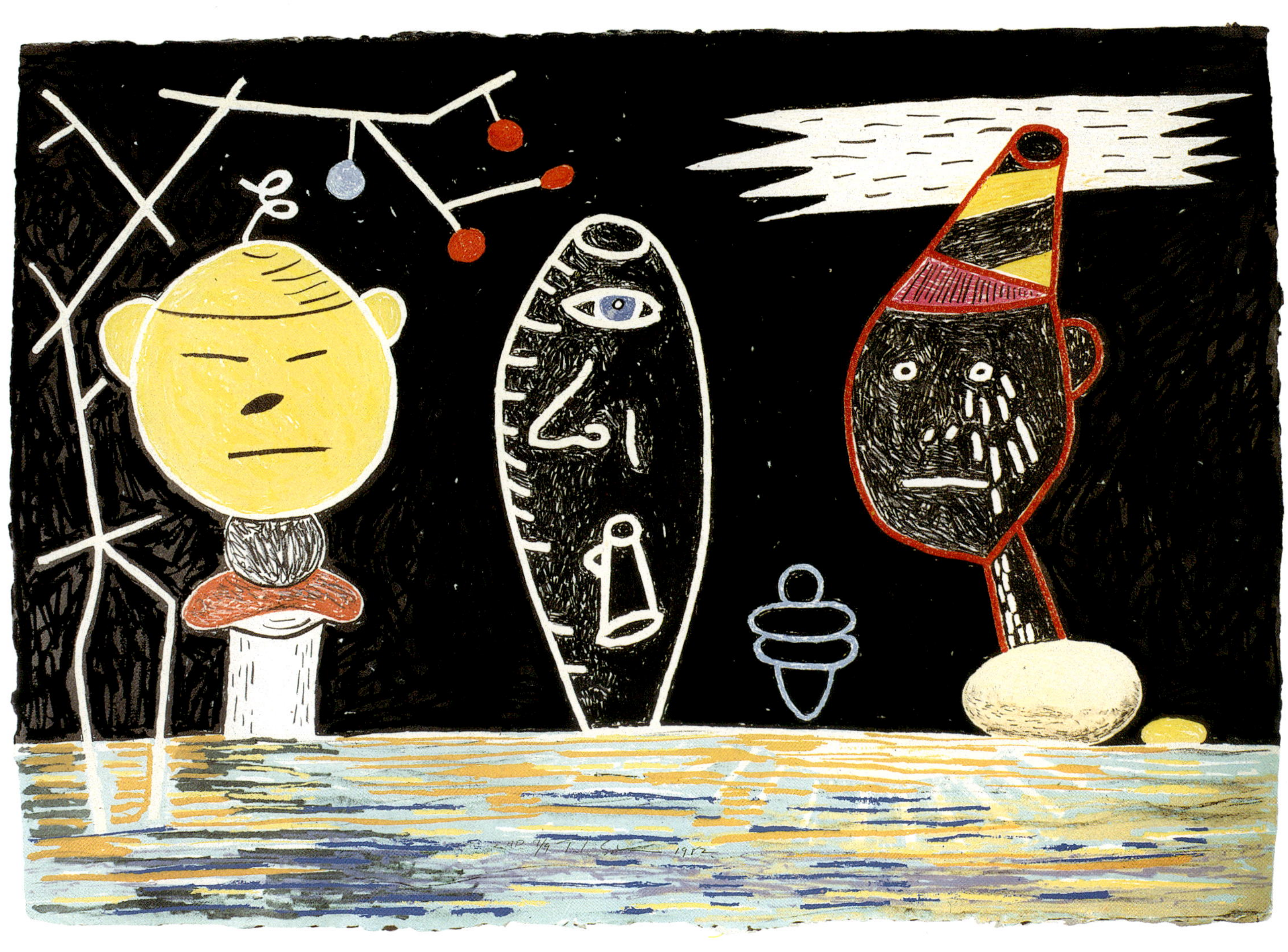

T. L. Solien *The Three Sailors* 1982
lithograph, intaglio, screenprint (cat. no. 97)

Terry Winters

born Brooklyn, New York   1949

Terry Winters' decision to make prints at ULAE was an easy one. Though he had never worked in the medium, he had a long-standing theoretical interest in printmaking, as well as a special attraction to ULAE publications. According to the artist, Jasper Johns and Robert Rauschenberg, who had produced their early prints at ULAE, set a particularly positive example because they "used the medium to make things that to me felt like *real* work."[1] Winters' first two lithographs, *Ova* (1982) and *Factors of Increase* (1983; p. 19), can likewise be considered real work.

Winters knew before starting his lithographs that he did not want to use them to rework previous images. Thus, aside from a few preliminary drawings, especially for *Ova*, he allowed his experiments with the lithographic process to determine the imagery. He drew on both plates and stones with tusche and crayon until, as he recalls, "at one point it all came together . . . and the drawing, proofing, and printing were all done in one day."

Ova evolved out of the botanical forms that became significant for Winters in the early 1980s. In the print the eponymous central figure rests atop a narrow stem—quite a feat considering its apparent weight. In form, it roughly resembles a halved tomato with a large core. Winters drew the ova in crayon and wash to achieve a finely textured surface. The irregular contours of the lithographic stone emboss the paper to give the ova a life of its own, separate from the activity of the two little balloon forms, which, floating in the lower-left corner, inevitably suggest sperm making their way toward an ample egg. A limited supply of the special English moldmade paper used for *Ova* accounts for its edition of only seven prints.

Winters prefers to think of *Factors of Increase* as his first full-fledged print since it fruitfully represents everything he was then learning. Its imagery was new for him, and, like *Ova*, it evolved out of the procedures unique to lithography—particularly experimentation with different stones and plates and work in progressive states. Cautiously enough, Winters terms the imagery of *Factors of Increase* "indescribable." Indeed, the print contains three club-shaped, honeycomb-patterned, apparently natural forms that somehow manage to defy comparison with any known organism. While they presumably belong to a common species, each is unique.

Although the images in both *Factors of Increase* and *Ova* were new for Winters, the technique employed—a building-up of contrasting layers and textures—is like that used in his drawings. There, he juxtaposes the barest areas of smudged charcoal with layers of crayon and charcoal markings. Similarly, he makes the most of contrasts between powdery, flat, and greasy textures in the lithographs. In *Factors of Increase* he uses the offset proofing press to achieve a richly evocative surface through repeated overprintings with transparent inks. Through these subtle layers, he creates a surface highly suggestive of a charcoal drawing. He further enhances this effect by making the image spread all the way to the rough edge of the sheet.

Winters actively participated in the production of *Factors of Increase* because, as he says, "it was all about it happening on the plates and stones." He adds that the making of this print helped him in nonprint projects, for it increased his awareness of his working methods. "With printmaking," he asserts, "you have to be conscious about *all* of your decisions."

—S.M.

---

1. The artist in a conversation with the author, 11 March 1988. All subsequent Winters quotations here are also taken from this conversation.

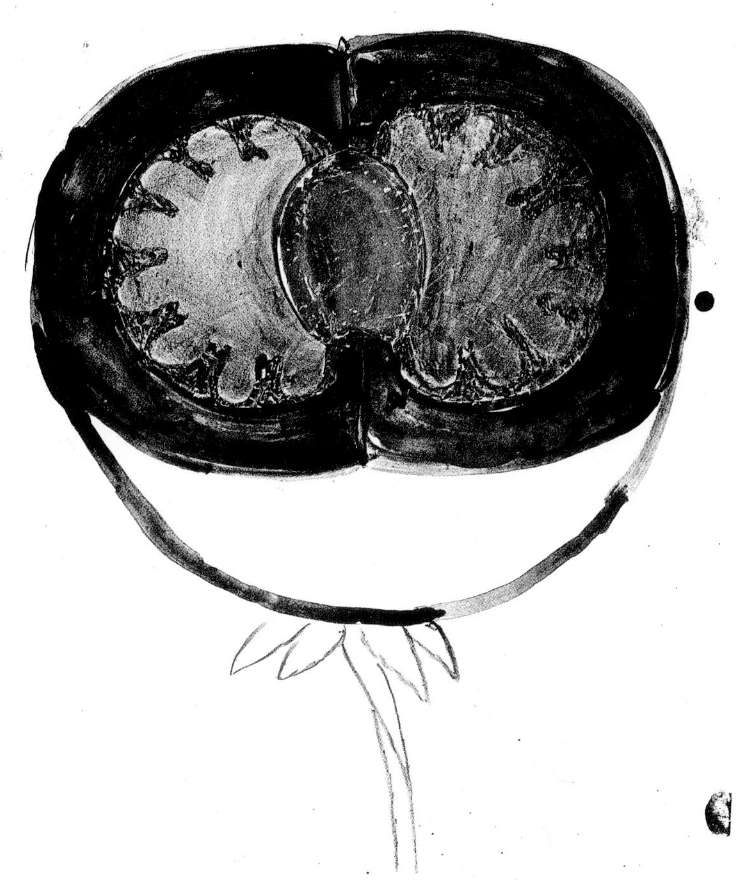

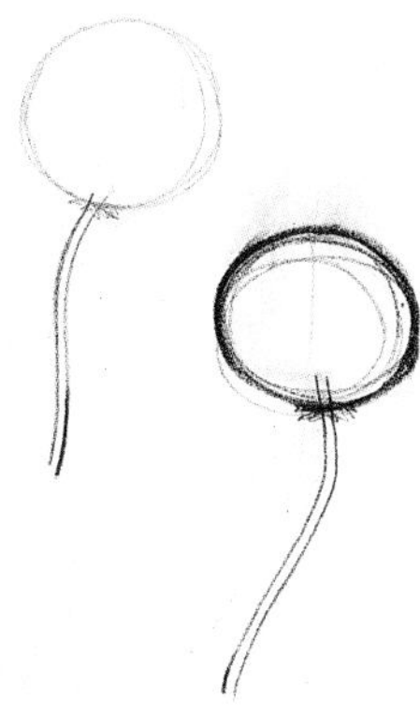

Terry Winters *Ova* 1982
lithograph (cat. no. 99)

Robert Longo

Robert Longo's versatility is evidenced in his performances, films, videos, sculptures, paintings, drawings, and prints. He commits himself to all of them—separately and in mixed-media pieces—to make timely statements about contemporary life, culture, and politics. From 1977 to 1981 he made nearly sixty large-scale graphite and charcoal drawings of men and women, their strained poses suspending them between agony and ecstasy. The black-and-white drawings, collectively known as Men in the Cities, sometimes reached heights of nine feet, Longo using large scale to emphasize the struggle and isolation in contemporary urban existence.[1]

Invitations from print publishers Brooke Alexander and Jörg Schellmann to make prints based on Men in the Cities gave the artist the opportunity to codify the ideas he had been grappling with in the drawings as well as a way to "entomb" the series once and for all.[2] He agreed to produce six large-scale, full-figure lithographs for Alexander and six even larger cropped-figure lithographs for Schellmann.

Working on these series with the printer Maurice Sanchez, at Derrière L'Etoile Studios in New York City, made it possible for Longo to explore printmaking in depth for the first time.[3] At the outset he attempted to draw on the lithographic plates in the same way he would on paper, but he soon realized that different types of marks would be necessary. "So," he said afterward, "I decided to accept the glitches that come with the medium," and to "hold back a bit in the more complex areas, to put in just enough detail to imply everything else."[4] By reducing his marks in the lithographs, he obtained even more neutral surfaces in the prints than in the graphite drawings. A limited selection of black and gray inks provided just enough nuance for the skin tones and heightened the dramatic contrast of black and white that was so important to these images.

In 1982 and 1983 Longo produced three lithographs of single figures—*Jules, Gretchen,* and *Mark*—which were not part of the proposed large-scale series. Although each print was published individually by Alexander, it was critical to Longo that they be experienced as a group. As with his large drawings, he felt strongly that the tensions, movements, and pressures inherent in each

figure were most fully realized in relationship to each other, so he printed the three images side by side to make the striking *Jules, Gretchen, Mark, State II* (1982–1983). The spasmodic falling gestures of Jules and Mark set off the relatively cool stability of the central figure, Gretchen, whose movement is limited to an evasive turn of the head and slightly thrown-back shoulders. An embossed line frames the threesome, drawing these psychologically distant figures physically together.

Concurrently Longo also began work on two large-scale lithographic series, which, owing to their size and his schedule, took more than three years to complete. For the artist the large lithographs are "highly tuned archetypes" of the Men in the Cities drawings. The majority of them represent variations on his favorite poses from the series, although "one or two of them never existed in full-scale drawings." One of his most familiar images, the dramatic figure of an agonized man reeling backward and grasping his lower back, makes its final appearance in the lithograph *Edmund* (1985), a figure based on a photograph Longo took of Brooke Alexander.

—S.M.

---

1. For further reading on the Men in the Cities, see Robert Longo, *Men in the Cities: 1979–1982* (New York: Harry N. Abrams Publishers, 1986), which includes an interview with the artist by Richard Price.

2. The artist in a conversation with the author, 9 May 1988. Unless otherwise noted, all subsequent Longo quotations here are also taken from this conversation.

3. Longo had taken a printmaking class at the State University College at Buffalo, New York, in the mid-1970s but, at the time, had little interest in pursuing the medium further. In 1981 he made a silkscreen, *Empire,* to raise funds for one of his performances—also called *Empire*—at the Kitchen in New York City. The same year he transferred a drawing, *Gretchen,* to a photo-silkscreen for a poster to benefit the Kitchen on its tenth anniversary.

4. Quoted in Carter Ratcliff, "Robert Longo: The City of Sheer Image," *The Print Collector's Newsletter* 14 (July–August 1983), p. 95.

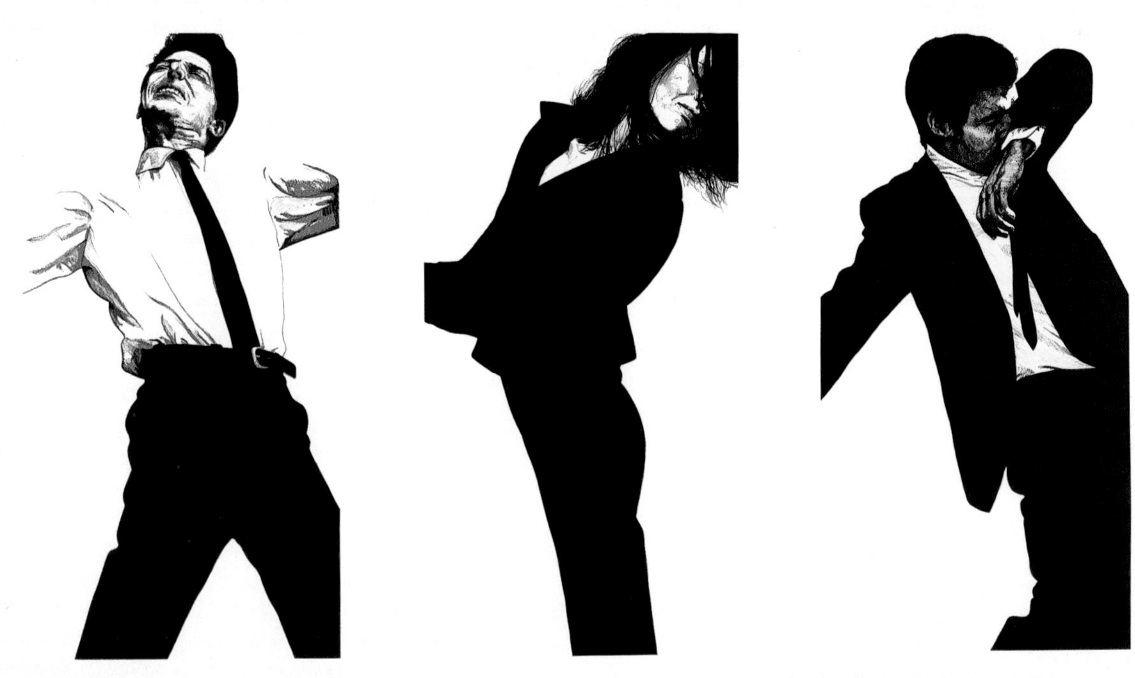

Robert Longo *Jules, Gretchen, Mark, State II* 1982–1983
lithograph with embossing (cat. no. 101)

David True

David True once described his art as emanating from an inner spirit that projects visions or ideas "essentially all at once, configured in my mind as fairly complete visual constructions."[1] His images include such familiar subjects as animals, plants, cars, houses, and boats, which, pared down to their essence, have a mystical quality. More symbolic than narrative, these haunting forms are emblematic of deep-seated emotions, and True acknowledges the unconscious as an important source for his work.[2]

True explored his imagery in sculpture, painting, and drawing before he considered making prints. Karen McCready, director of the New York City office of the California print shop Crown Point Press, had followed his work for some time and thought it would translate well into etching; Kathan Brown, Crown Point's director, agreed and, in 1982, invited the artist to make prints at their studio in Oakland. True was intrigued by the offer, figuring the process might be a valuable one. During his first visit, in February 1983, he tried a range of etching techniques and became particularly drawn to aquatint, which he learned under the direction of printer Marcia Bartholme.[3]

At the time of this visit, True was working on landscape paintings. He brought a transparency of one of these with him to provide a starting point, and he completed one landscape print, *Late* (cat. no. 103), a generalized view of rolling fields, jagged hills, and a rocky mountainside, all rhythmically joined. The velvety blues and blacks of the image, achieved through aquatint, reveal a propensity for dark, moody color. Two other prints, *Lifting Ascent* and *Sour Mistress*, are both very delicate images, drawn from True's evolving lexicon in his painting, and reflect his experimentation in hard-ground and soft-ground techniques. A fourth print, *Savannah Sea*, brings together rich aquatint, soft ground, and spitbite in a signature image of a simplified boat riding the high seas.

The boat is a particularly potent symbol that has appeared again and again in True's work and has, in the process, assumed numerous manifestations. Its archetypal form, striving to make headway against the formidable power of the sea, can be read as representing man's struggle to navigate life and his inevitable journey toward death. While many of True's representations of the boat convey a sense of anticipation and foreboding, the vessel in *Savannah Sea* sets a relatively optimistic tone. Its hull, cresting high above the water, is buoyantly afloat. True's sketchlike application of aquatint to depict water mimics the swelling movement of the rough seas, a swelling that becomes a sort of pedestal for the small, noble craft.

When True returned to Crown Point Press, in 1985, he made seven large-scale prints, including two more images of the boat. His skillful manipulation of aquatint, already evident in *Savannah Sea*, comes fully alive in these highly accomplished etchings, which extend the boat into a more ambiguous realm of perilous waters and shadowy night.

True's work in the medium broadened his approach to painting; his canvases now reflect the looser, more gestural style he had used when first experimenting with aquatint at Crown Point. True was surprised that printmaking proved so catalytic. Although his experience with the medium had been "a very profound one," he had not expected it "to be the springboard."[4]

—E.A.

1. Quoted in Richard Marshall, *New Image Painting*, exh. cat. (New York: Whitney Museum of American Art, 1978), p. 62.

2. Gerrit Henry, "David True: Poetry as Print," *The Print Collector's Newsletter* 16 (September–October 1985), p. 124.

3. Ibid., p. 125.

4. Quoted in an interview with Margaret Wrinkle at Crown Point Press, in *View* 4 (Spring 1988), p. 9.

David True *Savannah Sea* 1983
aquatint, soft ground, spitbite (cat. no. 102)

In 1977 James Turrell purchased the Roden Crater, an extinct volcano on the eastern margin of the San Francisco Volcanic Field in the Painted Desert.[1] Located some forty miles from Flagstaff, Arizona, the volcano is the artist's chosen site for an ambitious installation project intended to heighten perceptions of light and how it inhabits different spaces. His work around the time he bought the crater involved projecting light on gallery walls to create the illusion of physical objects as well as installations that probed the effects of natural and artificial light on specific sites. When completed, Turrell's Roden Crater will comprise a series of underground rooms, cut into the volcano's fumarole (the hole from which hot gases and vapors once issued), that will receive and interact with light generated by various celestial events, some that occur daily, some biennially, and some only infrequently—for example, lunar alignments and eclipses.[2]

Turrell's first prints comprised a portfolio of seven aquatints, entitled *Deep Sky* (1984), which focus on Roden Crater. Turrell had not previously made prints nor sold any of his drawings because he wanted to be known solely for his light installations and environmental projects.[3] After several invitations from publisher Peter Blum in New York, however, he agreed to make these aquatints in order to draw attention to the project and help raise funds for its construction.

Collaborating with printer Paul Kneubühler in Zurich, Turrell began the portfolio with specific images in mind. These, he later acknowledged, "proved to be quite naïve," owing to the unpredictable results of aquatint. "When you start working with it," he says of the process, "you definitely change your thinking because you may have one idea in your mind, and the acid and the copper have their own ideas." Despite Kneubühler's explanations and demonstrations, Turrell admits, he ruined many plates before completing the richly tonal aquatints, which depict the projected effects of both moonlight and artificial light on the created rooms and spaces at Roden Crater.

Predominantly black, the aquatints show the volcano's spaces as Turrell envisions they will look from deep night to early morning. The first print of the *Deep Sky* set reveals the dark silhouette of the looming volcano isolated against a starlit sky. A dawning of light over the horizon line at the far edge of the Painted Desert in the second aquatint represents the opening of the volcano's eastern

room. Several of the other prints show cross-sections of specific areas—the entrance to a fumarole space, light entering a fumarole space, and the west room—and emphasize the sculptural aspect of the project. *Deep Sky* culminates in an image of the open bowl of the crater, which Turrell had reshaped to heighten the sense of the sky's curvature. This view captures the moment when the visitor will pass from a lengthy tunnel into the vast, open crater.

At Blum's suggestion, Turrell also agreed to have a book published to accompany the *Deep Sky* aquatints. In that limited-edition volume, *Iconographia Coelestis* (1985), the poet and gallery owner Mario Diacono eloquently relates Roden Crater to " 'primitive' sites for observing celestial phenomena"[4] and warns against simplistically grouping this project among the earthworks that were artistically fashionable in the late 1970s. Besides commissioning Diacono's book, Blum had carpenter Chuck Endo handcraft a wooden box to house each copy of the *Deep Sky* portfolio.

In his conclusion to *Iconographia Coelestis*, Diacono writes of the Roden Crater project that "it exists not as a megastructure, inserted in the landscape as a potential monumental object of contemplation, but rather as a natural 'temple' invented to the ends of a higher, extra-historical experience of being on the part of an eventual observer."[5] Until the project is completed, *Deep Sky* and Turrell's recent group of five etchings with aquatint, *Mapping Spaces* (1987–1988), provide the best imaginative means of entering the volcano's mysterious spaces.

—S.M.

---

1. The Roden Crater project was initially financed by the Dia Foundation and later by the MacArthur Foundation, the National Endowment for the Arts, and Turrell himself. In 1982 Turrell formed the Skystone Foundation to raise additional backing. Turrell hopes that the project will be completed sometime in the 1990s.

2. For more information about the project, see Julia Brown, ed., *Occluded Front: James Turrell* (Los Angeles: Fellows of Contemporary Art and the Lapis Press, 1985).

3. The artist in a conversation with the author, 8 July 1988. All Turrell quotations here are also taken from this conversation.

4. Mario Diacono, *Iconographia Coelestis* (New York: Peter Blum Edition, 1985), p. 20. This book was printed by the Kelly/Winterton Press, New York, in an edition of one hundred fifty. The text was translated from the Italian by Meg Shore.

5. Ibid., p. 23.

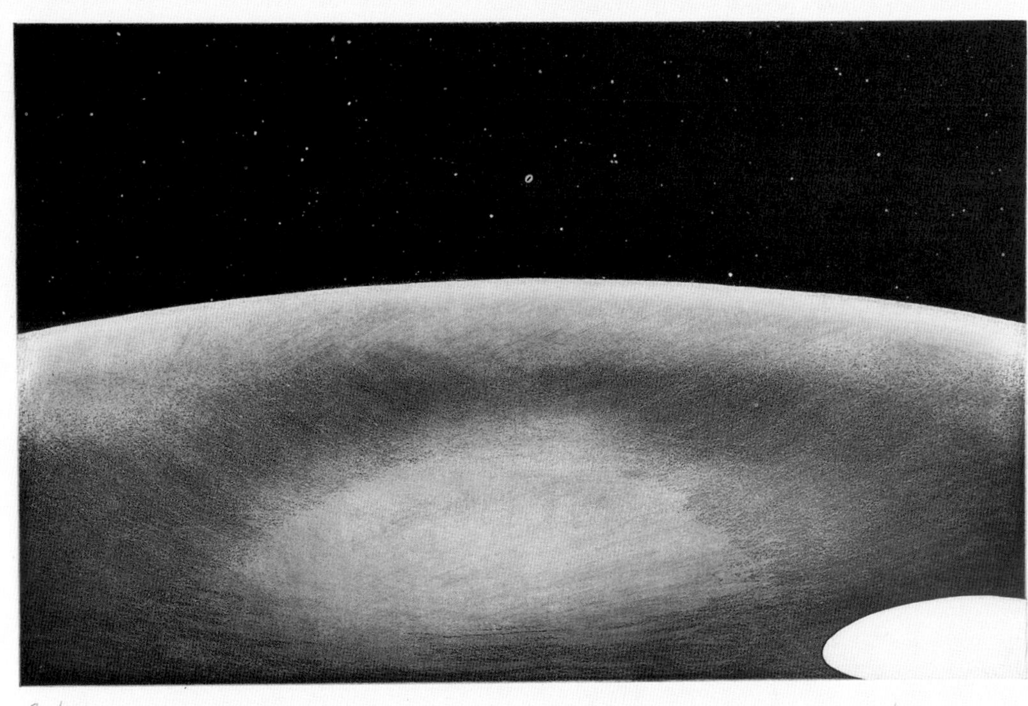

James Turrell *Deep Sky* 1984
aquatint (cat. no. 104)

Carroll Dunham

Since 1982 Carroll Dunham has made paintings on wood as well as drawings on veneered paper and thin sheets of wood. He regularly utilizes the wood's natural grain to determine, in part, the configuration of his compositions. Humorously wild colors such as Day-Glo green, hot pink, and bright lemon yellow frequently embellish highly charged organic forms. Critics have called Dunham's output "psychedelic" and "funky," and the overtly erotic overtones of his invented shapes prompted one writer to describe his imagery as a "writhing dance of organs."[1]

Dunham's first three lithographs, produced at ULAE in 1984 and 1985, are characteristically full of sexual energy. A collection of organic forms, scribbles, washes, and lines activates their surfaces. The sheer exuberance of the imagery and the accomplished use of several lithographic techniques in these prints belie his inexperience with the medium.[2] Bill Goldston, director of ULAE, brought a lithographic stone to Dunham's studio so the artist could experiment with the medium at his leisure. After six weeks of extensive drawing on the stone, he needed to see his marks printed on paper, so they moved the stone to the ULAE workshop in West Islip, New York. There, Dunham collaborated on this and another lithograph with printer Keith Brintzenhofe. He says he approached the project knowing that he wanted to make his prints "specifically about printmaking—about marks specific to working on stone."[3]

The relationship of the stone's edge to the paper's edge also intrigued Dunham. In his first lithograph, *Untitled* (1984–1985), he outlined a rectangular area within the sheet that functioned as a page-within-a-page, a "page" whose boundaries are violated by an explosion of squirting, twisting, spiraling, and springing forms. In the second published print, also called *Untitled* (1985; cat.

no. 106), a huge black torpedo/penis rips through the surface and ejects a flow of bubbles that spills out of a drawn page and onto the real one.

Dunham next produced a more complex lithograph, *Accelerator* (1985; cat. no. 107), printed in four different blacks from a combination of stones and plates. Far more fascinated by the lithographic process than he had anticipated, the artist became actively involved in the many stages of making this print, which included transferring the patterns of ball-shaped forms, seen in the lower-right corner, to sheets of transparent Mylar to achieve subtle layering effects.

Dunham has repeatedly returned to ULAE, making twelve prints there since 1984. He has begun exploring colored inks and working on a larger scale. Acknowledging that printmaking encourages him to think more analytically about his paintings and drawings,[4] Dunham has made it a significant element of his art.

—S.M.

---

1. Klaus Kertess, "Carroll Dunham: Painting against the Grain—Painting with the Grain," *Artforum* 21 (June 1983), p. 53.

2. Dunham was familiar with the basic concepts involved in printmaking as he had studied screenprinting and photography at Trinity College in Hartford, Connecticut, and worked for *Time* magazine for seven years; however, he had never experimented with lithography. The artist in correspondence with Elizabeth Armstrong, 15 March 1988.

3. The artist in a conversation with the author, 7 July 1988.

4. Artist correspondence, supra, note 2.

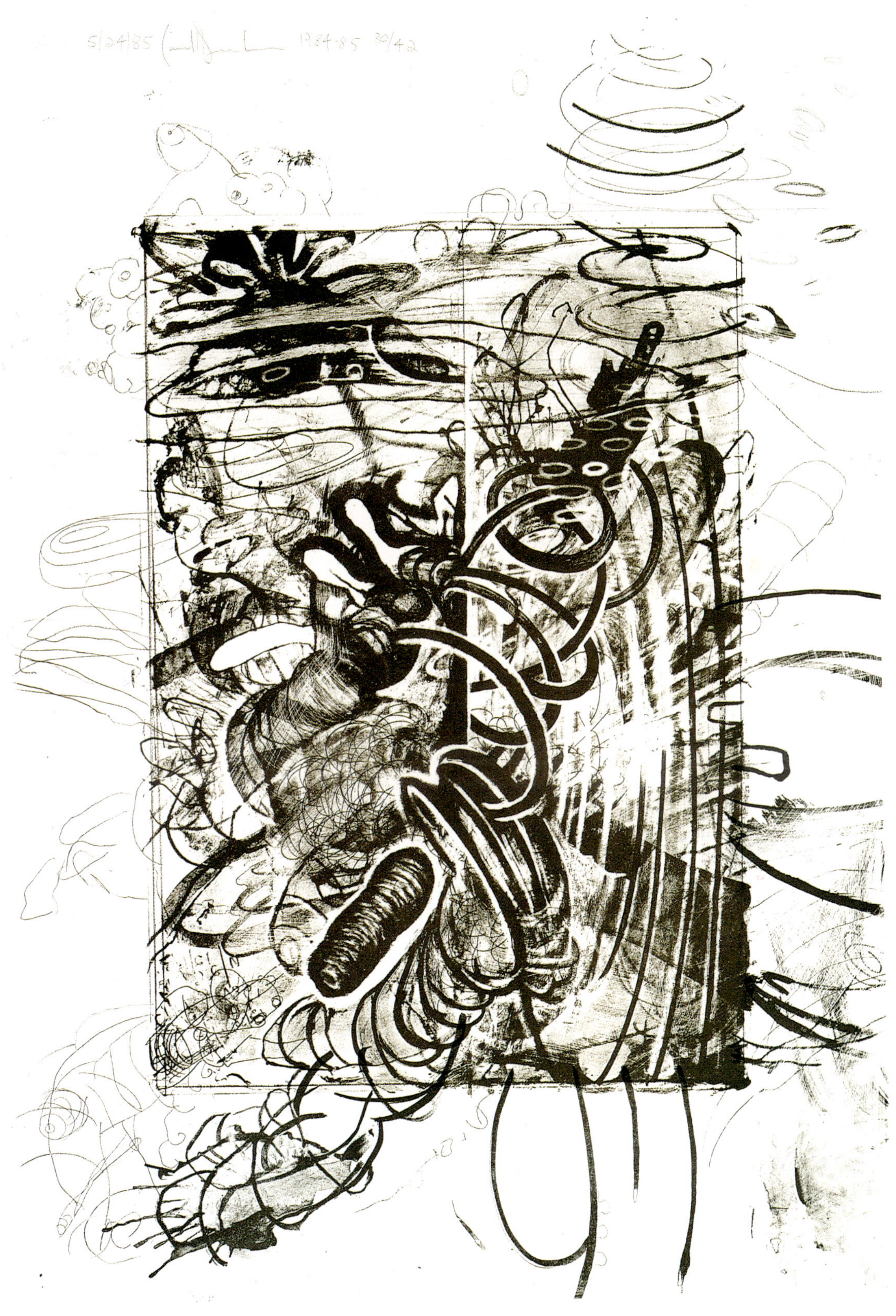

Carroll Dunham *Untitled* 1984–1985
lithograph (cat. no. 105)

Checklist

Larry Rivers

1. *The Bird and the Circle*, State IV   1957
lithograph
edition: 5
13 × 20
Printed and published by Universal Limited
Art Editions, West Islip, New York
Collection The Art Institute of Chicago, ULAE
Collection, acquired through a challenge grant
of Mr. and Mrs. Thomas Dittmer, donations
of supporters of the Department of Prints and
Drawings, and the Centennial Endowment

Larry Rivers and Frank O'Hara

2. *Stones*   1957–1959
twelve lithographs
edition: 25
18¾ × 23½ each
Printed and published by Universal Limited
Art Editions, West Islip, New York
Collection The Art Institute of Chicago,
William McCallin McKee Fund

Jasper Johns

3. *Target*   1960
lithograph
edition: 30
22⅝ × 17⅝
Printed and published by Universal Limited
Art Editions, West Islip, New York
Collection Walker Art Center, Minneapolis,
gift of Judy and Kenneth Dayton, 1988

4. *Coat Hanger I*   1960
lithograph
edition: 35
36 × 27
Printed and published by Universal Limited
Art Editions, West Islip, New York
Collection Walker Art Center, Minneapolis,
gift of Judy and Kenneth Dayton, 1988

5. *Coat Hanger II*   1960
lithograph
edition: 8
35½ × 24¾
Printed and published by Universal Limited
Art Editions, West Islip, New York
Collection Walker Art Center, Minneapolis,
gift of Judy and Kenneth Dayton, 1988

6. *Coat Hanger Variation*   1960
lithograph with embossing
trial proof
36 × 26¾
Printed by Universal Limited Art Editions,
West Islip, New York
Collection The Art Institute of Chicago, ULAE
Collection, acquired through a challenge grant
of Mr. and Mrs. Thomas Dittmer, donations
of supporters of the Department of Prints and
Drawings, and the Centennial Endowment

7. *0–9*   1960–1963
ten lithographs
edition: 10
20½ × 15¾ each
Printed and published by Universal Limited
Art Editions, West Islip, New York
Collection Walker Art Center, Minneapolis,
gift of Judy and Kenneth Dayton, 1988

8. *0–9*   1960–1963
notebook of forty-two lithographic proofs
25½ × 20½ × 2¼
Collection the artist

9. *0–9*   1960–1963
notebook of fifty-four lithographic proofs
25½ × 20½ × 2¼
Collection the artist

Jim Dine

10. *Car Crash I–V*   1960
five lithographs
edition: 33
32 × 20 each
Printed by Pratt Graphic Art Workshop,
New York
Published by Martha Jackson Gallery,
New York
Courtesy Petersburg Press, New York

11. *End of the Crash*   1960
lithograph
edition: 32
39¹³⁄₁₆ × 26
Printed by Pratt Graphic Art Workshop,
New York
Published by Martha Jackson Gallery,
New York
Courtesy Petersburg Press, New York

12. *These Are Ten Useful Objects Which No
One Should Be Without When Traveling*
1961
ten drypoints
edition: 6
12¹⁵⁄₁₆ × 10¹⁄₁₆ each
Printed by Pratt Graphic Art Workshop,
New York
Published by Martha Jackson Gallery,
New York
Collection The Museum of Modern Art,
New York, John B. Turner Fund

Claes Oldenburg

13. *Orpheum Sign*   1961
from *The International Avant-Garde: America
Discovered*, Volume 5   1964
etching, aquatint
edition: 60
10 × 7¹¹⁄₁₆
Printed by Atelier Georges Leblanc, Paris
Published by Galleria Schwarz, Milan
Collection Walker Art Center, Minneapolis,
gift of the artist, 1988

14. *Legs*   1961
etching
edition: 12
11⅛ × 15
Printed by Pratt Graphic Art Workshop,
New York
Published by the artist
Collection Walker Art Center, Minneapolis,
gift of the artist, 1988

Roy Lichtenstein

15. *On*   1962
from *The International Avant-Garde: America
Discovered*, Volume 5   1964
etching
edition: 60
11¾ × 9½
Printed by Atelier Georges Leblanc, Paris
Published by Galleria Schwarz, Milan
Courtesy Judith Goldberg Fine Art, New York

James Rosenquist

16. *Certificate*   1962
from *The International Avant-Garde: America
Discovered*, Volume 5   1964
photoengraving, etching
edition: 60
11¾ × 9½
Printed by Atelier Georges Leblanc, Paris
Published by Galleria Schwarz, Milan
Collection The Museum of Modern Art, New
York, gift of Peter Deitsch Gallery

Andy Warhol

17. *Cooking Pot*   1962
from *The International Avant-Garde: America
Discovered*, Volume 5   1964
photoengraving
edition: 60
11¾ × 9½
Printed by Atelier Georges Leblanc, Paris
Published by Galleria Schwarz, Milan
Courtesy Judith Goldberg Fine Art, New York

Robert Rauschenberg

18. *Abby's Bird*   1962
lithograph
edition: 50
22½ × 17½
Printed and published by Universal Limited
Art Editions, West Islip, New York
Collection The Art Institute of Chicago, ULAE
Collection, acquired through a challenge grant
of Mr. and Mrs. Thomas Dittmer, donations
of supporters of the Department of Prints and
Drawings, and the Centennial Endowment

19. *Merger*   1962
lithograph
edition: 16
22½ × 17½
Printed and published by Universal Limited
Art Editions, West Islip, New York
Collection The Art Institute of Chicago, ULAE
Collection, acquired through a challenge grant
of Mr. and Mrs. Thomas Dittmer, donations
of supporters of the Department of Prints and
Drawings, and the Centennial Endowment

20. *Urban*   1962
lithograph
edition: 38
41¼ × 29¾
Printed and published by Universal Limited
Art Editions, West Islip, New York
Collection The Art Institute of Chicago, ULAE
Collection, acquired through a challenge grant
of Mr. and Mrs. Thomas Dittmer, donations
of supporters of the Department of Prints and
Drawings, and the Centennial Endowment

Edward Ruscha

21. *Twentysix Gasoline Stations*   1962
book of twenty-six offset photographs
first edition: 400
7¹⁄₁₆ × 5½ × ¼
Printed by Henry Geiger, Los Angeles
Published by the artist
Collection Walker Art Center, Minneapolis

22. *Gas*   1962
lithograph
edition: 10
17½ × 14
Printed by Kanthos Press, Los Angeles
Published by the artist
Collection Modern Art Museum of Fort
Worth, anonymous gift in memory of Sam B.
Cantey III

23. *Standard Station*   1966
screenprint
edition: 50
25⁹⁄₁₆ × 39¹⁵⁄₁₆
Printed by Art Krebs, Los Angeles
Published by Audrey Sabol, New York
Collection Modern Art Museum of Fort
Worth, anonymous gift in memory of Sam B.
Cantey III

Ellsworth Kelly

24. *Red/Blue*
from *Ten Works by Ten Painters*   1964
screenprint
edition: 500
24 × 20
Printed by Scirocco Screenprinters under the
supervision of Ives-Sillman, Inc., New Haven,
Connecticut
Published by the Wadsworth Atheneum,
Hartford, Connecticut
Collection Walker Art Center, Minneapolis,
gift of Mr. and Mrs. Arnold Glimcher, 1986

25. *Green*
from *Suite of Twenty-seven Color
Lithographs*   1964–1965
lithograph
edition: 75
35¼ × 23⅝
Printed by Imprimerie Maeght, Levallois-
Perret, France
Published by Maeght Editeur, Paris
Collection National Museum of American Art,
Smithsonian Institution, Washington, D.C.,
gift of anonymous donor

26. *Yellow over Black*
from *Suite of Twenty-seven Color
Lithographs*   1964–1965
lithograph
edition: 75
35⅛ × 23⅜
Printed by Imprimerie Maeght, Levallois-
Perret, France
Published by Maeght Editeur, Paris
Collection National Museum of American Art,
Smithsonian Institution, Washington, D.C.,
gift of anonymous donor

27. *Cyclamen III*   1964–1965
from *Suite of Plant Lithographs*   1964–1966
transfer lithograph
edition: 75
35½ × 24¼
Printed by Imprimerie Maeght, Levallois-
Perret, France
Published by Maeght Editeur, Paris
Collection National Museum of American Art,
Smithsonian Institution, Washington, D.C.,
gift of anonymous donor

Alex Katz

28. *Luna Park*   1965
screenprint
edition: 30
40 × 29¾
Printed by Chiron Press, New York
Published by Fischbach Gallery, New York
Collection the artist

Bruce Conner

29. *Thumb Print*   1965
lithograph
edition: 20
41⁷⁄₁₆ × 29¹³⁄₁₆
Printed and published by Tamarind
Lithography Workshop, Inc., Los Angeles
Collection Thomas Garver and Natasha
Nicholson, Madison, Wisconsin

30. *Mandala*   1965
lithograph
edition: 20
18⅛ × 17
Printed and published by Tamarind
Lithography Workshop, Inc., Los Angeles
Collection The Grunwald Center for the
Graphic Arts, Wight Art Gallery, UCLA, gift of
Mr. and Mrs. Jack E. Libaw

31. *Rain*   1965
lithograph
edition: 20
26¹⁄₁₆ × 22¼
Printed and published by Tamarind
Lithography Workshop, Inc., Los Angeles
Collection The Grunwald Center for the
Graphic Arts, Wight Art Gallery, UCLA, gift of
Mr. and Mrs. Jack E. Libaw

32. *This Space Reserved for June
Wayne*   1965
lithograph
edition: 20
7⁹⁄₁₆ × 17½
Printed and published by Tamarind
Lithography Workshop, Inc., Los Angeles
Collection The Grunwald Center for the
Graphic Arts, Wight Art Gallery, UCLA, gift of
Mr. and Mrs. Jack E. Libaw

33. *Cancellation*   1965
lithograph
edition: 20
21⅛ × 32¼
Printed and published by Tamarind
Lithography Workshop, Inc., Los Angeles
Collection The Grunwald Center for the
Graphic Arts, Wight Art Gallery, UCLA, gift of
Mr. and Mrs. Jack E. Libaw

Leon Golub

34. *Wounded Sphinx*   1965
lithograph
edition: 20
29¹³⁄₁₆ × 41¹⁄₁₆
Printed and published by Tamarind
Lithography Workshop, Inc., Los Angeles
Collection The Grunwald Center for the
Graphic Arts, Wight Art Gallery, UCLA, gift of
the UCLA Art Council

35. *Running Man II*
from *Agon*   1965
lithograph
edition: 20
30⅛ × 22⅜
Printed and published by Tamarind
Lithography Workshop, Inc., Los Angeles
Collection The Grunwald Center for the
Graphic Arts, Wight Art Gallery, UCLA, gift of
the UCLA Art Council

36. *Wounded Warrior*
from *Agon*   1965
lithograph
edition: 20
22³/₁₆ × 29¾
Printed and published by Tamarind
Lithography Workshop, Inc., Los Angeles
Collection The Grunwald Center for the
Graphic Arts, Wight Art Gallery, UCLA, gift of
the UCLA Art Council

37. *Running Blue Sphinx*
from *Agon*   1965
lithograph
edition: 20
22⅜ × 30
Printed and published by Tamarind
Lithography Workshop, Inc., Los Angeles
Collection The Grunwald Center for the
Graphic Arts, Wight Art Gallery, UCLA, gift of
the UCLA Art Council

Frank Stella

38. *Star of Persia I*   1967
lithograph
edition: 92
25¹⁵/₁₆ × 31¹⁵/₁₆
Printed and published by Gemini G.E.L.,
Los Angeles
Collection Walker Art Center, Minneapolis,
gift of Kenneth E. Tyler, 1985

39. *Star of Persia II*   1967
lithograph
edition: 92
25⅞ × 31⅞
Printed and published by Gemini G.E.L.,
Los Angeles
Collection Walker Art Center, Minneapolis,
gift of Kenneth E. Tyler, 1985

40. *Arundel Castle*
from *Black Series I*   1967
lithograph
edition: 100
15 × 22
Printed and published by Gemini G.E.L.,
Los Angeles
Collection Walker Art Center, Minneapolis,
gift of Kenneth E. Tyler, 1985

41. *Delphine and Hippolyte*
from *Black Series II*   1967
lithograph

edition: 100
15 × 22
Printed and published by Gemini G.E.L.,
Los Angeles
Collection Walker Art Center, Minneapolis,
gift of Kenneth E. Tyler, 1985

Alan Shields

42. *c,b.a.r.l.a.a.(old)y.(odd)o.*
from *New York 10/69*   1969
screenprint with stencil, watercolor
edition: 100
18¹³/₁₆ × 17⅞
Printed by Maurel Studios, New York
Published by Tanglewood Press Inc.,
New York
Courtesy Rosa Esman Gallery, New York

Richard Artschwager

43. *Locations*   1969
six objects in Plexiglas, redwood, mirror glass,
Formica, and rubberized horsehair
edition: 90
dimensions range from 6¾ × 3½ × 3½ to
15 × 10⅝ × 4¾
Fabricated by the artist and assistants; cover
screenprinted by Dave Diao, New York
Published by Brooke Alexander, Inc., New
York, in cooperation with Leo Castelli,
New York
Collection Walker Art Center, Minneapolis,
Walker Special Purchase Fund, 1988

Bruce Nauman

44. *Studies for Holograms*   1970
five screenprints
edition: 150
25¾ × 25¾ each
Printed by Aetna Studios, New York
Published by Castelli Graphics, New York
Collection University Art Museum, University
of California, Berkeley, purchased with the aid
of funds from the National Endowment for
the Arts

Sol LeWitt

45. *Composite Series (Set of 5)*   1970
five screenprints
edition: 150
20 × 20 each
Printed and published by Sarah Lawrence Art
Press, New York
Collection Walker Art Center, Minneapolis,
donation of Virginia Dwan, 1987

Vito Acconci

46. *Kiss-Off*   1971
lithograph
edition: 50
30⅛ × 22⅜

Printed and published by Lithography
Workshop, Nova Scotia College of Art and
Design, Halifax
Courtesy Lithography Workshop, Nova Scotia
College of Art and Design, Halifax

47. *Trademarks*   1971
lithograph
edition: 50
20⅛ × 20
Printed and published by Lithography
Workshop, Nova Scotia College of Art and
Design, Halifax
Collection Walker Art Center, Minneapolis,
gift of Dayton Hudson Corporation,
Minneapolis, 1978

Ronald Davis

48. *Cube I*   1971
photo-offset with laminated Mylar overlay,
mounted on plastic
edition: 100
29⅝ × 39¾
Printed and published by Gemini G.E.L.,
Los Angeles
Collection Walker Art Center, Minneapolis,
gift of Kenneth E. Tyler, 1985

49. *Cube II*   1971
photo-offset with laminated Mylar overlay,
mounted on plastic
edition: 114
29⅝ × 39¾
Printed and published by Gemini G.E.L.,
Los Angeles
Collection Walker Art Center, Minneapolis,
gift of Kenneth E. Tyler, 1985

50. *Cube III*   1971
photo-offset with laminated Mylar overlay,
mounted on plastic
edition: 125
29⅝ × 39¾
Printed and published by Gemini G.E.L.,
Los Angeles
Collection Walker Art Center, Minneapolis,
gift of Kenneth E. Tyler, 1985

Edward Kienholz

51. *Sawdy*   1971
car door, mirrored window, screenprint,
fluorescent light, galvanized sheet metal,
automotive lacquer, polyester resin
edition: 50
39½ × 37½ × 8
Fabricated and published by Gemini G.E.L.,
Los Angeles
Collection Walker Art Center, Minneapolis,
gift of Kenneth E. Tyler, 1985

52. *Documentation Book: Five Car Stud and Sawdy*   1972
book of photographs, offset reproductions, magazine clippings, printed text
edition: 55
11½ × 10½ × 2½
Printed and published by Gemini G.E.L., Los Angeles
Collection Walker Art Center, Minneapolis, gift of Kenneth E. Tyler, 1985

53. *Souvenir License Plate for Sawdy*   1972
die-stamped painted license plate with printed sticker, chrome frame, plastic reflectors, polyester resin
edition: 55
6⅜ × 12¼ × 1
Fabricated and published by Gemini G.E.L., Los Angeles
Collection Walker Art Center, Minneapolis, gift of Kenneth E. Tyler, 1985

Ed Paschke

54. *Hairy Shoes*   1971
lithograph
edition: 30
18 × 24
Printed and published by Landfall Press, Inc., Chicago
Courtesy Landfall Press, Inc.

Nancy Graves

55. *Fra Mauro Region of the Moon*
from *Lunar Maps*   1972
lithograph
edition: 100
22½ × 30
Printed by Landfall Press, Inc., Chicago
Published by Carl Solway Gallery, Cincinnati
Collection Walker Art Center, Minneapolis, Art Center Acquisition Fund, 1973

56. *Maestlin G Region of the Moon*
from *Lunar Maps*   1972
lithograph
edition: 100
22½ × 30
Printed by Landfall Press, Inc., Chicago
Published by Carl Solway Gallery, Cincinnati
Collection Walker Art Center, Minneapolis, Art Center Acquisition Fund, 1973

57. *Julius Caesar Quadrangle of the Moon*
from *Lunar Maps*   1972
lithograph
edition: 100
22½ × 30
Printed by Landfall Press, Inc., Chicago
Published by Carl Solway Gallery, Cincinnati
Collection Walker Art Center, Minneapolis, Art Center Acquisition Fund, 1973

58. *Maskeyne DA Region of the Moon*
from *Lunar Maps*   1972
lithograph
edition: 100
22½ × 30
Printed by Landfall Press, Inc., Chicago
Published by Carl Solway Gallery, Cincinnati
Collection Walker Art Center, Minneapolis, Art Center Acquisition Fund, 1973

59. *Sabine D Region of the Moon, Lunar Orbiter Site IIP-6, Southwestern Mare Tranquilitatis*
from *Lunar Maps*   1972
lithograph
edition: 100
22½ × 30
Printed by Landfall Press, Inc., Chicago
Published by Carl Solway Gallery, Cincinnati
Collection Walker Art Center, Minneapolis, Art Center Acquisition Fund, 1973

Chuck Close

60. *Keith*   1972
mezzotint
edition: 10
50¹⁵⁄₁₆ × 41¹³⁄₁₆
Printed by Crown Point Press, Oakland, California
Published by Parasol Press, Ltd., New York
Collection The Museum of Modern Art, New York, John B. Turner Fund

61. *Keith's Mouth*   1972
mezzotint
trial proof
6½ × 11¾
Printed by Crown Point Press, Oakland, California
Collection Kathan Brown, San Francisco

62. *Keith's Eye*   1972
mezzotint
trial proof
9½ × 11¾
Printed by Crown Point Press, Oakland, California
Collection Kathan Brown, San Francisco

63. *The Chuck Close Mezzotint "Keith" 1972*   1972
bound portfolio with letterpress and photographic etchings
edition: 20
15⅜ × 11¾ × ¾
Printed by Crown Point Press, Oakland, California
Courtesy Parasol Press, Ltd., New York

Richard Estes

64. *Grant's*
from *Urban Landscapes I*   1972
screenprint
edition: 75
19¹³⁄₁₆ × 27⅝
Printed by Domberger KG, Stuttgart
Published by Parasol Press, Ltd., New York
Collection Museum of Art, Rhode Island School of Design, Providence, National Endowment Fund, 1973

65. *Danbury Rubber Tile*
from *Urban Landscapes I*   1972
screenprint
edition: 75
19¹³⁄₁₆ × 27⅝
Printed by Domberger KG, Stuttgart
Published by Parasol Press, Ltd., New York
Collection Museum of Art, Rhode Island School of Design, Providence, National Endowment Fund, 1973

66. *Ten Doors*
from *Urban Landscapes I*   1972
screenprint
edition: 75
19¹³⁄₁₆ × 27⅝
Printed by Domberger KG, Stuttgart
Published by Parasol Press, Ltd., New York
Collection Museum of Art, Rhode Island School of Design, Providence, National Endowment Fund, 1973

67. *560*
from *Urban Landscapes I*   1972
screenprint
edition: 75
19¹³⁄₁₆ × 27⅝
Printed by Domberger KG, Stuttgart
Published by Parasol Press, Ltd., New York
Collection Museum of Art, Rhode Island School of Design, Providence, National Endowment Fund, 1973

William T. Wiley

68. *Moon Mullings*   1972
lithograph
edition: 80
22 × 30
Printed and published by Landfall Press, Inc., Chicago
Courtesy Landfall Press, Inc.

69. *Thank You Hide*   1972
lithograph
edition: 80
35 × 48
Printed and published by Landfall Press, Inc., Chicago
Courtesy Landfall Press, Inc.

70. *Coast Reverse*   1972
two lithographs
edition: 35
27½ × 30 and 33 × 46
Printed and published by Landfall Press, Inc.,
Chicago
Courtesy Landfall Press, Inc.

Yvonne Jacquette

71. *Traffic Signal*   1973
lithograph, hand-colored with watercolor
edition: 27
19½ × 26
Printed by Paul Narkiewicz, New York
Published by Brooke Alexander, Inc.,
New York
Private collection, courtesy Brooke Alexander,
Inc.

72. *Traffic Signal*   1973
lithograph, hand-colored with pastel
edition: 27
21½ × 27¼
Printed by Paul Narkiewicz, New York
Published by Brooke Alexander, Inc.,
New York
Private collection, courtesy Brooke Alexander,
Inc.

73. *Traffic Signal*   1973
lithograph, hand-colored with pastel
edition: 27
21½ × 27¼
Printed by Paul Narkiewicz, New York
Published by Brooke Alexander, Inc.,
New York
Private collection, courtesy Brooke Alexander,
Inc.

Pat Steir

74. *Roll Me a Rainbow*   1974
lithograph
edition: 35
22 × 29½
Printed and published by Landfall Press, Inc.,
Chicago
Courtesy Landfall Press, Inc.

75. *Between the Lines*   1974
lithograph
edition: 50
27½ × 32
Printed and published by Landfall Press, Inc.,
Chicago
Courtesy Landfall Press, Inc.

Michelle Stuart

76. *Tunyo*   1974
lithograph
edition: 15
18⅞ × 16⅞

Printed and published by Tamarind Institute,
Albuquerque, New Mexico
Courtesy the artist and Max Protetch Gallery,
New York

77. *Tsikupuming*
from *Tsikomo*   1975
lithograph
edition: 24
13½ × 11
Printed and published by Tamarind Institute,
Albuquerque, New Mexico
Courtesy the artist and Max Protetch Gallery,
New York

78. *Tsikomo*
from *Tsikomo*   1975
lithograph
edition: 24
15¾ × 15
Printed and published by Tamarind Institute,
Albuquerque, New Mexico
Courtesy the artist and Max Protetch Gallery,
New York

79. *Okuping*
from *Tsikomo*   1975
lithograph
edition: 24
20⅝ × 14¾
Printed and published by Tamarind Institute,
Albuquerque, New Mexico
Courtesy the artist and Max Protetch Gallery,
New York

Susan Rothenberg

80. *Untitled*   1977
lithograph
edition: 18
12 × 15½
Printed by Derrière L'Etoile Studios,
New York
Published by Prestige Art Limited,
Mamaroneck, New York
Courtesy the artist

81. *Untitled*   1977
hand-colored lithograph
edition: 18
12 × 15
Printed by Derrière L'Etoile Studios,
New York
Published by Prestige Art Limited,
Mamaroneck, New York
Collection Janie C. Lee Gallery, Houston

82. *Untitled*   1977
hand-colored lithograph
edition: 18
12 × 15½
Printed by Derrière L'Etoile Studios,
New York
Published by Prestige Art Limited,
Mamaroneck, New York
Collection Shirley and Sidney Singer,
Mamaroneck, New York

Jenny Holzer

83. *Truisms*   1977–1979
various media, including photo-offset,
photostats, T-shirts, electronic billboards
edition: unlimited; first printing: 1,000
various dimensions; first printing:
16¹⁵⁄₁₆ × 13¹¹⁄₁₆
Printed by Millner Brothers, New York
Published by the artist
Courtesy Barbara Gladstone Gallery,
New York

Steven Sorman

84. *The First Building Project According to
What Plan*   1978
lithograph, etching, aquatint, collage
edition: 45
26 × 76
Printed by Vermillion Editions Limited, Inc.,
Minneapolis
Published by Bird Island Publishing,
Minneapolis
Collection Walker Art Center, Minneapolis,
gift of Russell Cowles, 1984

Lynda Benglis

85. *Lagniappe I*   1978
cast paper with acrylic
edition: 26
35½ × 11½ × 5
Fabricated by Exeter Press, New York
Published by Paula Cooper Editions,
New York
Courtesy Paula Cooper Gallery, New York

86. *Lagniappe II*   1979
cast paper with acrylic, glitter, gold leaf,
polypropylene
edition: 16
38 × 13 × 8
Fabricated by Exeter Press, New York
Published by Paula Cooper Editions,
New York
Collection Julie Graham, New York

Jennifer Bartlett

87. *Day and Night*   1978
two drypoints and one etching
edition: 35
15 × 11 each
Printed by Aeropress, New York
Published by Multiples, Inc., New York
Courtesy Brooke Alexander, Inc., New York

88. *Day and Night*   1978
three drypoints
edition: 35
30 × 20 each
Printed by Aeropress, New York
Published by Multiples, Inc., New York
Collection Cincinnati Art Museum, gift of
Janet Lehr, Inc.

Donald Sultan

89. *Water under the Bridge*   1979
eight aquatints
edition: 45
18 × 18 each
Printed by Crown Point Press, Oakland,
California
Published by Parasol Press, Ltd., New York
Collection Walker Art Center, Minneapolis,
Walker Special Purchase Fund, 1985

Nicholas Africano

90. *The Shadow*   1979
four etchings with aquatint, spitbite,
embossing
edition: 45
11 × 14 each
Printed by Aeropress, New York
Published by Barbara Gladstone Editions,
New York
Courtesy Barbara Gladstone Gallery

Elizabeth Murray

91. *Untitled, States I–V*   1980
five lithographs
edition: 35
22¾ × 17¹³⁄₁₆ each
Printed by Derrière L'Etoile Studios,
New York
Published by Brooke Alexander, Inc., and
Paula Cooper Gallery, New York
Collection First Bank System, Inc.,
Minneapolis

Richard Bosman

92. *Man Overboard*   1981
woodcut
edition: 36
26⅝ × 16½
Printed by Chip Elwell, New York
Published by Brooke Alexander, Inc.,
New York
Collection Walker Art Center, Minneapolis,
T. B. Walker Acquisition Fund, 1984

93. *Polar Bear*   1981
woodcut
edition: 14
30 × 25½
Printed by Chip Elwell, New York
Published by Brooke Alexander, Inc.,
New York
Courtesy Brooke Alexander, Inc.

John Buck

94. *Les Grande Eclipse*   1982
woodcut
edition: 20
75 × 38
Printed and published by Landfall Press, Inc.,
Chicago
Courtesy Landfall Press, Inc.

Eric Fischl

95. *Digging Kids*   1982
etching, aquatint
edition: 40
54 × 38
Printed by Aeropress, New York
Published by Corinthian Editions, New York
Courtesy First Bank System, Inc., Minneapolis

96. *Beach Balls*   1982
etching, aquatint
edition: 40
48 × 34¾
Printed by Aeropress, New York
Published by Corinthian Editions, New York
Collection William Van Straaten, Chicago

T. L. Solien

97. *The Three Sailors*   1982
lithograph, intaglio, screenprint
edition: 43
32½ × 46¼
Printed and published by Vermillion Editions
Limited, Inc., Minneapolis
Courtesy Vermillion Editions Limited, Inc.

98. *Fragments of Hope*   1982
six drypoints
edition: 21
13¼ × 17¼ each
Printed and published by Vermillion Editions
Limited, Inc., Minneapolis
Courtesy Vermillion Editions Limited, Inc.

Terry Winters

99. *Ova*   1982
lithograph
edition: 7
29½ × 21½
Printed and published by Universal Limited
Art Editions, West Islip, New York
Courtesy Sonnabend Gallery, New York

100. *Factors of Increase*   1983
lithograph
edition: 30
31 × 22
Printed and published by Universal Limited
Art Editions, West Islip, New York
Collection John and Sheila Stoller, courtesy
John C. Stoller and Co., Minneapolis

Robert Longo

101. *Jules, Gretchen, Mark, State II*
1982–1983
lithograph with embossing
edition: 30
36½ × 68
Printed by Derrière L'Etoile Studios,
New York
Published by Brooke Alexander, Inc.,
New York
Courtesy Brooke Alexander, Inc.

David True

102. *Savannah Sea*   1983
aquatint, soft ground, spitbite
edition: 35
25¾ × 33
Printed and published by Crown Point Press,
Oakland, California
Courtesy Crown Point Press, San Francisco
and New York

103. *Late*   1983
aquatint
edition: 35
29¾ × 44
Printed and published by Crown Point Press,
Oakland, California
Courtesy Crown Point Press, San Francisco
and New York

James Turrell

104. *Deep Sky*   1984
seven aquatints
edition: 45
21 × 27 each
Printed by Peter Kneubühler, Zurich
Published by Peter Blum Edition, New York
Collection Walker Art Center, Minneapolis,
Art Center Acquisition Fund, 1985

Carroll Dunham

105. *Untitled*   1984–1985
lithograph
edition: 42
27¹⁵⁄₁₆ × 19
Printed and published by Universal Limited
Art Editions, West Islip, New York
Collection Walker Art Center, Minneapolis,
Walker Special Purchase Fund, 1986

106. *Untitled*   1985
lithograph
edition: 31
24¹³⁄₁₆ × 18¼
Printed and published by Universal Limited
Art Editions, West Islip, New York
Collection Walker Art Center, Minneapolis,
Walker Special Purchase Fund, 1986

107. *Accelerator*   1985
lithograph
edition: 51
41½ × 29¾
Printed and published by Universal Limited
Art Editions, West Islip, New York
General Mills Art Collection, Minneapolis

Brooke Alexander, Inc., New York

The Art Institute of Chicago

Kathan Brown

Cincinnati Art Museum

Paula Cooper Gallery, New York

Crown Point Press, San Francisco and New York

Rosa Esman Gallery, New York

First Bank System, Inc., Minneapolis

Thomas Garver and Natasha Nicholson

General Mills Art Collection, Minneapolis

Barbara Gladstone Gallery, New York

Judith Goldberg Fine Art, New York

Julie Graham

The Grunwald Center for the Graphic Arts, Wight Art Gallery,
    University of California, Los Angeles

Jasper Johns

Alex Katz

Landfall Press, Inc., Chicago

Janie C. Lee Gallery, Houston

Lithography Workshop, Nova Scotia College of Art and Design, Halifax

Modern Art Museum of Fort Worth

Museum of Art, Rhode Island School of Design, Providence

The Museum of Modern Art, New York

National Museum of American Art, Smithsonian Institution, Washington, D.C.

Parasol Press, Ltd., New York

Petersburg Press, New York

Max Protetch Gallery, New York

Susan Rothenberg

Shirley and Sidney Singer

Sonnabend Gallery, New York

John C. Stoller and Co., Minneapolis

University Art Museum, University of California, Berkeley

William Van Straaten

Vermillion Editions Limited, Inc., Minneapolis

Three private collections

Reproduction Credits

Courtesy Brooke Alexander, Inc., New York   129
Courtesy The Art Institute of Chicago   24, 43, 44
Courtesy Richard H. Axsom   48
Courtesy The Brooklyn Museum   36, 51
Jian Chen, courtesy Shirley and Sidney Singer   99
Courtesy Paula Cooper Gallery, New York   105
Courtesy Crown Point Press, San Francisco and New York   131
Courtesy Rosa Esman Gallery, New York   63
Courtesy Barbara Gladstone Gallery, New York   100
Courtesy Grunwald Center for the Graphic Arts, Wight Art Gallery, University of California,
   Los Angeles   55, 59
Steven Kasher, courtesy Brooke Alexander, Inc., New York   90, 91
Courtesy Landfall Press, Inc., Chicago   79, 87, 88, 93, 121
Courtesy Janie C. Lee Gallery, Houston   16
Courtesy Mount Holyoke College Art Museum, South Hadley, Massachusetts   107
Courtesy Museum of Art, Rhode Island School of Design, Providence   85
Courtesy Museum of Fine Arts, Boston   127
Courtesy The Museum of Modern Art, New York   15, 31, 37, 39, 41
   (reproduction © 1989 The Estate and Foundation of Andy Warhol), 83
Courtesy The New York Public Library   18
Bill Orcutt, courtesy Barbara Gladstone Gallery, New York   113
Eric Pollitzer, courtesy Brooke Alexander, Inc., New York   106
Pollitzer, Strong and Meyer, courtesy Castelli Graphics, New York   66, 67
Adam Reich, courtesy The Brooklyn Museum   52
Larry Travis and Dick Lane, courtesy Modern Art Museum of Fort Worth   46, 47
Courtesy Universal Limited Art Editions, Inc., West Islip, New York   23
Walker Art Center, Minneapolis   10, 12, 14, 17, 19, 27–29, 32, 33, 35, 45, 49, 56,
   61, 65, 70, 71, 73, 75, 77, 81, 95–97, 101, 103, 110, 111, 119, 123, 125, 133, 135
Courtesy Yale University Art Gallery, New Haven, Connecticut   115–117